GREEK WHISKY

.

Food, Nutrition, and Culture

Series Editors:　Rachel Black, Boston University
　　　　　　　　　Leslie Carlin, University of Toronto

Published by Berghahn Books in Association with the Society for the Anthropology of Food and Nutrition (SAFN).

While eating is a biological necessity, the production, distribution, preparation, and consumption of food are all deeply culturally inscribed activities. Taking an anthropological perspective, this book series provides a forum for thought-provoking work on the bio-cultural, cultural, and social aspects of human nutrition and food habits. The books in this series bring timely food-related scholarship to the graduate and upper-division undergraduate classroom, to a research-focused academic audience, and to those involved in food policy.

Volume 1
GREEK WHISKY
The Localization of a Global Commodity
Tryfon Bampilis

Titles in preparation:

RECONSTRUCTING OBESITY
The Meaning of Measures and the Measure of Meanings
Edited by Megan McCullough and Jessica Hardin

TASTEFUL TRENDS
Identity, Power and Mobility of East Asian Food
Edited by Kwang-ok Kim

THE REINVENTION OF CHEESE
Food Cultures between Tradition and Modernity at the Foot of the Alps
Cristina Grasseni

Greek Whisky

The Localization of a Global Commodity

By Tryfon Bampilis

berghahn
NEW YORK • OXFORD
www.berghahnbooks.com

Published in 2013 by

Berghahn Books

www.berghahnbooks.com

© 2013 Tryfon Bampilis

Library of Congress Cataloging-in-Publication Data

Bampilis, Tryfon.
  Greek whisky : the localization of a global commodity / by Tryfon Bampilis. —
1st ed.
      p. cm. — (Food, nutrition, and culture vol. 1)
  Includes bibliographical references.
  ISBN 978-0-85745-877-3 (hardback : alk. paper) —
  ISBN 978-0-85745-878-0 (institutional ebook)
  1. Whiskey—Social aspects—Greece. 2. Whiskey industry—Greece.
3. Drinking of alcoholic beverages—Greece. 4. National characteristics, Greek.
5. Greece—Social life and customs. I. Title.
  GT2895.B36 2013
  394.1'309495--dc23

                                                          2012032449

British Library Cataloguing in Publication Data

A catalogue record for this book is available from the British Library.

ISBN 978-0-85745-877-3 (hardback)
ISBN 978-0-85745-878-0 (institutional ebook)

Για την Άννα Σοφία

Το Anna Sophia

Contents

✠ ✠ ✠

Acknowledgments

This book has been the effort of over seven years of research and writing, and any errors or omissions are entirely my own responsibility. During this period various colleagues, friends, and companions read parts of the book and discussed them with me. I owe them a great deal, as their generous assistance, guidance, and encouragement kept the spirits high and helped me with the completion of the project. I would like to thank them all and especially my mentors Peter Pels, Peter Geschiere, Giorgos Aggelopoulos, Roger Just, Pieter ter Keurs, and Charles Stewart. A lot of gratitude goes also to Peter Loizos, Eleni Papagaroufali, Dimitra Gefou-Madianou, Leonidas Oikonomou, Ratna Saptari, Patricia Spyer, and Sabine Luning for their comments and inspiration. Many thanks also to the three anonymous reviewers who read and commented on versions of this book. A lot of friends, colleagues, and interlocutors have also supported me during this long endeavour, and I would like to thank them all: Umut Azak, Marco Beltrame, Erna Van der Berg, Vincent Breugem, Vicky Brousali, Giannis Christopoulos, Christos Chrissoulis, Giorgos Ekseltzes, Els van Dongen, Giannis Fergadis, Stathis Katsarelias, Anastasios Kavasis, the "Kokalenia" family and especially Thodoris, Nikos Kondynopoulos, Maria Kouloumbi, Aliki Labrou, Alecos Lamprou, Miriam Lang, Guy Loth, Anastasia Makri, Roland Moore, Aris Perperoglou, Girogos Portokalidis, Maarten Onneweer, Christos Sakkas, Panagiotis Sotiropoulos, Andronicos Theoharidis, Dimitris Tsakopoulos, Giannis Venardis, and Martijn Wienia. I am also thankful to the owner of Rodon bar, Takis Georgoudis, who unfortunately passed away before the completion of this book, for the endless nights we shared in Rodon next to the wooden stove in an empty bar, full of music, *kefi,* and lively discussions.

My grandmother, Efrosini Christodoulou, has helped enormously by commenting on the ethnography of Skyros and by answering patiently all my queer questions. Without her, I cannot imagine what the progress of my work would have been. My gratitude goes to all my family and especially Emmanuella, Michalis, and Anna for their kind support and assistance.

Financial support for research and writing was provided by the endowment of social anthropology by the National Scholarship Foundation of Greece (IKY), the School of Asian, African and Amerindian studies in Leiden (CNWS), and the department of cultural anthropology in the faculty of social sciences in the University of Leiden.

Above all, I am deeply indebted to those Athenians and Skyrians who opened up their lives and introduced me to cultural appropriation and freedom. Finally, I would like to thank my partner, Amber Gemmeke, who has been next to me during this long effort and has supported this project with her affection, patience, encouragement, and lively humour. The company of my cats, Zahra, Muffin, and Cookie, helped also in a lot of stress relief and brought creativity, enjoyment, and warmth. With them, the everlasting editing process became a *gezellige* experience. This book is devoted to my daughter, Anna Sophia, who fills my life with happiness and enthusiasm.

Illustrations

Figures

Tables

Maps

Note on Transliteration

The book has adopted a simplified method of transliteration, which makes the word recognizable and easily understood without losing the pronunciation. Although a few Greek keywords or passages are written in Greek, this system of transliteration follows each word to make it easier for the reader to pronounce the language.

Consonants

For this I follow the convention followed by most Greeks of attributing letters γ with g, δ with d, and χ with ch. Ξ is represented by ks. Similarly, the phonetics ντ, γκ/γγ, and μπ are represented by d, g, and b. However, the pronunciation of phonetics in the Greek language requires a good command of the language, and the sounds cannot by any means be interpreted totally correctly with this transliteration system.

Vowels

All vowels ι, η, υ and phonetics οι, ει are represented with i. O and ω are represented by o. Phonetics αι and ου are represented by e and ou. Αυ and ευ are represented by av and ev, respectively, but their pronunciation changes depending on the word. All words indicated follow the *monotoniko* system of modern Greek.

All translations are my own.

Preface

When I first began with this research in Greece, there was a general optimism about the country and the lives that most people had. There was a sense of freedom and independence from a rational westernized modernity while at the same time there was an assurance that Greece was becoming more and more European. That was a time that consuming excessively was seen, by some, as a denial of a constructive economic planning, and within this context Scotch whisky had become a negation of the economic and social responsibilities of the middle class. Gradually, modernization fantasies pushed the Greek economy to growth until 2008 and then soon vanished with the deep recession that Greece encountered. People who once spent enormous sums of money on clothing and entertainment now found it increasingly difficult to feed themselves. Therefore, a deep sense of disappointment and failure has replaced the optimism of past lives. Nevertheless, the urge of independence from "modernity" is more present than ever before, and Greeks continue to drink Scotch in smaller quantities while they boycott German or Dutch commodities in an effort to show their discomfort about the pressure of the implementation of the modernization program to the two countries.

Nowadays, "The party is over" or "consumerism is over" various international media are declaring in an effort to denote the inability of people to consume and the constriction of the lavish Greek styles. In fact, some argue, this mentality of spending excessively is responsible for the current crisis in Greece and consumption has to be controlled. Greeks have been guilty of spending, and now they have to save and reinvest their savings to develop their country. Even better, they can borrow massively to pay their interest rate debts and continue saving. Even major Greek politicians now state guiltily that the era of consumption is over. Why then has this view of spending lavishly as the ultimate sin been so prominent? Why is there such a big fuss over consumption, one of the driving forces of capitalism and neoliberal ideals? And why is squandering portrayed as the source of all evil? This book takes an ethnographic stand to the meanings of consumption and squandering in an effort to contextualize the meaning of these terms and their relationship to culture in Greece. This ethnography is related to a period that the crisis was not yet part of Greece, and as such, it is time specific and contextual. Nevertheless, it records a time of sociocultural transformation and excessive consumption. My point of departure is Scotch whisky and the local or global claims that conglomerates, commercial films, advertisements, and consumers make.

Drawing on fieldwork in the center of Athens and on the Aegean island of Skyros, this book discusses, among others, bars, *bouzoukia* venues, shepherds country houses, *kafenia,* and private homes in an effort to understand the position of Scotch in such locations and the extent that cultural worlds are affected by a seemingly imported, modern commodity. *Greek Whisky* examines the appearance of Scotch in Greek commercial cinema in the 1950s and 1960s and its profusion in the post-authoritarian Greece in the 1970s driven by marketing and the rise of transnational capitalism.

Smashing plates or glasses while dancing a Greek popular song, throwing massive amounts of napkins on the air or throwing tens of baskets filled with red carnations to a singer, one might wonder how such practices relate specifically to Scotch whisky. Even more importantly, how Scotch has come to represent a culture of spending excessively and an out of control party atmosphere is a question that haunts most of this book.

During the course of this research, many friends and interlocutors persisted in how Greek whisky is and how important has been in their lives. It was therefore my obligation to title this book with this local claim in mind. On the other hand, marketing and advertising have also presented Scotch as a Greek beverage dressed with a national aesthetic as well as a global commodity. As a result, one of my first questions was the extent that the cultural industry shared or shaped a similar perception about Scotch with my interlocutors.

Therefore, in this historical ethnography I explore the differences between global and local claims and practices and their relationship to the processes of localization. The way I use the term *localization* is not related to theories that claim an absorption of the global into the local or the other way around; or simply an imposition of a commodity over a culture; or a false consciousness constructed by the cultural industry. Localization is not one half in a dichotomy but an activity of connecting the global and local scales, a strategic or tactical practice that, depending on the context, has different causes and motives.

The subject is extremely important for anthropologists, sociologists, or scholars of culture, as there is a wide recognition that larger forces are affecting the small communities or groups that we study. Especially in this time of an economic crisis, the terms *global, local, modernization,* and *consumption* become burning matters. How are we to interpret such terms then and examine them methodically during the course of practice of our interlocutors? Are these dynamics changing the cultures we study, and if this is the case, what are the effects? Are globalization and modernity just fashionable terms, or are we to take them seriously in our studies of culture and comprehend them ethnographically and historically?

Greek Whisky makes an effort to take such theoretical discussions seriously through the quaint study of alcoholic beverages. By bringing along the discussions and outings with my schoolmates and friends from Athens, the experiences with the shepherds and laborers of Skyros, and the interviews of marketers and heads of global corporations, I hope to draw a vivid portrait of the perplexities of commodity consumption and the struggle of those who try to negate modernity or reinvent it.

Introduction
The Social Life of Whisky

"We have had a mania for the *kseno* (foreign) for a long time. We wanted to drink whisky instead of Greek-produced beverages. As a result, whisky has come to be a Greek beverage and ouzo a European one. We drink *ksena pota* (foreign beverages). We look down on Greek drinks. You can't go to a bar and ask for *ouzo*. They'll snub you. You'll say, give me a whisky."

—Vagelis, owner of Makedonia coffeehouse on Skyros Island

Whisky is one of the favorite beverages of Karolos Papoulias, the latest President of Greece, and of most prime ministers of the last three decades, including Andreas Papandreou and Kostantinos Karamanlis. In public discourse and lifestyle magazines, whisky has been characterized as the "the national drink of Greece" in contrast with retsina, which has been called pure "folklore" (Greek *Playboy* Magazine January 1990: 136–141).[1] It is apparent that signs of modernity have developed at the expense of other objects that are thought traditional, backward, or Greek. Furthermore, the consumption of this imported commodity has clear connections with popular culture and music.[2] Apart from this, Greek sailors are always offered a bottle of whisky and some boxes of American cigarettes by the companies that employ them before they embark on their next voyages. Whisky can be found at high society parties and in *bouzoukia* music venues, in alcohol stores and supermarkets, and in the household cupboards of Kypseli and Kolonaki. Whisky is not only a prestige good anymore; it has become a mass beverage that is part of the lives of Greeks.

In the summer of 1986, as a result of increased consumption (Stewart 1989: 99), the Greek government imposed a strict quota on the amount of whisky that could be imported into the country. The whisky boom was at its height, with thousands of bottles consumed every night in a variety of spaces such as bars, nightclubs, and households. Between 1981 and 1991 alone, the consumption of whisky in Greece increased by 279 percent (*Kathimerini* newspaper, 12 October 2002).

In 1969, per capita whisky consumption in Greece was only 0.39 liters per year, but by 1980 this had risen to 4.55.[3] Within a decade, the consumption of spirits had increased elevenfold, while the consumption of wine and beer remained steady and *ouzo* and *raki* had gradually declined.[4] More specifically, the total consumption of Scotch whisky in 1981 was 5.4 million liters and by 2001 had risen to 23.274 million liters.[5] The increased consumption resulted in the production of whisky by Greek companies, which named their spirits Scots whisky.[6] These companies tried to present the whisky they produced as Scottish and used several Scottish symbols on the labels of their bottles of Scots, blended, and Greek whisky. Lions, fake kilts, and horseshoes were only a few of the so-called Scottish symbols. As a result, the Scottish Whisky Association petitioned the Greek court of justice to prohibit the production of any beverage marketed as Scots or blended.[7]

Nowadays, popular culture and popular music have appropriated the beverage, which has become the main drink of choice in music venues where popular Greek music is performed live. Bottles of whisky can be found everywhere—in small music halls on the highways, in coffeehouses, in bars, in rural and urban spaces, and inside and outside homes—and whisky is consumed by both men and women.

Most of the whisky consumed in Greece comes from Scotland, and brands such as Johnnie Walker, Chivas Regal, Dimple, Famous Grouse, and Cutty Sark are widely available. Almost twenty years after the whisky boom, whisky is still one of the most preferred drinks and (in Athens) one of the most frequently consumed ones.[8] Greece is also one of the countries in Europe with the highest consumption of spirits and whisky.[9] In 2003 alone, 33.9 million bottles were sold in a country with a population of fewer than 11 million people.[10] Greece is one of the top three markets for Scotch, with the average person consuming nearly three liters per year.[11] In recent research by the National Statistical Service of Greece, it was shown that when most households in Greece spend on alcohol, their first preference is to buy spirits, specifically whisky (ESIE 2007). This is striking if one recalls that before World War II, Greeks hardly consumed any whisky or other imported beverages at all. Nowadays, Greek brandy and *ouzo* have declined, whereas imported beverages have become the major celebratory symbols. Whisky is still institutionalized in Athens in music venues with live popular music, where singers perform Greek popular songs. Visiting such a place requires literally booking a bottle of whisky. The first time I visited such a place a few years ago, I was surprised. There were many tables, some full, some empty, but each with a bottle of whisky on it. I was wondering what happens if a person does not drink whisky. A friend from my group answered:

"When I go to these places, I have to drink whisky even though I don't like it. It's a way of socializing. I avoid going there with my friends for that reason. But whisky is not only there. Even if I go to a birthday party, this is often the only drink that people serve and drink."

The price of whisky in *bouzoukia* music venues (music halls with live Greek popular music) ranges from 150 to 200 euros a bottle, whereas the price of whisky in supermarkets is only 10 to 15 euros a bottle. Despite the high prices at evening entertainment venues, some Athenians spend money there as part of their leisure and as part of a performative way of spending. People can also buy small baskets of flowers (ranging from 20 to 50 euros each) for throwing at the singers. The consumption of whisky and alcohol in general in modern Athens is thus embedded in excessive spending and is a symbol of lavish or slightly out-of-control entertainment.

On Skyros Island, in contrast, where the other major part of the research took place, the consumption of whisky is associated with specific bars, coffeehouses, and *poka,* a Greek version of poker played by men. Generally speaking, it is more a conspicuous performance of modernness, which stands opposed to the commensal exchange of wine and *tsipouro.* Within this context persons make themselves through the beverage, the beverage is identified with specific networks. Surprisingly enough, there was no whisky on Skyros until the 1960s. Wine, *tsipouro, ouzo,* and beer were the major alcoholic beverages in cafes and restaurants.

These processes of localization on Skyros Island and in Athens have been taking place side by side with the establishment of large multinational corporations, which have adapted their marketing to local tastes and have taken over most of the beverage market. Generally speaking, the commercialization of the Greek economy in recent decades can be interpreted as a success of multinational capitalism and an adoption of neoliberal economic policies by the state. The values that have shaped contemporary consumption are certainly influenced by the general context of the economy. However, this in itself would not be enough to explain the success or failure of a commodity that has been thought of as Greek, national, part of the contemporary Greek popular music scene, or as representative of the values of laborhood on Skyros. In this study, I propose to use whisky as a symbol of connections (with a focus on Greece and, more specifically, on Athens and Skyros) that companies, consumers, and the cultural industry use as a vehicle to negotiate their own styles. As such, the use of the term *global* expresses the process of global connectivity of a commodity that is globally traded, projected, and used and the scale-making of globality by various agents.

In addition, this study takes an ethnographic approach to terms such as *modern, Western,* or *European,* which have hitherto tended to be used with a positive valuation. These terms are understood here within the context of larger political and historical processes that have been taking place in the Greek nation-state. The case of whisky and imported beverages constitutes one element of these consumer goods that have been associated with the distinction of different classes. Nowadays, the consumption of these things is related to the reproduction of different social identities, whether popular, national, or local. Such commodities are not necessarily homogenizing our globalized world, as they are interpreted and used in different ways in different parts of the world.

Focusing on the consumers of imported alcoholic beverages—and more specifically on one category, whisky users—thus enables me to describe the production of meaning in various contexts: multinational corporations, the films of the golden age of Greek cinema, and contemporary Athens and Skyros.

Although whisky in Greece is one of the most preferred alcoholic beverages, various other drinks can be offered, ordered, or consumed in a variety of social settings. Generally speaking, alcohol occupies a central position in the social lives of most Greeks, as in many other cultures. However, until recently in Greece, there was no culture of drinking alcohol without eating. This would take place only in cases of extreme poverty or in family rituals. The gradual establishment of imported beverages (and for our purposes, whisky) coincided with the development of a culture of drinking without eating or snacking, a definite influence from modern Western European/American modes of consumption. By following Scotch whisky, I wish to research the extent to which the habit of consuming Scotch has affected the cultural worlds of the users I encountered and, in general, to discover if the relationship between the cultural industry and the consumers has fulfilled the disciplining desire to become a modern European emancipated person.

To illustrate the cultural meanings of the beverage in the fieldwork locations of this ethnography, it is necessary to draw first a historical context of the importation of the beverage in Greece and its position in the postwar cultural industry. Scotch was firstly presented to the Greek audiences through commercial Greek cinema and later became widely promoted through marketing and advertising. As such, the modernization of Scotch became gradually associated with the high consumption levels of Greeks who were possibly understood as mere imitators of modern forms of consumption. Although this is a discussion that will be coming up in different parts of the book, the aim of the long ethnographic chapters is precisely the understanding of the alcohol modernity and the extent that Scotch is affecting the social life of my interlocutors.

Further, the ethnography investigates two settings where performances of whisky consumption are highly appropriated and used in various ways. By examining the self-representations and the outings of my networks in the center of Athens, I draw upon the specific types of consumption that are interrelated with whisky, its relationship with popular culture and the locations where the beverage is localized. Similarly, I follow the beverage on the island of Skyros, focusing on a network of laborers who express their masculinity through drinking whisky and who use whisky to perform the nondomesticated aspects of their values.

By choosing these two ethnographic settings, the book aims to examine the limits of transnational capitalism, modernization, Westernization, and symbolic domination. The ethnography of reception is not simply an effort to understand how appropriation and social practice intertwine but draws on the complicated fluxes of modern, national, local, and gender making of identity. The presentation of this multiplicity of possibilities in appropriation tests therefore the larger theoretical schemas that have been haunting anthropological and sociological theory since its foundations.

The specificity of each ethnographic case and the multiple layers of understanding required to asses the trajectories of tactical cultural appropriation would not be sufficient though without the short historical context. As a result, the book is dealing with two levels of analysis—one focusing on macro processes and history and the other on micro processes and ethnography.

The major point, however, is that through this study I am trying to understand the meanings and the processes of meaning formation in relation to the beverage on different levels and in different spaces. The major analytical concepts are (but are not limited to) trajectory, style, and consumption. These anthropological concepts are used with particular reference to their respective authors, Appadurai (1986), Ferguson (1999), and Miller (1995a, b). These concepts will be briefly discussed in this introduction; they will be unfolded and further elaborated in the following chapters.

Materiality

The first study along the contemporary lines of following a thing or a commodity was the influential work of Fernadno Ortiz on the history of tobacco and sugar in Cuba, *Contrapunteo Cubano del Tabaco y el Azúcar* (1940). This present study is also situated within the wider field of material culture and anthropology, which has produced a number of monographs on the world history of commodities and has stimulated research on the social lives of things. Investigations of the histories of sugar (Mintz 1985), alcohol (Douglas 1987), Coca-Cola (Foster 2008, Miller 1998), and tea (Moxham 2003) are only a few of the many studies produced in recent times. This interest has also pushed popular genre writers to investigate commodities such as cod and salt (Kurlansky 1997, 2002), potatoes (Zuckerman 1998), and tobacco (Gately 2002) in a so-called follow-the-thing approach (Marcus 1995).

This approach is a response to a growing literature on the effort to understand globalization and the fast movements of things across the globe (Foster 2008: 15). By following objects, anthropologists are able to construct and understand the networks created in motion as well as the shifting meanings of commodities in various cultural contexts. A large part of this discipline is based on prior work done on the social life of things and, more specifically, on the seminal essays found in the book *The Social Life of Things: Commodities in Cultural Perspective* (Appadurai 1986). A major contribution has been the introduction by Appadurai, who argues that the source of value of commodities can be found in the "things in motion" (Appadurai 1986: 5). The notion of "things in motion" includes the potentiality to transform during their social lives, and for this reason they have distinctive trajectories. Appadurai argues that tracing the course of these trajectories allows us to estimate the human agency that becomes materialized in these things.

One major advantage of this approach is the recognition that the same thing can potentially enter into a wide range of exchanges and practices, exactly as in the case of Scotch whisky in Greece. In this manner, this study follows three distinct trajectories of the object with a major aim of unraveling the human motivations, calculations, and intentions that activate and become embedded in Scotch.

Moreover, Appadurai's analysis of the commodity in *The Social Life of Things* demonstrates that the commodity is not defined by its materiality or production. On the contrary, the commodity is a stage that things come into and out of by changing their value and status in the process. By analyzing what kind of exchange commodity the exchange is, he explores the trajectories that things take when they enter and exit commodity status.

In this sense, things can become commodities, and commodities can move out of their commodity-hood. In parallel to Appadurai's approach, Kopytoff argues that we should also examine the career of the thing to be able to overcome the problematic relationship of thing and person (1986: 66). By tracking the culturally and historically specific "biographies of things," Kopytoff is able to define the ways that things become culturally constructed and are classified as things. Moreover, the analysis of Kopytoff on things is not only related to their commodity-hood and cultural signification. The author argues that things can be much more than indicators of social exchange and cultural meaning; things are able to constitute the social person (1986). In a similar vein, the last two trajectories of my analysis (on Skyros and Athens) research this possibility and inscribe the meaning of the trajectory with the cultural biography of things. Consequently, the meaning of trajectory in the course of this study is not only related to the work of Appadurai (and commodity-hood) but also to the implications of things in the constitution of social persons.

Another methodological strategy of following commodities has been the research on commodity chains or total trajectories (production, distribution, consumption), such as Ortiz's work in Cuba (1940) and Mintz's work on the sugar trade in the Caribbean (1985). Ortiz developed his book on Cuban history in two sections, the first of which is presented as an allegorical tale between tobacco and sugar and the second as a historical analysis of their development as the central agricultural products of Cuba. By treating both tobacco and sugar as commodities and as social vehicles in a historical process, Ortiz examined the changes in their roles within the context of transculturation, a critical term that he developed to understand the complex transformation of cultures in the context of colonial and imperial histories. Similarly, Mintz focused on sugar in a political and economic framework in the Caribbean. By tracing the commodity chain of sugar, Mintz analyzed the ways in which capitalism and colonialism influenced the Caribbean. Through the expansion of a system of agro-industry, a system of hierarchy was constructed. Such approaches have become valuable tools for analyzing economic changes that are related to wider processes.

A usual way of thinking about objects in Western Europe and North America has been the differentiation between things as objects and persons as subjects. Things are seen as matter that gain significance only through social actors while itself being denied a social life. This perspective has been criticized by a current thread of anthropology that places an emphasis on objectification, holding that "through making things people make themselves in the process" (Tilley 2001: 260). This particular perspective tries to transcend simple dualisms to place the emphasis on transformation and process.

Material culture studies investigate how things become important in an anthropological way (Miller 1998). Commodities that seem trivial and not central to social life might have influential effects in the lives of people. Things therefore become a central point of analysis for the study of culture. Interdisciplinary approaches are usual in such studies, combining a variety of disciplines, such as media, marketing, history, and social geography.

According to Tilley, "[M]aterial culture is a relational and critical category leading us to reflect on object-subject relations in a manner that has a direct bearing on our understanding of the nature of the human condition and the social being in the world" (2001: 258). The proliferation of studies of this kind has led to a wider trend toward an anthropology of material culture or materiality (Bampilis and Ter Keurs 2013, Buchli 2002, Miller 2005, Tilley 2006). Things have become a central point of analysis in any approach toward the cultural, and their trajectories have brought together religious, political, and social relationships. Studies range from ethnographic approaches to modernity (Miller 1994, 1995) to the politics of landscape (Bender 2001b), science and nature (Latour 1993), religion (Keane 2008, Spyer 1998), materiality and cultural heritage (Rowlands 2002), border fetishisms and trade (Spyer 1998, 2000), art (Küchler 2002), the senses (Seremetakis 1996), alienable and inalienable wealth (Weiner 1992, Yalouri 2001), the relationship between the local and the global (Appaduari 2001, Foster 2008, Miller 1995, Wilk 1995), and consumption (Miller 1994, 1995a, 1995b).

The example of whisky in Greece demonstrates the persistence of films, advertisements, and consumers in producing meanings, styles, or dreams through materiality. Furthermore, it is my intention to use materiality as a point of departure for an understanding of the "webs of significance" of my interlocutors (Geertz 2000: 3–32). The bottle of whisky is not only a thing but also a material with which consumers imagine their lives, express their taste for modernity, and negotiate their own styles. As such, the beverage connects, in various ways, networks that might look unconnected at first sight: films and marketing, consumers and multinational corporations, and an island and the center of a city.

Mass Commodities: The Things of Modernity

Various authors have demonstrated that "a singular modernity was never an empirical, historical fact except as a Eurocentric ideology of a universal teleology of the evolution of social systems" (Pels 2003: 29).[12] Therefore, theories that reduce human agency to a unilinear social model such as modernization or even globalization should be criticized and their inconsistencies should be exposed ethnographically (Ferguson 1999, Tsing 2000). An anthropology of modernity needs to account for both the ideological and the practical effects of modernity, whether one takes modernity to refer ideologically "to the global (but not hegemonic) spread of a consciousness of radical temporal rupture" (Pels 2003: 30) or, practically, to social changes understood by Foucault's theory of discipline, Marx's theory of commodity production and consumption, Durkheim's collective consciousness, or Weber's shells of rationalization and bureaucratization (Pels 2003: 30). Consequently, the study of mass commodities within the context of modernity has two dimensions: one refers to their ability to express the ethnographic perceptions about modernity and the other, a historical dimension, refers to their history of production, circulation, and consumption. It is the aim of this study to address both processes and discuss wider theoretical issues in relation to mass commodities.

The choice of this study to follow a mass-produced commodity was influenced by the intellectual paradigm of material culture studies that trace the social life of things in an effort to understand the processes of globalization and diffusion in late modernity as well as the position of specific commodities in the lives of people. However, the specific choice of whisky was based on the persistence of my interlocutors in making themselves through the consumption of the beverage and its appropriation in various contexts. I should, therefore, note that not all commodities are fetishized in the same way; they do not have the same symbolic efficacy or the same results. To make clear the key concepts employed, I should start with a short analysis of these discussions. This discipline is placed within a wider debate about commodities, which has a long history and strong arguments.

The two key texts that have formulated our understanding of commodities are *The Gift* by Mauss (1954) and "The Fetishism of Commodities" in Marx's *Kapital* (1867). Both texts investigate how specific objects incorporate a social life beyond their materiality and argue that the characteristics of commodities and gifts relate to social practice. More specifically, Marx argues that commodities are part of capitalist production and that they conceal the relationships of production, as they are able to stand apart from this sphere and relate to other commodities and consumers. This independent agency is expressed by Marx as fetishism. Fetishism arises out the peculiarity of capitalistic production and exchange and mystifies real social relations. As a result, commodities become objectifications of the social and material conditions in which they are produced. According to Keane, Marx's "fetish" is not a way of misunderstanding goods but a way that humans misunderstand themselves (Keane 1998: 13). In Keane's words, "[I]n the process of attributing life to things, they lose some of their own humanity and come to treat themselves as objects in turn" (Keane 1998: 13). Furthermore, Burke has proposed that fetishism is

> More than (but includes) the meanings invested in goods; it is also the accumulated power of commodities to actually constitute, organize and relate to people, institutions, and discourses, to contain within themselves the forms of consciousness through which capitalism manufactures its subjects. (1996: 5)

It is this agency in the form of fetishism that manifests itself in the conceptualizations about Scotch whisky in modern Greece. However, this fetish is intimately linked to the history of trade in twentieth-century Greece as well as to the establishment of transnational capitalism. As such the fetish expresses relations of power that might not be visible at first sight. The meanings invested in Scotch whisky by the scenarios of the cinematic genre and the cultural industry in general and more importantly the marginality of Athenian *bouzoukia* and Skyrian laborhood are clearly expressing its fetishization.

However, other forms of exchange (such as gift exchange) might represent different forms of relationship. For Mauss, gifts in certain sociocultural contexts carry a part of a person's identity and obligations of return to the giver. Gifts are viewed as objects that are not alienating as certain moral obligations and relationships exist between givers and receivers. Other institutions, such as the potlatch, are also understood as religious representations that are centered on specific forms of gifts that orient social relationships.

These two approaches led to further debates in anthropology and other social sciences focusing on the dichotomies of gift/commodity, use/exchange value, and inalienable/alienable wealth. More specifically, Mauss's concern with the gift in non-Western societies has affected cultural anthropology at large. Many anthropologists have tried to understand the societies they studied as gift-oriented, while the capitalistic Euro-American world was viewed as a commodity-based one (Gregory 1980). This distinction further influenced a view of gift economies as ruled by inalienable objects and commodity economies by alienable ones. However, the coexistence of both types of objects and relationships that is evident in most societies poses serious questions about such dichotomies.

The terms *use value* and *exchange value* were at the center of an anthropological theory of commoditization that reproduced the problematic dichotomies of Western and non-Western societies. Though Marx never argued clearly that these two terms described only capitalistic or precapitalistic societies, several anthropologists tried to understand gifts and commodities in relation to the production process. These views reproduced the idea that precapitalist societies are based on exchange and capitalistic societies on commodities (Taussig 1980).

Both views and dichotomies are highly problematic because they essentialize the gift in archaic societies and the commodity in the Western industrial world (Carrier 1995). This has further complications, as the gift/archaic/inalienable/use-value and commodity/Western/alienable/exchange-value distinctions are mixed up in most fields of research and usually by the same actors. As a result, the processes of alienation and inalienability or of gift and commodity exchange are evident in any given society and they exist side by side.

A major critique of both arguments is made by Appadurai in relation to Mauss's gift theory, which holds a central position in the anthropological analysis of commodities (1986: 3–63). Although many anthropologists have seen the commodity and the gift as separate and oppositional, Appadurai argues that commodities are not the monopoly of modern industrial economies and should be understood and examined within their exchangeability in each situation.[13] In this framework, the paths of objects and the diversions of objects from these paths are affected by strategies, while the production of their value is a political process. Appadurai concludes by suggesting that commodities exist in various forms of exchange and that their tournaments of value and calculated diversions lead to new paths of commodity flow, thus giving space to value shifts that express contestations of power, especially among the elites. Such contexts are the politics of diversion, display, knowledge, connoisseurship, and so on. Appadurai argues, in other words, that value is not intrinsic to things but is contextually defined through exchange.

Another major contribution to the debate is by Kopytoff, who argues that "the same thing may be treated as a commodity at one time and not at another. The same thing may, at the same time, be seen as a commodity by one person and as something else by another" (1986: 64). Therefore, commodities can be understood as things in a commodity phase, one stage of their careers in their social lives.

From their production to their consumption, objects might change state and are not necessarily considered commodities. Tracing the cultural biography of things is a way of understanding that things can have radically different meanings according to the stages they have reached in their "life-cycles" (Tilley 2001: 264). It is from this perspective that the career of whisky is traced in this book and the phases of its cultural biography are analyzed, especially when the impersonal commodity of whisky transforms into a drinking or birthday gift.

Weiss has further contributed to our understanding of the anthropology of commodities by arguing that although the collapsing of the opposition between gifts and commodities is valuable, it has obscured real differences in the potential of objects to embody value (Weiss 1996: 14). Among Haya, for example, there are specific practices that are intended to prevent certain objects being equated with other kinds of commodities. Certain objects have different potentialities in the lives of people and distinct social lives. Thus "all objects have the potential for alienation or personification, for diffusing or condensing value. But not all objects do so in the same way" (Weiss 1996: 14). Commodities and commoditization are used in such a way as to pinpoint processes of sociocultural change in relation to particular objects. Commoditization is understood as a process that creates the capacity for equivalence or commensurability of objects, similar to the qualities of money. However, it cannot be applied universally because the cultural conception of specific objects does not always allow them to be candidates for commoditization. In Weiss's view, commoditization includes not only market forces and diffusion of commodities but also the possibility to make any object into a commodity insofar as it is transacted, whether in an appropriate or inappropriate manner. From such a perspective, commoditization is not viewed as alienating the lived world, "for commoditization emerges within the process of inhabiting the world and commodities themselves derive their significance from being engaged in practices that make up this process" (1996: 8).

Anthropologists who have been more influenced by Marxist definitions of commoditization as a result of the influence of capitalistic processes use the term *resistance* (Comaroff 1985). Resistance is a way of localizing the commoditization processes under the gradual spread of capitalistic values and has to be understood contextually. It is a process of rejection when commoditization is at work and is demonstrated by a variety of ethnographic cases. Resistance can take the form of gift giving or the transformation of money into local cosmological systems, as most cases in the edited work of Bloch and Parry (1989) also describe. From this perspective, money is seen as a threat and as such has to be transformed into something different through kinship and ritual.

As Burke has argued, scholars who have studied Marx have followed "an interpretative tradition that sees fetishism as a process by which 'false needs' are made and 'real' relations concealed by the conscious agency of the ruling classes" (1996: 6). This present study differentiates itself from such a tradition and is positioned within the field of material culture that places emphasis on the process of cultural appropriation and self-creation. Moreover, by following Burke (1996) and Weiss

(1996), I argue that Marx's definition of fetishism could be widened and should not be confined to the social relations of production alone. Other relations of domination are also concealed and differ by place, time, and consumer (consumers having different cultural backgrounds). As such, the notion of commodity fetishism can be extended to incorporate those social relations that are reified through exchange.

However, use values are socially and culturally constructed. Within capitalism, such use values have complex meanings that move beyond their exchange value, and their cultural position might be a consequence of noneconomic factors. Therefore, objects do not arrive in the market as blank signifiers to receive their use values, but they are also influenced by specific cultural patterns.

Moreover, by following Miller (1987) and Weiss (1996), I argue that the potentiality for personification and alienation is inherent in the process of objectification. However, objectification is not inherently alienating. That means that commodities in the context of hegemonic capitalism do not necessarily lead to alienation (Miller 1987). On the contrary, commodities might be entwined with the persons who posses them, and they might be associated with processes of personification (Weiss 1996). Webb Keane, for example, has argued that anthropologists should "take seriously the materiality of signifying practices and the ubiquity and necessity of conceptual objectification as a component of human action and interaction." (2003: 223). In this sense, he suggests that objectification is integral to human activity because "far from being only a disease of social science [objectification] is the very politics of everyday awareness and interaction" (2003: 239). In that sense, objectification is neither good nor bad, not necessarily negative and alienating; the results of objectification depend on human action.

Moreover, fetishism in a Marxist sense does not correspond to the complexity of value formation of the commodity in the modern capitalistic system. As Foster has argued, value formation is a process by which various agents evaluate a product. This

> [i]nvolves more than the labor of producers; it requires the (evaluative) work of consumers as well. Value creation occurs as a product circulates through the multiple hands of both producers and consumers. Likewise, the extraction of surplus value requires more than deploying the labor power of wage workers; it also requires capturing the use values attributed to products by consumers. (2008: xviii)

Similarly, Greek cinema and marketing have overcommunicated a fetishization of whisky and have produced various sets of meanings, consciously or unconsciously targeting their audiences. Although on Skyros and in Athens commoditization has been more evident in recent decades, money and commodities have long careers in these areas as a result of a general monetary system that existed in the Byzantine and later Ottoman empires. Within this context, commodities might be transformed into "inalienable wealth" (Weiner 1992) as well as payment for labor. The commercialization of the economy and the advent of multinational capitalism brought new branded products and alcoholic beverages which, depending on the context, became appropriated. Cigarettes and alcoholic beverages especially became central symbols of style employed in social life and were embraced as hallmarks of modernity. To understand these processes, I now turn first to an anthropological understanding of consumption.

Commodity Consumption and Globalization

The consumption of commodities characterizes commoditization and the spread of capitalistic values, and as such it has been portrayed as a negative and non-socializing process. As Miller has argued, already from the 1950s commodities were seen by various anthropologists as changing forces for culture and local cosmologies (1995a). The study of commodity consumption as an anthropological subject has resulted in a transformation of the discipline because it has brought various new arguments and debates. Modernity is no longer understood as a force of cultural extinction but rather a process of objectification that results in the appropriation of things (Miller 1995b).

Consumption is intertwined with globalization primarily because globalization has been thought of as McDonaldization (Ritzer 2004), which entails the following: a world connected by trade and information technologies (Barber 1995: 4); a global village that consumes similar images and shapes similar identities (McLuhan 1964); a process of "time-space compression" with a major goal of speeding up globally the production and consumption of transnational capitalism (Harvey 1989: 147); and processes of disembedding, which enables the circulation of commodities, the proliferation of consumption of the same products, and reembedding that makes meaningful the appropriation of commodities (Giddens 1991: 21). As Inda and Rosaldo have put it,

> Globalization can be seen as referring to those spatial-temporal processes, operating on a global scale, that rapidly cut across national boundaries, drawing more and more of the world into webs of interconnection, integrating and stretching cultures and communities across space and time, and compressing our spatial and temporal horizon. It points to a world in motion, to an interconnected world, to a shrinking world. (2008: 12)

Commodities such as Coca-Cola and whisky can be found almost anywhere in the world; music is becoming increasingly globalized; youth movements follow similar styles; and issues of global meaning, such as the environment, circulate around the world. At the same time, the Internet and communications technology, airplanes, and fast trains have made it possible to communicate and travel anywhere in the world, at any time. There are fears of an intensification of a global culture and a prevalence of one homogenous modernity of capitalism, individualism, and state power (Erickson 1999: 297).

The cultural economy of globalization has been viewed in the light of the theory of cultural imperialism and the homogenization of the world. These scenarios claim that "the spread of American/Western cultural goods is leading to the absorption of peripheral cultures into a homogenized global monoculture of consumption" (Inda and Rosaldo 2008: 16). Furthermore, it has been claimed that globalization is a Western global hegemony that designates a unification of styles, attitudes, institutions, ideas, values, and goods (Inda and Rosaldo 2008: 17). Goods such as branded clothes and beverages are circulating, appropriated and consumed by more and more people; music, films, and news have global audiences; and international institutions such as the Olympic Games or the International Court of Justice have a global reach.

According to some authors, mass consumption in this global world is nothing but a consumerism that assimilates different cultures and turns them into models of profit (Baudrillard 1990, Bauman 2000, Featherstone 1990). Other authors have argued that globalization is instead a double-sided process that on the one hand promotes global identities and creates consumers, but on the other produces difference and localization or "flow and closure" (Appadurai 1996, 2001, Meyer and Geschiere, 1999, Miller 1995b). According to Tilley,

> The effects of globalization have in fact turned out to be cultural differentiation, 'revivals' and inventions of ethnicity. It has been shown that localized processes intersect in an increasingly creolized and hybridized world of people and experiences in which a search for cultural 'authenticity' seems particularly fruitless. (2001: 267)

In recent years anthropological studies have shown a world where globalization results in reinventions of ethnicity, cultural differentiation and hybrids or "bricolage" rather than well defined homogenized entities (Appadurai 2001, Geschiere 1999, Miller 1998, Wilk 1995). The dialectics of "flow and closure," as Meyer and Geschiere have put it, are simply an aspect of globalization in which goods and people might circulate more easily but identities tend to be imagined and reproduced much more as closed entities (1999: 2).

In addition, Hannerz has argued that here is a new space of interaction among cultures, a "global ecumene" (Hannerz 1989, 1996): a space where flows from the center to the periphery come together, a process carried out by cosmopolitans who travel and live around the world. Such cosmopolitans, as they are on the move, bring along their cultural frameworks and these influence as well as integrate with other cultures.

In terms of economic capital, globalization has resulted in a spatialization of the world economy and, more particularly, in movement that occurs across national and political boundaries (Trouillot 2003: 48). This internationalization is nothing new (Bampilis 2012), but the speed of the circulation of capital, commodities, and markets is surprising and unique. Capital, labor, and consumer markets create entangled spatialities and shape the world economy. Furthermore, the domination of financial capital shapes the main directions and trends globally and leads to increasing inequalities across countries. As Appadurai has noted, globalization indicates the circulation of people, capital, images, and concepts across the globe along certain trajectories (1996). These trajectories (scapes) do not extend to all parts of the world, but their increasing presence characterizes global processes. Financescapes, for example, include capital flows; ethnoscapes include migrant flows; mediascapes include media and film flows; technoscapes are about technology flows; and, finally, ideoscapes relate to the flow of state or subaltern ideologies. Such flows constitute paths in which imagined communities or networks influence their own sense of belonging and social identity.

One of Appadurai's most important points is to do with de-territorialization, the idea that space has become less important and that this has brought about new sociocultural concepts. As Harvey has argued, it was within the twentieth century that the compressions of space and time as well as the fast movement of people, capital, and technologies came to influence our existence to a great extent (1989). The flow of ideas and values around the world, especially through print capitalism but also through other media, has also resulted in nationalism and the creation of imagined communities (Anderson 1983). It is through these processes that identities such as ethnicity, gender, and class are redefined and negotiated on different levels. Consequently, ethnoscapes and mediascapes with their interdependence on imagination have become the most decisive trajectories of globalization as they construct and reproduce social and cultural identities (Appadurai 1996).

A series of studies have tried to illustrate the process of the indigenization, or localization of objects. Abu-Lughod has described how a scene from an American soap opera can be more relevant to villagers in Egypt than one based on the issues with which local elites are concerned (1995). Michaels has demonstrated how Hollywood videotapes among Warlpiri Aborigines are perceived in relation to the local meanings of fiction and how, as a consequence, interpretations are highly localized (Michaels 2002). In a similar manner Wilk has examined the production of local difference on a global level through beauty contests (1995). He states, "[W]e are not all becoming the same, but we are portraying, dramatizing and communicating our differences to each other in ways that are more widely intelligible" (1995: 118). Miller has argued in his study of Coca-Cola in Trinidad that in local perception the drink is part of a wider classification of black drinks and as such has come to represent Black African identity (1997). Research in East Asia and Moscow has demonstrated how adaptations of McDonalds suit local circumstances (Watson 1997, Caldwell 2008). O'Hanlon's research in New Guinea argues that foreign advertisements or products are used to express issues of particular local character (1993), and research in Nigeria has demonstrated how Bollywood films have shaped other genres, such as Nollywood (Larkin 2008). Another important contribution is Gandoulou's study (1984) of the Congolese sapeurs in Paris and their consumption habits. Such migrants manage to reach Paris after many difficulties, and once they arrive, they work to collect a large amount of money to be spent on expensive fashion clothes. The clothes will be worn later on the streets of Brazzaville to express status in a country where the sapeurs have no access to power. This conspicuous consumption has been characterized as "a way of challenging power by overcommunicating one's own superiority and success" (Eriksen 2001: 308).

Consumption has been analyzed as part of a cultural perspective in opposition to the homogenization, Americanization, or commoditization argument (Appadurai 1996). According to Appadurai, "what these arguments fail to consider is that at least as rapidly as forces from various metropolises are brought into new societies they tend to become indigenized in one or the other way" (1996: 32). The views criticized also tend to overlook the fact that Westernization or Americanization is only one perspective in a world in which a politics of cultural assimilation has been promoted by states such as China, Indonesia, and Brazil and smaller states such as Greece and Turkey. Anti-consumption movements coexist with organizations that protect the rights of the consumer. Therefore, there are reverse processes, and for that reason it is useful to study the perceptions of consumption as different cultural perspectives—an anthropological task.

Along the same line of thought, Miller argues for an anthropology of consumption and commodities to avoid essentialization of these categories (1995a: 141–161). Miller suggests that to moralize in relation to commodities and commoditization is simplistic and that a closer anthropological examination should take place while keeping a critical stance vis-à-vis theories of modernization. In much ethnography, the authenticity of the so-called other has been represented as existing far from the noise and pollution of consumption. Miller, however, draws attention to "the equality of genuine relativism that makes none of us a model of real consumption and all of us creative variants of social processes based around the possession and use of commodities" (1995a: 144). Thus, the examination of commodities within the context of consumption should be understood as a part of mass consumer societies that leads to a heterogeneous comparative modernity instead of a global homogenization (1995b).

This view privileges an anthropological approach to global commodities. The most important implication is that actors/consumers are not portrayed as passive beings who imitate consumer practices and consumption is conceptualized as secondary production (de Certeau 1984). The idea of using things creatively, dressing them with new cultural meanings, and making them at home (or not) has important implications for a theory of commodities and globalization. Furthermore, anthropologists recognize that commodities have cultural biographies even if they are mass-produced, and as such they enter into a commodity phase and come out of it again (Kopytoff 1986). This idea of Kopytoff's makes clear the qualities of things even when they move into global trajectories and contextualizes the relationship of the so-called other with imported commodities that has often been viewed as problematic.

Whereas Miller puts forward a view of consumption based on creative freedom, Foster is more careful to differentiate his own approach from Miller's (2008: 8). He claims that consumption within the globalization process should be understood as a creative adaptation by which people make themselves, under circumstances of not entirely free choice. As he states, "[T]he challenge for anthropologists considering the relationship among globalization, commodity consumption, and culture is to hold world historical structures and contingent, creative agency—as well as pessimism and optimism—in tension with each other" (Foster 2008: 10). My study also avoids viewing the processes of globalization as a naïve celebration of the creativity of people in localizing imported things and tries to take a critical stance toward what the terms *local* and *global* mean and under what conditions they are produced. Although the establishment of multinational capitalism and the proliferation of advertisements might influence consumers, the media projections of the cultural industry are not always aimed at a certain result (as in Greek cinema) and are not intended to produce consumers and sell the product. Neither are they interested in creating bonds and trust with the consumers. The genealogy of whisky in Greek media demonstrates how fetishism was reproduced in Greek films.

My research identifies clearly with Burke's (1996) and Weiss's (1996) argument that the reception and use-value of a certain product are influenced by the culture of a group. Burke's point, for example, is demonstrated by his research on Lifebuoy soap and Pond's lotion, products that have value in the cultural conceptualization of aesthetics and hygiene. It is this point that makes us think that commodities should not only be understood in their life cycles or career but that they also include (or not) a set of meanings historically accumulated as categories. As a result, "[d]ifferent commodities thus have different histories and require different accountings, both of prior meanings that shape their reception and of the competing supply—side interests that promote their production and consumption" (Foster 2008: 14).

This study is also set within a general framework of an anthropology of consumption (Miller 1995a, Appadurai 2005) and shares the view that "today consumption is at least as important as the practice through which people potentially make themselves (Miller 2005: 44). As Appadurai has stated, the discipline is in need of an equivalent sociology of consumption to the one that Marx gave us for production (2005: 61), because classes are no longer created on the basis of production alone but also on the basis of consumption. In modern mass consumer societies, where people face the alienability of production under objectification, consumers appropriate commodities to make sense of their own self.

Performances of Consumption in Relation to Style

In his study of workers in the copper belt of Zambia, Ferguson used an interesting term to understand social and cultural differences among people residing in the same settlements and cities (1999: 93–122). As he stated,

> The concept of style can serve as a quite general analytic tool by being extended to include all modes of action through which people place themselves and are placed into social categories. Specifically I use the term cultural style to refer to practices that signify difference between social categories. (1999: 95)

Style in Ferguson's formulation refers to the accomplished performative qualities of the actor and as such has to be understood in the context of performance theory. For example, the ability to shift from a local dialect when at home to a widely used accent elsewhere expresses the learned capacity of the actor to negotiate and embody such performances.

Ferguson's approach enables a study to research commonalities and differences in the same group and to make sense of the shared consumption patterns in stylistic terms, relating to the performances and the practices associated with consumption. As he notes,

> Conceiving of cultural style in this way thus means significantly bracketing off, or at least holding open, questions of identities or commonalities of values, beliefs, worldview, or cognitive orientation within stylistic categories. That members of culturally-stylistically distinctive subgroups of a society share such commonalities is an unexamined assumption of great deal of subculture theory in anthropology and sociology. Such groups *may* of course have such commonalities. But the assumption that they *must*, or that shared experiences and values are logically or temporally prior to stylistic practice, is unwarranted and has caused an enormous amount of confusion. It is a way of turning specific shared practices into a posited shared "total way of life," "culture," or "way of thought," a way of converting particular stylistic practices into badges of underlying and essential identities. (1999: 97)

Although the similarities of consumers of whisky in Skyros and Athens are evident in terms of style, the beverage is intertwined with mentalities and practices that are more distinctive in the two settings. Ideas about popular music, entertainment, and Scotch whisky in Athens, for example, bring together different kinds of people; on Skyros, ideas about shepherhood and laborhood are expressed in the consumption of alcoholic beverages and, more importantly, Scotch. As such, style expresses the consumption habits of the interlocutors.

The style of the male interlocutors is also related to an expressive masculinity in both settings. This masculinity and its relationship to whisky are further elaborated in expressive forms of Greek contemporary popular music. Style is able to connect the categories of gender and consumption. In the words of Butler, "consider gender as a corporeal style, an 'act,' as it were, which is both intentional and performative, where 'performative' suggests a dramatic and contingent construction of meaning" (Butler 1990: 139, quoted in Ferguson 1999: 99). In this view, gendered style is an enduring practice that has to be understood as more dynamic than essentialized understandings of gender and expressing the strategies and conscious negotiation of social identity, without leaving aside unconscious learned and embodied habits.

This view implies that styles have continuity over time and that long and difficult processes are involved in acquiring or rejecting them. Developing a style is a long, sometimes painful activity that requires devotion and concentration. The cultivation of a style encompasses ideological, aesthetic, and corporeal qualities, and style is an asset or an investment that relates to the immediate social and economic contexts (Ferguson 1999: 100).

Sustaining a style is therefore partly an economic issue, and as such, style is limited to the resources of the actor. As Ferguson states, "cultivating a viable style thus requires investment, in a very literal sense, and the difficulties of cultivating more than one stylistic mode at the same time are formidable. Economic constraints thus work in favor of stylistic specialization" (1999: 100). This aspect of developing a style is immediately related to consumption, as several times when I asked specific interlocutors why they were not regular drinkers of whisky, they replied that they could not afford it. Similarly, the consumption of whisky in Athens as part of leisure in music venues with contemporary live Greek popular music is a practice that not all persons are able to afford. In such a context, consumption is understood as a major part of sustaining a viable style and, to expand on Miller's (1998) idea, a way of making oneself at home with style.

Finally, the localization process should not be examined as if it were an abstract absorption of the global into the local, as already noted. Localization is a process of locale creation, and any appropriation is a form of style negotiation in a given context. Style can therefore be a useful analytical tool for studying commodities.

The Cultural Context of Consuming Alcohol in Greece

Recent History

During the twentieth century, the development of the Greek economy was based on liberal ideas and (especially after World War II) on the foreign aid, foreign investment, and remittances that flowed into Greece. However, the end of World War II in 1945 was not received with the same enthusiasm in Greece as in the rest of Europe. The civil war between liberals and communists continued until 1950 and resulted in the killing of thousands of people. The postwar reconstruction plan was pursued at the beginning by Britain and carried on by the United States. This had a destructive effect on the communist groups, but, conversely, a long development plan helped the country's economy to start anew. That affiliation placed Greece within the sphere of Western European capitalism until 1990, far from Eastern European communist influence (Close 2005: 18). The British and American partnership deeply influenced the political life of the country from the end of World War II, when it became dominated by a powerful king and a politically active army. This form of democracy was bound to collapse in 1967 when the so-called colonel's regime took over. This Cold War dictatorship brought a deep political crisis, oppressed the people, and remained in power until 1974.

The period between 1952 and 1972 can be described as one of the most successful economically, with sustained growth and low inflation (Koliopoulos and Veremis 2002: 172, Stathakis 2007). From 1950 to 1974, Greece developed economically in the style of Western European liberalism. The majority of the population moved into cities, migration increased, production and consumption rose considerably, and Greek industrialism was established. Although these processes were received positively, they had shattering effects for rural Greece. Although a large part of social life had formerly been connected with rural production and relatively large communities, from the 1950s, large populations left their villages and islands to go the city. This was the period when most Greeks became acquainted with imported commodities and consumerism.

In terms of social change, the period of the dictatorship (1967–1974) was the most decisive. According to Stathakis, the Greek economy shifted to a service-oriented form, which came after a long period of agriculture-based economy (2007: 7). Internal migration intensified, and within a few years, Athens was booming into a huge metropolis. This change had devastating effects on the countryside, which was left without resources and employment. The city became the center of Greece, economically and in terms of population. This period was also when the new Greek consumer society emerged, with the ideal example being the first supermarket, Sklavenitis in Piraeus St, in 1970 (Stathakis 2007: 12). New products such as Coca-Cola, cars, and blue jeans were massively imported and consumed by the emerging low-income professionals who migrated to Athens.

The petrol crisis of 1973–1974 impacted on the economy, and during the dictatorship, an economic recession occurred. The succeeding Karamanlis government was faced with many problems and adopted a state intervention program to manage the crisis and create a healthy economic environment. Despite the fact that Karamanlis's program did not manage to solve Greece's economic problems, he succeeded in gaining Greek accession to the European Economic Community (EEC) in 1980 (Koliopoulos and Veremis 2002: 175). After 1974, a new period began in Greece that became known as postauthoritarian or, in Greek, *metapolitevsi* (Close 2005: 18–23). The decline of the dictatorship and the arrival of Karamanlis, the first postauthoritarian prime minister, brought new hope and faith in democracy among the majority of Greek citizens. The democratization process resulted in the gradual control of political power by the parliament, the absence of any political influence from the army, and the abolition of the monarchy after a referendum. Democratic citizenship, political freedom, a renegotiation of the relationship between church and state, a new educational system, independent universities, and independent local government were among the most important postauthoritarian policies.

In 1981, the socialistic policies of PASOK (Pan-Hellenic Socialistic Party) under the government of Andreas Papandreou ameliorated the lives of many women and absorbed a large number of leftists who had been politically marginal until this period. Although mass consumption began during the 1970s, it was not until the beginning of the 1980s that it rose considerably. Despite the controversial mixed socialistic and liberal economic policies of PASOK, middle-class incomes rose. Moreover, PASOK had come into power with the slogan "Greece belongs to the Greeks" as an answer to Karamanlis' "Greece belongs to the West" (Clogg 1992: 179), and thus it differentiated its position from European capitalism.

With time, the large political gap between left and right diminished while the center of power remained with two parties. The political debates during the postauthoritarian period (1974–1989) continued to be structured as left-wing and right-wing arguments, especially in relation to the economy. However, both sides agreed that a transfer of power from the state to the other constitutional bodies should take place. These changes were possible in the last year of *metapolitefsi* in 1989 that resulted in the free establishment and distribution of a private press and private television channels, along with the transfer of power to the Greek parliament, the Greek justice system, local government, and independent state and EEC institutions (Close 2005: 22). In the marketplace, the end of *metapolitefsi* resulted in a new form of neoliberalism under the auspices of the EEC and later the European Union (EU). Most members of the Greek parliament agreed on liberalization of the market forces without the patronage relationships between state and market agents that had been evident in former times. Scotch whisky, for example, had a huge tarrif as an imported good, as it was taxed until the 1980s, as luxury good, and since the EU ascension, such tariffs had to be lowered. In addition, the decline of socialism brought insecurity to left-wing members of parliament and weakened their resistance. The neoliberal policies of the 1990s finalized the economic structures of the country and, despite the fact they had a large negative impact on middle- and lower-class Greeks, stabilized inflation. That success met the requirements for EU membership, and Greece was admitted to the Eurozone on 19 June 2000 (Close 2005: 20). According to Clogg, "an unspoken assumption underlying the enthusiasm of many Greeks for Europe was that membership would somehow place the seal of the legitimation on their country's somewhat uncertain European identity" (1992: 177). Although Greece is geographically part of Europe, its identity has been highly debated, as various authors have demonstrated (Skopetea 1992, Herzfeld 1989). As Nikos Dimou notes, "the roots of Greek unhappiness are two national inferiority complexes. One temporal—in the face of the ancestors, and one spatial—in the face of 'Europeans.' Maybe unjustifiable, but all the same real, complexes" (Dimou 1976: 34, quoted in Petridou 2001: 40).

The fact that both middle-class incomes and consumption rose in the 1980s does not explain people's preference for whisky, imported drinks, and Western consumer goods in general. The expression *megla* is associated with the mentality of consuming imported goods. In particular, this term refers to a product that is of high quality, and *megla* effectively means made in England. In popular conceptualizations, when something is made in the United Kingdom, it is viewed as having high quality and usually also as expensive. However, as the example of whisky will demonstrate, the place of production can be misinterpreted and a product of Scottish origin can be conceptualized as American or Western.

Moreover, the belief that any foreign commodity is much better than a Greek one is prevalent among many Athenians. More particularly, middle- and higher-class Athenians prefer to spend money on imported products, which are available in most neighbourhoods of Athens. This mentality is related to a long history of imported products in Greece and can be traced back to the first high-class import shops in Athens, such as the famous department store Sidney Noel in the 1920s.

The mania for imported foreign commodities was so apparent in the 1980s that the Greek government decided to start a campaign against the consumption of imported commodities to support the consumption of Greek products. In 1984, the Association for the Promotion of Greek Products along with the Ministry of Economics started a campaign with the slogan *o epimenon elli-nika,* meaning "s/he who insists in a Greek way." The government's realization that Greeks were living in a consumer society, which would gradually have to follow EEC guidelines on free trade along with the increased consumption of imported products, raised fears about the future of Greek products. In the advertisements, the word *elli-nika* was strategically spelled in that way, meaning not only *Greek* but also *winner.* The television advertisement of that campaign presented a famous actor claiming that he wore and consumed only Greek products (see figure 0.1). At the end of the advertisement he would ask, "Who am I? Am I imported?" (*"Ma pios ime, isagomenos ime?"*). His role was intended as a representation of the new low/middle class Athenians, but the advertisement's message was much wider and nationally encompassing. The overall conclusion was that the consumer had to insist on consuming Greek products, which would result in the

Figure 0.1. Epimenon Ellinika, "The One Who Insists on Greek" campaign (1984) (Source: Ministry of Interior).

victory of the underdeveloped Greek economy. The advertisements, presented in all media, pointed out the preference of Greeks for foreign goods and their *xenomania,* a word that expresses the Greek practice of "adopting foreign products, ideas and manners and attributing to them superior value" (Petridou 2001: 43). This mentality is evident in the lifestyle of many Greeks who prefer to identify with imported products, international cuisine, ethnic music, or American clothes. Therefore, the notion of the West is bound up with certain consumption patterns that have emerged over the last decades, and the West is a concept that carries diverse meanings and modes of representing one's identity. The concept of being modern is almost synonymous with the West and often carries with it certain national concepts that are expressed through the localization of products in popular culture or media (as it will be demonstrated).

In general the fascination with globalized commodities and products that might be conceptualized as Western or European can also be understood under the theory of *disemia* developed by Herzfeld. According to Herzfeld, Greek identity is based on two representations, the Hellenic and the Romaic (1989). The Hellenic identity has been projected toward the world situated outside Greece since the creation of the nation state and is related to the ancient Greek heritage. The Romaic is the internal aspect of Greek culture, and it is associated with the history of Byzantium, Greek-speaking orthodoxy as part of the Ottoman Empire, and orthodoxy in general. It is not accidental that the opposition of West and East has been central to Greek modernity. The ambivalence of Greek identity and the paradox "of being the ancestor of Europe" and at the same time "situated at its margins" (1989: 1–27), as Herzfeld has pointed out, has been a continuing argument in various discourses in Greece. However, the effort to modernize Greece has been based solely on representations of Westernization and Europeanization, processes that are expected to develop the country economically and increase the standard and the quality of living. From the beginning of the Greek enlightenment, the West has been closely associated with the civilized and the modern and the East with backwardness (Skopetea 1992). These conceptualizations of modernity in contemporary Greece should be understood in relation to Europe and the West. Greece has been placed at the periphery of the modernizing processes taking place in Europe, including the Renaissance and the Reformation, and as a result did not become modernized and progressive. As a result, modern Greek civil society was seen as in need of Europeanization because Europeanization is taken as synonymous with modernization and progress (Kontogiorgis 2006: 71). Generally speaking, the modern nation-state was seen as in need of modernity to be a state and in need of tradition to be a nation, a fundamental paradox of modernity (Herzfeld 2005). These are views that Greeks share widely in contemporary Greece.

Europeanization has been a long process from the beginning of the century, as is evident in various spheres of social life such as literature and food.[14] The famous cookbook by Tselementes Europeanized Greek gastronomy (Bakalaki 2000: 76), and Delmouzos stated in 1927 that

> Progress is to follow anything new in the European market, whether it suits us or not, whether our stomachs can digest it or not. Like this we get modernized; progress and modernization become one thing … as far as bringing from the West all the superior elements of its civilization even if we cannot assimilate them. (Alexandros Delmouzos 1927: 54 quoted in in Tziovas 2006: 56)

As Tziovas demonstrates, it was in the period between the two world wars that the terms *modern* and *modernization* were adopted into Greek discourse and came to express a wider debate in Greek society about the dichotomies of Greek and European, foreign and familiar, or old and new (2006: 20–25). This debate was to influence further the well-known literary generation of the 1930s, who imagined itself as the carrier of national visions and the gatekeepers of the modern Greek language, the demotic language known as *dimotiki*.

In contemporary Greece, European images of modernity continue to carry powerful associations. On Lesbos island, for example, the French restaurant was characterized as a successful Western-style one and quickly became a successful point of socialization for middle- and higher-class islanders (Bakalaki 2000: 76). In general the consumption of what is considered Western has been a form of symbolic capital (Bakalaki 2000: 76) and has resulted in the popularization of Western things among most social strata. This intensification of value formation in relation to imagined Western products has characterized the postauthoritarian period and the last two decades. More importantly, these processes of consumption should be placed in the general context of EU integration, which is related to political, economic, and consumerist agendas as well as market imperatives (Yiakoumaki 2006: 415).

All of these subjects that I have briefly discussed here will reemerge in later parts of the book and will be continuously analyzed. The aforementioned topics—the associations of the West with the modern, advertising, the media, and the political and economic situation—and their relationships to the consumption of alcoholic drinks will be central throughout most chapters. It will become clear that these larger processes that I have mentioned have been influencing the social life within the settings of Athens and Skyros and have also affected the ways in which whisky, imported drinks, and consumption goods in general are conceived and consumed.

Drinking Alcohol in Greek Ethnography

Although alcoholic beverages are not necessary for human survival as food is, they constitute one of the most culturally significant and social objects in the lives of humans. In many ways, they are the glue of society. As such, the ideas that relate to their consumption and the choices that people make express larger issues at stake. For example, Christianity embraces wine as a holy ingredient that transforms into the blood of Christ (Iossifides 1992), and Scottish mythology associates whisky (*usquebaugh* in Gaelic or *aqua vitae* in Latin) with the prolongation of life, a sort of panacea.

One of the first books in anthropology that focuses on alcohol consumption from a socially constructive perspective is Douglas's *Constructive Drinking* (1987). In that edited work, some authors stress that alcohol might construct the world as it is (Gusfield 1987), whereas others focus on the ways in which drinks create an ideal world (Bott 1987). In particular, Gusfield stresses that a change in drink also represents a shift in time and space. In Gusfield's analysis, coffee, for example, is usually related to a working environment whereas whisky is part of leisure.

The view of alcohol drinking as constitutive of commensality has influenced most of the ethnographers of modern Greece (Cowan 1990, Damer 1988, Herzfeld 1985, Gefou-Madianou 1992, Papataxiarchis 1991). As Cowan has stated, "A centrally important context within contemporary Greek society for expressions of personhood, both as ideally conceived and as practically negotiated, is that of commensality, the sociable sharing of food and drink" (1990: 182). More importantly, the analysis of the drinking of alcohol found in the ethnographies of Greece is rarely outside of the context of commensality (except Abatzi 2010, Papagaroufali 1992, Papataxiarchis 1989), to the extent that Damer claims after his research in Sfakia that "as elsewhere in Greece, alcohol is never drunk without food" (1989: 298). Even if that is not true, it seems that a part of the anthropology of Greece would like to imagine Greeks as traditional beings who exchange Greek-produced food and drinks only commensally. Although a general criticism of folklore studies has questioned the role of that discipline in the essentialization of national tradition (Herzfeld 1982), it is worth stating that the role of anthropology in such processes of objectification has been neglected. For example, the major focus on Greek alcoholic products—despite the fact that people make themselves through various imported beverages—has produced rather contradictory understandings of contemporary Greece. In the literature, most of the drinks in focus are *ouzo, raki,* and wine. New modes of consumption, such as drinking without eating, are rarely mentioned, and alcohol is rarely approached in relation to excess or excessive behavior despite the fact that in certain contexts this connection is evident (Abatzi 2004).

Another problem of various approaches in Greece in relation to alcohol is the clear separation of the drinking gift, or *kerasma,* and the commodity, or *emporefsimo agatho.* Usually, local, nonimported beverages are portrayed as drinking gifts (Damer 1988, Herzfeld 1985, Gefou-Madianou 1992, Papataxiarchis 1991) versus the imported beverages/commodities. This division has further influenced two more ethnographic dichotomies, namely, small community/city, local beverages/imported beverages, and inalienable/alienable relationships.

The focus of many anthropologists of Greece has been on gender and alcohol in a socially constructive commensal perspective (Gefou-Madianou 1992, Papataxiarchis 1991, Papagaroufali 1992).[15] Papataxiarchis and Gefou-Madianou have stressed the point that drinking, as a social practice in Greece, is a space of gender negotiation. In particular, Gefou-Madianou has illustrated how the consumption of sweet wine and retsina unites or excludes men and women. According to her account, "Wine creates boundaries between genders, separating them from one another, and defines the nexus between the mundane and spiritual worlds. It also indicates the unification of the genders" (1992: 124). The sphere of retsina reproduces masculine styles by excluding women from its production and consumption. As a result, women negotiate their own position with the production of sweet red wine and the offering of it to men. It follows that red wine transforms female sexuality to fertility and reproduces the household and the community.

Papataxiarchis has pointed out the importance of drinking gifts or treats in contemporary Greece (1991, 1998). In his study of the coffeehouse, he examines *raki* as a real gift that might not include the Maussian obligation to return it. *Kerasma* does not follow the calculations of daily life and is a way to express the real self. This is the reason that the men of the *kafenion* view *kerasma* as a right, not as an obligation.[16] These drinking practices take place among men and create a certain emotional atmosphere that corresponds to Turner's communitas. This kind of real gift is an opportunity to share the same gender identity. Moreover, the real "friends of the heart" are those who will enter into *kefi*, an emotional state of freedom that suggests "an ideal mood of joy and relaxation achieved when the worries and concerns of this world are banished" (1991: 170–171). In this context, *raki* is a major ingredient that initiates this transformation of sentiment and reproduces masculinities.

Cowan is more interested in the reproduction of gender identity through dancing, but states that "gender difference is codified through the foods and drinks that appear in these everyday exchanges. The association of men with pungent and salty substances and women with sweet substances is pervasive" (1990: 183). These drinks are referred to as "sharp, strong, red wine" or *ouzo* for men. *Ouzo* in particular is central to an understanding of male conviviality and is opposed to the womanly drink, the category of sweet brandies or sweet wine. Men drink *ouzo* with salty foods, whereas sweet liqueurs are offered by women to women accompanied by sweets.

In a recent ethnography, Sutton has investigated how food and commensality are intertwined with memory (2001). More specifically, Sutton argues that the stories of Kalymnian islanders in relation to past, present, and future events construct this relationship. The act of eating and drinking are understood as embodied practices that through synesthesia (the intersection of sensory experiences) become meaningful entities that express social, local, and national identities, especially among migrants living abroad. The author contrasts the foreign exotic foods as a result of globalization to local products and concludes that they are not integrated or associated with memory in the same way (2008). However, Sutton does not sufficiently analyze the imported exotic commodities or their disconnection from memory. In this way, the reader is left with a presupposed sociocultural transformation that assumes the alienation of the consumer by foreign, nonindigenous commodities and the disassociation of memory from imported goods.

One of the few studies on imported beverages has been conducted by Papagaroufali. According to Papagaroufali, drinking practices can be a medium for gender redefinition (1992). Feminist women use drinking as "a violation, or resistance, or reversal, or transformation of the 'Establishment' and the legitimation of these women's actual and dreamed of interest: to become culturally visible the way they 'wished'" (1992: 66). In this way, imported alcohol drinking becomes an arena for a negotiation of gender identity. The space of the bar or the associations of women develop into spaces where drinking styles are expressed in various forms to challenge dominant views of womanhood.

Stewart has also conducted a short research project in relation to the position of imported beverages, and more specifically whisky, in Greece (1989: 77–104). In his analysis, whisky should be understood in terms of Gramsci's theory of hegemony, as in his view the beverage is no longer used by the higher classes, whereas in the past it was considered a prestigious good. Following Bourdieu, he argues that the general tendency of social groups with different access to economic resources, wealth, and generally power is to distinguish themselves by presenting different styles in everyday action and thought. However, these trends stand in relation to each other because each social group makes sense of its own identity in opposition to the others. According to Stewart, the relationship between these trends implies a historical dynamic, "for if one group's style changes then other groups are likely to adjust their style to account for that change" (1989: 78). The dynamic can be understood in Gramsci's terms, because hegemony implies consent with the powerful in the modern capitalistic world. This consent, however, does not guarantee the distinctiveness of the elite. Once a trend is appropriated by the majority, then the dominant groups embrace a new one to be differentiated.

Abatzi has examined the commoditization of sexuality in the bars of Athens that are known as bars with women (2010). By establishing a role as a woman who provides company in exchange for alcoholic drinks in a specific bar, she is able to describe thickly the ways in which commoditization is produced in such contexts. Abatzi describes a highly commoditized culture of drinking gifts of imported beverages to the women who work in the bar. The company of women is exchanged for alcohol that might represent excessive spending. The customers, who are usually whisky drinkers, negotiate their masculinity in the process of seduction, and by buying drinks for them, they try to influence the women working in the bar.

Only recently have scholars in Greece begun to research how consumption is entangled with social identities and materiality in the context of recent socioeconomic transformations (Bakalaki 2000: 67–90, Dimitriou Kotsoni 2003, Petridou 2006, Yalouri 2001: 101–135, Yiakoumaki 2006: 415–445). Yiakoumaki, for example, has examined how the projections of ethnic, rural, and local foods operate as a medium for negotiating the monocultural aspects of national Greek identity. The commoditization of locality within the project of a multicultural and diverse Europe and the political, economic, and consumerist agendas of the EU are intertwined with these transformations.

Petridou has examined the commoditization of dairy food products and their association with the construction of Greek identity (2001). By following the commodity chain of these products, she traces the production of meanings in various locations: the marketing administration, the retail sector, and the spaces of consumption. In this way, she outlines the agency of these products and their roles in the reproduction of social relationships in the commodity chain.

A further contribution in material culture studies in Greece comes from Yalouri, who approaches the site of the Acropolis as major arena of global and local claims of heritage, identity, and history. This contested monument emerges as a site of agency that informs the ways Greeks view their national identity. In Yalouri's words, her study "investigates the way Greeks and the Acropolis are engaged in a dialectic process of objectification, forming, transforming or reproducing each other" (2001: 17). Furthermore, the inalienability of the Acropolis does not necessary mean that is not capitalized or consumed massively. One evident form of its commodification is in the sphere of marketing in which global commodities such as Coca-Cola try to appropriate the symbol and dress it with civilization and harmony.

To "Follow the Thing"

The Scope of Following Things and Commodities

Research by "following the thing" refers to a wide spectrum of anthropological inquiry (Marcus 1995, 1998). According to Marcus, "This mode of constructing the multisited space of research involves tracing the circulation through different contexts of a manifestly material object of study, such as commodities, gifts, money, works of art and intellectual property" (Marcus 1998: 91). This chiefly requires the involvement of the anthropologist in a number of different contexts and spaces. The anthropologist follows the object or the commodity in motion through its various trajectories, phases, or paths and in this way is able to understand the various aspects of the career of the thing. As Kopytoff (1986) has argued, things have cultural biographies. As he states,

> In doing the biography of a thing, one would ask questions similar to those one asks about people: What, sociologically, are the biographical possibilities inherent in its 'status' and in the period and culture, and how are these possibilities realized? Where does the thing come from and who made it? What had been its career so far, and what do people consider to be an ideal career for such things? What are the recognized 'ages' or periods in the thing's 'life,' and what are the cultural markers for them? How does the thing's use change with its age, and what happens to it when it reaches the end of its usefulness? (Kopytoff 1986: 66)

Studies range from research in laboratories to cyberspace and might involve investigation of commodity chains, artifacts, buildings, or any other kind of object. One particular reason that an anthropologist might become involved in such a project is the expectation that objects are able to link a number of different spaces, communities, or periods of time. In addition, such methodology emphasizes the problems of locally bounded ethnographies in a period in which processes such as globalization, a global market, and imagined communities have become increasingly significant (Comaroff and Comaroff 2003, de Pina-Cabral 2005). This kind of methodology can therefore be a productive tool for approaching localization.

This methodology is a reaction to a major question in recent anthropology about the ability of the anthropologist to study the complex movement of people and things across the globe within the context of globalization processes. The theoretical and methodological challenges that such research poses can be overcome by following objects, as Marcus has suggested (1998). This suggestion is inspired by earlier thinkers who have worked in this manner, such as Mintz (1985), and who have built upon world system theory (Wallerstein 2004). The capitalistic system has expanded and become highly complex and therefore more difficult to grasp (Comaroff and Comaroff 2001). Most market processes in this context are not bounded to one locale but to various interconnected places, and therefore the need to pursue multisited research is imperative. It follows that identity formation is constructed by multiple agents and in multiple contexts and places (Marcus 1998: 52). Ethnography is purposefully multisited so as to be able to illustrate more complex connections and multiplicities. Following the thing is part of a strategic construction of multisited fieldwork that brings the commodity into focus and illustrates the processes of capitalism.

Such methodologies are useful because, as Foster has argued, these tracking exercises aim to make visible the "sometimes obscure and often unanticipated networks through which everyday objects of consumption move, thereby mapping the linkages between people and places that define the social organization of globalization" (2008: 16). It is in such a context that an understanding of a whisky network might be useful. Furthermore, a multisited research on whisky in Greece is meaningful especially because it tries to overcome a strictly bounded form of ethnography. Petridou, for example, has demonstrated by following dairy products in various sites how these commodities "constitute mechanisms of cultural negotiation and change" (2001: 12). More specifically, by investigating the case of feta within the context of the commoditizing mechanisms of the EU, she furnishes a clear example of food nationalization. Moreover, her extended research into the production of marketing illustrates how the competition between Greek and foreign companies has produced a discourse about the dairy industry as an agent of progress and modernization.

Furthermore, my study includes what Foster has called "extended apt illustration," which is the investigation of a single commodity to trace cultural, economic, and political aspects of globalization (2008: xiv). These aspects might include the consumption of branded commodities, the history of transnational capitalistic corporations, and the formation of consumer citizenship, but they are not limited to these. The overall aim is to describe "in a combination of historical, ethnographic and journalistic terms a particular instance of complex connectivity, of the actually existing and variously imagined linkages among people and things unevenly distributed across large swatches of space and time" (Foster 2008: xiv). Similarly, this study investigates the various linkages of whisky in Greece in time and in space. Although spaces in this type of research might be distant, the two field locations that I have chosen, Skyros and Athens, are relatively close.

Moreover, it is worth stating that in recent years "the anthropological study of Greece's highly urbanized contemporary society is often set either in cities and large towns or is comparative and multi-sited" (Karakasidou and Tsibiridou 2006: 219). In late modern Greece, the modernization processes, Europeanization, and the neoliberalism of the market have pushed anthropologists who study Greece to take a critical stance and challenge dominant views of fieldwork. Probably another major factor has been the long line of research projects mainly on small communities on islands and villages that have produced high-quality ethnographies but with limited horizons.

Finally, a follow-the-whisky methodology pinpoints the influence of the contemporary economy in creating possibilities of identity formation and style. By focusing on the production of the value of the commodity in various contexts, my study aims to shed light on the multiplicity of meanings produced by the various agents and the emerging relatedness of the consumers who make themselves through the beverage.

Research and Fieldwork

The material for the study was collected from December 2004 to September 2007. The information was gathered on Skyros and Athens from different kinds of sources such as libraries, import companies, nightclubs, and bars. Several methods were used for gaining data, depending on the occasion. My central interest was to discover under what conditions whisky and other imported alcoholic beverages were consumed, how they were established, and what kind of perspectives people had regarding the drinks. However, I could not neglect the history of the alcohol industry in Greece and the role of advertising in localizing the drink. I therefore decided to gather as much material as I could on these subjects. A good reason for focusing on whisky and alcohol in Greece has been the centrality of drinking in people's lives. As one might expect, alcohol occupies a central position in many communities throughout the world, as numerous studies have demonstrated. Even more importantly, the focus on whisky has been legitimated by the increasing consumption in Greece and the localized character of the drink.

My choice of sites was based on numerous factors. The conscious choice to situate this ethnography in two fields by following the thing (Marcus 1998) and to illustrate some of the distinct trajectories of Scotch whisky (Appadurai 1986: 5) goes against the long tradition of a strictly bounded form of ethnography, which has been carried out in Greece by a line of anthropologists. Cowan has correctly commented on this issue by suggesting that anthropologists working in Greece have to reexamine the categories of local and indigenous, otherwise they run the danger of objectifying them (1992: 129, 130). I would further suggest that the reexamination has to include the categories of urban and rural, which have also been central in the anthropological enterprise and have therefore obscured other power relations.

In ethnographic writing, the political and the poetical are inseparable—and social science is not objective or above the historical processes that influence human existence (Clifford and Marcus 1986: 2). Within this context, "culture is composed of seriously contested codes and representations," and ethnographic writing must be critical and ethical to highlight the "constructed, artificial nature of cultural accounts" (Clifford and Marcus 1986: 2).

My own position as a Greek Athenian and half Skyrian (from my mother's side) influenced my research and made things easier on several occasions. However, conducting research in a familiar place does not secure the position of the anthropologist. There is always the possibility that "interiority does not necessarily follow inclusion" (Panourgia 1995: 10). Issues of gender and class can always arise. In my position, for example, the fact that I am a man was extremely important in being accepted in the coffeehouse and in the bar and being excluded from several aspects of the female realm.

In addition, my relationship with Skyrians was developed over many summers of my life since my childhood, and my identity as half Skyrian influenced my research and had a positive effect in collecting information and negotiating my relationships as an anthropologist. Among other things, I operated as a semi-local informant for other colleagues (anthropologists) who were trying to write an ethnography of Skyros island. A division therefore between local and anthropological understandings of knowledge became highly intriguing during my fieldwork. As Agelopoulos has argued, "distinctions between ethnographers, natives, native ethnographers and ethnographic natives" are never clear-cut and are highly fluid (2003: 249–263).

Generally speaking, both of my research fields have been changing. The island of Skyros is small and close to Athens. In terms of tourism, it began developing on a small scale over the last twenty years. Inhabitants have been producing and drinking large amounts of wine for a long time. However, several groups of people have begun to consume other alcoholic beverages. Whisky in particular is consumed in coffeehouses, households, and nightclubs. It is notable that some groups do not like other spirits so much, and therefore they do not consume any spirits other than whisky.

Similarly in Athens there are networks that consume mainly whisky, entertain themselves in clubs where whisky is the central drink, and claim popular styles. My own acquaintances and my experiences as an Athenian were invaluable in approaching the consumers of whisky and discussing (as well as participating in) various aspects of social life. The main network that I followed on outings was based on friends from school in Kypseli, the center of Athens. However, I conducted interviews and participated in outings with various other groups and persons. In both ethnographic chapters and only in some cases, I have chosen not to use the real names of my interlocutors, as they might not be feeling comfortable with the publicity of their identity.

During my fieldwork, I stayed in Athens for six months from January to June 2006. The time spent on Skyros was from December 2004 to April 2005, from July 2005 to December 2005, and the summer months (June to September) of 2006 and 2007. During that time, I stayed in the house of my aunt Emmanuelle in the old town of the village. Skyros has always been a summer destination, and therefore it was not hard to reestablish my relationships with people who live on the island. However, it was somewhat difficult to explain to my interlocutors what exactly I was doing. I had endless discussions about whether I was a psychologist or a folklorist, and people did not seem to understand the term *anthropologist* very well. Therefore, I decided to adopt the term *sociologist*, which might have become familiar in recent years through discussions on television. As a sociologist, I was legitimately interested in a number of topics such as weddings, gender relationships, food and drinking habits, tastes, professional life, and local history. Thus, in daily discussions these themes were brought in without much resistance or skepticism.

Most material was collected through participant observation. I rarely spent time at home, unless I had people visiting. Consequently I spent many hours in the village market where I could have many different discussions with people in the coffeehouse, in bars, restaurants, and in the alcohol shop (*cava*), and in many instances I was invited to dinner parties that came to be the most rewarding and

enjoyable experiences. As a result, the period of my fieldwork was very pleas-
ant—in opposition to the stereotypical idea of the suffering anthropologist.

In terms of information, I gathered a number of different notes, interviews,
photographs, films, local books, and newspapers. As I already noted, the fact that
my mother is native to the island played a vital role in my own relationship the
inhabitants of Skyros. I was able to meet informants through my family network
and especially through my mother's brother, who was living on the island while I
was conducting my fieldwork.

While on Skyros, I was lucky enough to stay with a family who owned a tavern, Kokalenia. Through them I was able to extend my network and meet many
more inhabitants of Skyros who would go there to eat and drink. In addition,
this was apparently one of the most popular places for tourists, so I also had the
opportunity to meet visitors from Holland, Germany, France, and England who
went to Skyros regularly.

Besides gaining information from interlocutors, I was able to gather a lot of
material from the Skyrian Association in Athens. The association has published
a monthly newspaper since 1976, which I came to research in depth. Furthermore, the association owns a variety of books and papers about Skyros. All these
sources have been invaluable in the anthropological enterprise. A particular reason for researching this material was the expectation that I would find the voices
of people expressing their views on modernity, tourism, and the arrival of new
consumer values. In this way I came across many perspectives that I took into account. Through the association, I was also able to extend my network of Skyrian
immigrants in Athens.

In the capital of Greece, I was faced with several methodological problems.
Despite the fact that I grew up in Athens, I do not claim to have walked all its
streets. Athenians know better than anyone else how many neighborhoods and
thresholds the city has. The diversity of a city of more than four million people is
challenging enough for any kind of social research. Therefore, I used a rather un-
usual way of conducting fieldwork. I tried to discuss and interview as many people as possible from different social and economic backgrounds. These included
club owners, consumers of different ages, publishers, economists, historians, importers of alcohol, and local Athenians. I also received a great deal of information
from my own friends and former schoolmates. During these encounters, I took
notes and sometimes I used an mp3 recorder. The recorder was used when there
was a time limit for an interview and therefore it had to be as brief as possible.

The most difficult information to access was in relation to the import industry.
After considerable effort, I was given the opportunity to interview a few people.
However, the most important material was collected from economic reports and
from articles in newspapers, journals, and magazines. A possible explanation for
the relatively uncooperative attitude I encountered is the strong competition between the multinational import companies. In that sense, people were always

careful about the kind of information they provided. Despite several obstacles, I managed to come into contact with some importers and multinationals through the Greek industrial association related to alcohol.

I obtained advertisements from television, magazines, and newspapers from the 1970s onward to reconstruct the strategies of the import industry and understand the ways in which whisky was projected and promoted. *Kathimerini, To Vima, Eleftheorypia,* and *Eleftheros Typos* are the ones that I read and used the most. Much of my research on marketing took place in the archive of the Institute of Marketing and Communication. There, I managed to collect a number of advertisements from magazines such as *Ikonomikos Tahidromos, Status, Playboy, Athinorama, Gyneka, Man, Car, Marketing Age, Marketing Week,* and many more. I was also able to find additional material in the National Historical and Literature Archive of Greece as well as in antique shops in Plaka, the old part of Athens under the Acropolis.

During fieldwork, I also gathered a number of Greek films from the 1960s, the golden age of Greek cinema. After happening to see some films during participant observation, I became increasingly aware that whisky was the main drink of consumption and was projected as a symbol of modernity, class distinction, and Western elitist habits.

The fact that most of this study was written in Leiden helped me distance myself from the fields of research and think more reflexively about my fieldwork. I found this experience extremely rewarding, as my surrounding friends and colleagues were unaware of most of the things I was describing to them. My work and life in The Netherlands therefore shaped my ideas about this book.

Finally, this study has been enriched by the insights of a critical anthropology that intends to share coevaleness instead of denying it and producing an allochronic discourse (Fabian 1983). For that reason, the material is presented in historical form, but several ethnographic parts employ the ethnographic present. This usage is based on the realization that my own research is rooted in the present and my own presence as an ethnographer is contextual and time-specific, a kind of "temporal rootedness" (de Pina-Cabral 2000: 341–348). This strategy does not aim at detemporalization; rather, the researcher recognizes that it is a way of writing ethnography in the present tense while being conscious of changing sociocultural conditions. As de Pina-Cabral states, "[W]e do not presume that the sociocultural contexts we study are stopped in time. In fact, we have learnt that there is no means of achieving anything like synchronicity in ethnographic reporting, as sociocultural life is multi-layered" (2000: 343).

The Ethnography of Modernity and Cultural Transformation

The study deals with macro and micro processes of value formation. The first historical chapters offer the basis of the development of multinational capitalism in late modern Greece and the shift from small importers to large corporations that compete to establish their own brands in the Greek market. This change is related to a gradual displacement of *ouzo,* retsina, and brandy over several decades and an increase and final appropriation of whisky. I have chosen to begin with this outline, which makes clear the politics of importing and highlights their relationship to the emergence of consumer culture after the colonels's regime in Greece.

In addition, the study examines the first projections of whisky in the cultural industry from the 1950s onward. The drink was first presented significantly in the popular Greek cinema of the 1950s and became a vehicle for dreaming about modernity, especially among those who wanted to claim a middle-class style. The scenarios of consumption in Greek cinema are examined to demonstrate the multiple and sometimes conflicting values relating to the beverage. Whisky becomes a starting point for future imaginations of modernity and, as such, a tool for social differentiation. The projections of whisky in advertising continued massively after the beginning of the 1970s, when popular Greek cinema declined and gradually disappeared. In advertising, though, the commodity follows another aesthetic of modernity that has been gradually influenced by transantional capitalism as well as by culture.

The extent that such marketing or film imaginaries, within the context of transnational capitalism and the cultural industry, are transforming consumers into passive agents of gloabalizing forces is being examined in the largest ethnographic part of the book. While various claims of Greekness or middle classness are evident in the majority of these projected meanings by the cultural industry, they do not necessarily correspond to the views that interlocutors have about Scotch. On the contrary, whisky might operate at various levels as a symbol of a European or Euroamerican modernity and simultaneously as a denial of the efficiency, control, and discipline that this system demans from individuals.

The ethnography examines the position of whisky in the everyday life of people in the center of Athens and on Skyros, mainly within the sphere of entertainment and leisure. In the chapter dealing with the trajectory of Scotch in Athens, I demonstrate how people's sense of themselves in relation to contemporary Greek popular entertainment affects their cultural identity, their modernness or traditionality, and, therefore, their style that is habituated by the movement of commodities. This part also deals with interrelated themes that emerge within the consumption of whisky, such as the development of popular culture, the emergence of music venues with live Greek popular music and bars, and the excessive character of the consumption of whisky.

In addition, in the ethnography of the Greek island of Skyros, I follow the trajectory of whisky in the space of the *kafenio,* in which laborers make their own style by associating Scotch whisky with urbanness and modernness. Their use of Scotch is tactical, as it opposes the notions of shepherdhood expressed in the consumption of wine and *tsipouro.* By embracing Scotch as a symbol of Athens and popular culture, they try to negotiate their opposition to the matrilocal kinship obligations and the *soi*-based society of Skyros.

The selection of the two settings in Athens and Skyros aims to demonstrate the interrelation of specific networks with Scotch whisky and the association of social and gender styles with drinking alcohol. The drinking habits of both the Skyrians and the Athenians that I researched and the importance of alcohol in the lives of these people make whisky an ideal tool for investigating the issues of modernity and tradition, popular culture and style, and, finally, consumption.

Notes

1. Imerisisa : http: //www.imerisia.gr/article.asp?catid=12305&subid=2&pubid=575128&t ag=2617, Greek *Playboy* Magazine, Jan. 1990: 136–141, *The Independent,* 1-2-2003, "This Europe: Greece calls time on teens' taste for whisky," by Daniel Howden, *Kathimerini* daily Greek newspaper 13-3-04 "Ouiski to ethniko mas poto." Folklore in that context is related to traditionality instead of *laografia.*
2. Although the term *popular* might be highly misleading in Greek discourse, I use the term strictly ethnographically. *Popular culture* in Greece has been cited in relation to two major meanings, as various scholars have demonstrated; one is based on folklore studies (*laografia*) and the other on sociology (*kinoniologia*) (Herzfeld 1982, Damianakos 2003: 139–152). Oikonomou has also argued that popular music has been used in relation to the emergence of postwar *bouzouki* music (Oikonomou 2005: 363).
3. WHO Official Internet site for adult per capita alcohol consumption 1961–2000 http: // www3.who.ch/whosis/alcohol/alcohol_apc_data.cfm?path=whosis,alcohol,alcohol_ apc,alcohol_apc_data&language=english. Accessed 11 June 2004.
4. Information in *Kathimerini* daily Greek newspaper 13-3-04. "Ikonomia kai agores."
5. Information on *Kathimerini* daily Greek newspaper on 8-9-2008. "Alkool: To nomimo narkotiko."
6. Information on the case: http://www.kiortsis.gr/en/the_Scotch_whiskey_association.html. Accessed 17 June 2004.
7. Legal representation by Kiortsis Law Offices, cases No. 3581/87, No. 8077/76, No. 3155/76, No. 1261/76 of the Court of 1st Inst. of Athens.
8. *Kathimerini,* Greek daily newspaper in English, 28 April 2004, p. 21. Available on: http: // www.ekathimerini.com/4dcgi/_w_articles_economy_1641409_20/04/2004_41925.
9. WHO Official Internet site for adult per capita alcohol consumption 1961–2000. www3 .who.ch/whosis/alcohol/alcohol_apc_data.cfm?path=whosis,alcohol,alcohol_apc, alcohol_apc_data&language=english. Accessed 11 June 2004.
10. Scotch Whisky Association. Public Relations Department.
11. *The Independent,* 1.2.2003, "This Europe: Greece calls time on teens' taste for whisky," by Daniel Howden.
12. For a general critique see Mitchell (2000: 1–34).
13. Appadurai cites Bourdieu (1977) and Douglas and Isherwood (1979), among others, for their efforts to understand the cultural dimensions of exchange by being critical of the gift/commodity dichotomy. Burke (1996) and Weiss (1996) are also worth noting.

14. Nikolaos Tselementes was a Greek chef of the early twentieth century who tried to Europeanize and modernize the Greek kitchen. His effect on Greek cooking was very influential, as he published several cookbooks that became a synonym of the Greek kitchen.

15. The subject of alcohol in Greece has been examined in the past from a more medical perspective by various anthropologists such as Allen (1985) and Blum and Blum (1965).

16. *Kafenio* is a type of coffeehouse in which alcoholic and nonalcoholic beverages are served. It has been an institution in most parts of Greece, a classic place of male socialization in which political and other discussions take place and men play cards or *tavli,* and drink alcohol. Nowadays, a *kafenio* can at the same time be a mini-market, a tavern, telephone center, an Internet café, or any other kind of business, depending on the investment of the owner. Rodon on Skyros is a bar that during the winter operates much like a *kafenio.*

CHAPTER 1

The Imported Spirits Industry in Greece

Whisky in Greece usually refers to a broad category of Scotch. After the creation of the nation-state in Greece, British luxury goods became particularly prestigious and in certain cases were considered much better than domestic ones.[1] A similar mentality can be still found nowadays in the expression *afto ine megla,* which literally means "this is made in England" in Athenian slang, the connotation being that the product referred to is of high quality. This view of a British modernity is also related to a conceptualization of the West, which in many cases in Greece is tied to notions of high culture, style, and progress.

To understand the trajectory of the consumption patterns, it will be necessary to describe first the localization of whisky in terms of investment and trade. It is essential before the book proceeds to the ethnography of reception of the beverage to draw a short history of the importation of Scotch in contemporary Greece, which is deeply entangled with the development of the cultural industry, commercial Greek cinema, and marketing. As it stands, this short economic history would not be able to explain the specific success of Scotch in Greece without a cultural understanding of the beverage because the reception and use-value of a certain product are always influenced by culture. Therefore, commodities should not be understood only in their life cycles or career but because they also include a set of meanings historically accumulated as categories. As a result, different commodities have different histories and require different accountings, both of prior meanings that shape their reception and of the competing supply-side interests that promote their production and consumption.

This is by no means an effort to write a complete history of the importation of alcoholic beverages in Greece. On the contrary, a specific focus on Scotch and the shift from small Greek importation companies to large transnational corporations signals the capitalistic globalizing processes at the end of the twentieth century.

As Harvey has suggested, globalization is characterized by an intensification of social and economic life, a sort of time and space compression (1989: 141). Within this context, the shift to a post-Fordist regime of flexible accumulation is related to the appearance of new sectors in the economy, increasing and new consumption patterns, new sectors of production, new markets, and an intensification of information networks that aim to speed up the processes of consumption and production. In addition, in this era, the flexibility of production, consumption, and labor has been central in the establishment of a new form of capitalism. The speeding up of social and economic life has resulted in the expansion of large multinational corporations, especially since the 1970s. As will be demonstrated, Greece's beverage sector and the successful establishment of whisky can be interpreted in terms of the wide impact of flexible accumulation. The process of value formation of whisky from the side of the importers and the industry is intertwined with these economic and social shifts.

However, the ethnographic chapters of this book will be moving beyond economic globalization in an effort to examine the extent that globalization as a Western global hegemony designates a unification of cultures, styles, attitudes, ideas, values, and goods, including the processes of Westernization, Europeanization, and modernization in general.

In what follows, I examine how importers and producers of whisky established the beverage in Greece, especially after World War II, and expanded the trade. This set of local relationships was a prerequisite of multinational capitalism and ensured that the process of value formation of whisky would be an ongoing enterprise in the commercial sense. This chapter examines the strategies used by both the importers and the producers of whisky in Greece to establish their position in the market.

The Industry in the Twentieth Century: The Small Importers

Several symbols of Britishness appeared in Greece after the independence war. The landmark hotel Grande Bretagne, for example, next to the Greek parliament in the center of Athens, was founded in 1874 and became one of the city's most important buildings. Grande Bretagne became the central meeting place for those Greeks and foreigners who were shaping the political, economic, and social lives of the country. Industrialists, ship owners, diplomats, government officials, and journalists gathered daily in its reception rooms and restaurant while in the elegant apartments famous foreigners stayed and, in some cases, lived. The name of the hotel was carefully chosen and expressed the glory of the British Empire, a place where kings and queens could socialize and even sleep. English or French names expressed quality and style. Café Splendid was a coffeehouse in the center of Athens where high-class Athenians would socialize (Skoumpourdi 2002: 14).

The British store Sidney Noel was one of the first department stores in Athens in the 1920s (see figure 1.1), where all kind of British products (including whisky) could be found.

Figure 1.1. Advertisement for the British department store Sidney Noel in Athens in the 1920s. The text in the center reads "Sterling in quality and sterling in price—The most important English store in Greece" (Source: Skoumpourdi 2002).

Despite the fact that whisky has long been a part of Greek social life, the focus in this chapter is on the postwar era and, more specifically, 1960 and onward, when such beverages were widely imported, promoted, and massively consumed in Greece. In that time frame, the commodity trade has undergone numerous transformations, which continue up to the present day. Many small importing companies grew in size, and many were acquired by multinational corporations. As a result, the distribution chain became more efficient but less profitable for small Greek importers and less competitive. Whisky nowadays can be found in supermarkets, neighborhood shops, bars, clubs, and households. Most of the whisky consumed in Greece is Scottish in origin, and some of the more popular brands include the well-known Johnnie Walker, Chivas Regal, Dimple, Famous Grouse, and Cutty Sark.

In terms of production and consumption, two distinct periods can be identified. The first spans the time from the end of the nineteenth century to the end of the 1950s, whereas the other encompasses the development of the industry from the 1960s to the present. The primary characteristic of the first period was the production and consumption of brandy, ouzo, and beer. Among these drinks, brandy, liqueurs, and *ouzo* were projected as traditional and Greek because, according to their producers, they have been historically based on Greek ingredients such as grapes, Corinthian raisins, and Chios mastic. Furthermore, their production has a long history, and they are deeply embedded in Greek social and cultural life. Many of these beverages are still made today from recipes that have been passed on from generation to generation featuring special combinations of spices and aging techniques.

Ouzo was mainly produced and consumed by Greek-speaking populations living in Asia Minor and on the islands of Lesbos and Chios. Many family distilleries can still be found there, such as Ouzo 12 and Plomari. These distilleries date back many years despite the fact that nowadays they have evolved into commercial production units. *Ouzo* was also produced in Piraeus and in Athens but became even more popular and widely consumed after the arrival of the Greek-speaking refugees from Turkey in the 1920s, who brought with them a variety of new tastes and foods that became incorporated into Greek life.

The production of brandy was based mainly in the Peloponnese and Athens and was associated with the local types of grapes that are grown in these areas. Furthermore, there was a continuous trade of brandies and liqueurs from Greek communities that were living in Alexandria, Asia Minor, Thessalonica, Volos, and other cities on the Mediterranean. One of the first brandy companies was Metaxas, founded in 1888 by Spiros Metaxas. The brandy was made with grapes and spices and came in different ages. The drink became widely traded and consumed throughout Greece and abroad, and in 1900 it was exported to the United States, which was the major destination for Greek emigrants.

On the other hand, the consumption of beer in Greece is associated with the arrival of King Otto of Wittelswach of Bavaria in 1833. Otto was followed by a number of bureaucrats, civil servants, entrepreneurs, and troops when he first arrived in Greece. As one might expect, most of the newly arrived Bavarians were beer drinkers. One of them was Johan Ludwig Fix, who set up a brewery in Athens, followed in 1864 by his son Charles and the foundation of the modern Fix brewery, which coincided with the appointment of King George Christian Wilhelm Glyxbourg. Since then, beer has been widely produced and consumed in Greece and imported into Greece. An example of the social distinction conferred by the consumption of beer at that time is evident in the well-known sketch by the Bavarian Hans Hanke in 1836, copying the original by L. Kollnberger (Clogg 1992: 52). The watercolor (see figure 1.2) depicts the Orea Ellas café, which was for a long time the main center of political discourse and, like all cafes, a place of male leisure. On the left of the picture, a group of Greek men dressed in Western style drink beer like the Bavarian soldiers behind them. On the right, the Greek men dressed in local kilts (*fustanela*) are drinking *raki* or *tsipouro*.

At the beginning of the twentieth century, the negative performance of the Greek economy had a detrimental impact on commerce and trade (Kremidas 2003). The government at the time was struggling to meet its public debt obligations, which had been incurred pursuant to the creation of the modern Greek state. As a result of these conditions, the food and beverage industries came into crisis, much like the highly developed textile industry.

Figure 1.2. Orea Ellas coffeehouse, 1836 (Source: Skoumpourdi 2002).

However, during the war period the food and alcohol industry experienced growth. One of the first import companies of that time was Karakostas & Giannakos, which was founded in 1903 by Nikolaos Karakostas. The company started as a food and liquor store in the center of Athens, situated at the corner of Athinas and Geraniou Streets. The shop imported a variety of wines and spirits, which became very popular among the Western-oriented Athenians of the time. AMVIX is a similar company that was founded in the war period, specifically in 1917, by Albert Revah and two other partners. AMVIX imported luxury food products and beverages and soon became one of the leading import companies in the sector. However, this was one of the most difficult periods for the imported beverages sector.

Turkish nationalism and the war of Asia Minor resulted in the retreat of Greek troops and Greek refugees from central and western Turkey. At the time, the state had contracted with several companies for the provision of consumer goods for the army. Furthermore, the decline of international trade between 1914 and 1918 resulted in a sharp decline in imported commodities and a corresponding increase in domestic production. After 1922, 1.5 million refugees fled to Greece. Several among them decided to invest in the liquor industry, whereas others sought to continue their family businesses in Greece.

The period between 1923 and 1939 was characterized by the development of many small industries, which was a result of the arrival of the large number of refugees from Asia Minor during the Greek–Turkish war. The economic crisis of 1929 did not harm the Greek economy to the same extent as it did other countries, and this situation allowed industry to expand. Within this context, the food and alcohol industry also developed, for similar demographic reasons (Riginos 2000: 204). It was also during this period that small quantities of whisky were first produced and consumed in Greece. The famous Karoulias importing company was established in 1940 and imported a variety of foods and drinks to Athens.

During World War II, the Germans imposed a harsh regime, appropriating all available food and alcohol sources and forcing the country to pay for all occupation costs. The result of this policy was a famine during the winter of 1941–1942, which caused the deaths of 100,000 people. Despite the fact that food was in short supply, the wealthy continued to have access to British, French, and American luxury delicacies and specialty goods (Clogg 1992: 127). In 1944, when the war was almost over, Winston Churchill and Josef Stalin made the informal percentages agreement, which established British predominance in Greece and Russian predominance in Romania and Bulgaria (Clogg 1992: 138). Under these conditions, the British forces played an important role in the repression of the insurgent communist forces and the establishment of a new national political framework.

After the war, the British revived the economic life of the country by giving a loan of 10 million pounds to the Greek government. However, a result of this

ESTABLISHED 1840

THIS LABEL IS REGISTERED

FINEST WHISKY

SPECIAL OLD

FROM THE DISTILLERY OF
THE FIRM

Figure 1.3. Finest Whisky Kalos Bros. The first whisky label produced in Greece by the Kalogiannis Brothers. The label dates from the inter-war period (Source: National Literature and History Archive of Greece).

was its active involvement in the political economy of the country. The U.S. government, too, through the Truman doctrine, included Greece in their sphere of economic and political influence. Due to the difficult years of the war in combination with the Greek civil war (1946–1949), the efforts of the United States to compete with the influence of the British coupled with the fear of communism made Greece a major recipient of aid through the Marshall Plan. According to historians, "Between 1945 and 1950 Greece received U.S. \$2.1 billion in all forms of aid, a sum greater than the total of all foreign loans contracted between 1821 and 1930" (Koliopoulos and Veremis 2002: 172).

Under these conditions, liberalism was promoted as the core economic system of the postwar period. Within this perspective, the state should not interfere in the market but rather support and sustain the forces that enable supply and demand. Especially after 1954, this principle became central in the state's postwar policies (Hatziiosif 2003: 295).[2] Furthermore, the monetary reforms that took place during that time had a very positive effect on foreign investment. Through the effect of the Marshall Plan and the promotion of further plans for economic support, the Americans became important agents in Greece to the extent that "few major military, economic or indeed, political decisions could be taken without American approval" (Clogg 1992: 146). That client relationship would dominate most of the second half of the twentieth century in Greece. Under these conditions of British and (even more) American influence, trade between Greece and these two countries was further developed and expanded. It was no coincidence that after the war a massive flow of new products and commodities arrived from both Britain and the United States.

After World War II, the Greek alcohol and import industries developed massively. More particularly, the GNP per capita growth between 1952 and 1972 increased at an average rate of 7–8 percent, and remittances flowed into the economy as a result of the high level of migration of Greeks to countries such as Germany and Australia (Koliopoulos and Veremis 2002: 174). Consumption increased considerably, and new consumer goods appeared on the market. Furthermore, the companies that had traded in food and imported drinks before the war were further developed and became actively engaged in importing whisky. In 1951, for example, the company known as Karakostas & Giannakos was renamed GENKA. GENKA imported a variety of whiskies, such as Ballantine's and Canadian Club, into the Greek market after the 1960s.

In the 1960s, more companies that were principally focused on the production and importation of alcohol and whisky invested in the market. In 1963, the Athenian breweries contracted with Amstel beer, and a new factory was founded in Athens (Kerofilas 1997: 138). During that period, the economy was booming and the first supermarkets, such as Vasilopoulos and Marinopoulos, were established in Athens. Coca-Cola and other new soft drinks appeared on the market and a variety of standardized consumer goods became part of daily life. Athens started growing rapidly, and the first luxury hotels, such as the Monte Parnes and the Hilton, were founded. The Karoulias Company expanded further into the alcohol and beverages sector and moved out of the food sector. It was during this period that Karoulias became the representative of Cutty Sark Scottish whisky in Greece. A characteristic example of the developments in this period is the joint corporation of Lizas and Lizas, the unification of two family distilleries, one in Pireus port and one in Kalithea. The company was created in about 1965 and continued producing spirits for the Greek market, such as the liqueur Eoliki. During this period, the company became increasingly aware that imported drinks were also becoming more and more fashionable in Greece, and therefore they decided to import other beverages to sell on supermarket shelves.

The period after 1967 is known as the dictatorship, when the regime of the colonels took over the Greek democracy. After that period, nothing would resemble the Greece of the past, either socially, economically, or culturally. This was the time when Greece negotiated its political institutions and tried to develop and become modernized.

From the beginning of the dictatorship, the colonels arrested more than 10,000 people, including all major politicians. Other people left the country for different European destinations in self-exile. The main figure who could legitimize the group of the dictators was King Constantine. Under pressure, he agreed to cooperate. However, under constitutional changes that started in May 1968 and amid the increasing violence and torture of citizens, the King stated, "This is not my government" (Gallant 2001: 199). King Constantine left in exile as all efforts to change the situation, including the coordination of a counter military coup against the colonels proved fruitless.

The colonels who organized the so-called glorious revolution were Giorgos Papadopoulos, Nikolaos Makarezos, and Brigadier Colonel Stilianos Pattakos (Gallant 2001: 197). They were not so much interested in modernizing Greece as in saving the country from the communist threat and other hidden enemies who supposedly had as their target the glorious Greek civilization. The colonels' conservative policies included the banning of miniskirts and the imposition of a mandatory hair length for men. In addition, their overt nationalistic discourse was immediately expressed in their symbols. With the revolution, the mythical phoenix was reborn as the Greek nation. The colonels had no clear plan or policies or even a coherent ideology, and in that sense they could not articulate a future political economy (Koliopoulos and Veremis 2002: 174). Even so, the Greek economy went through a period of sustained growth and low inflation, the result of a longer process that had already started in 1952. Remittances flowed into the Greek economy from guest workers in Germany and other European countries (Koliopoulos and Veremis 2002: 174). During this period, tourism played an important role in raising people's incomes and strengthening the economy.

The regime wanted to attract foreign capital and industry to Greece and tried to bring Greek ship owners back to the country by offering generous privileges. These actions, though, were not enough to keep up with the work of their democratically elected predecessors. The regime borrowed heavily to finance its schemes, and doing this resulted in inflation that could only be kept under control by means of violent pressure on workers and trade unions, who could no longer negotiate their salaries and rights (Gallant 2001: 200).

The first country to accord official recognition to the regime of the colonels was the United States. Under Richard Nixon, the relationship between the two countries became tighter and Greece's position as part of NATO during the dictatorship became more important. The major reason for this diplomatic approach was the changing political and economic conditions in the Middle East and the Eastern Mediterranean, such as the coup of Gaddafi in Libya, the continuing Arab-Israeli conflict, and the increasing Soviet influence in the area (Gallant 2001: 201).

In Greece after 1973, performance in most sectors of the state and the economy worsened. This decline can be understood as a result of the seven-year dictatorship and the world petrol crisis. Foreign and domestic investment declined, and inflation increased (Close 2002: 170). The economic conditions favored importing, and as a result, the trade deficit became much bigger than before. Brands emerged everywhere; household shelves became packed with supermarket products, and marketing was found in many different contexts. American cigarettes became popular, and whisky was found at entertainment and social events. Vodka was not widely consumed, especially during the dictatorship, because it was considered "a drink for communists or for people who were leftist."[3] During the postauthoritarian period, more companies importing alcoholic beverages were established, and several importers made an effort to produce whisky in Greece. The company Boikos, for example, was founded in 1978 and represented William Grant whisky. Other imported drinks included Glenfiddich, the bourbon Old Huck, Whyte and Mackay, and Havana Club.

With regard to the production of whisky in Greece during the 1970s, the producer companies tried to present the whisky they made as Scottish and therefore depicted what they considered to be Scottish symbols on the labels of their bottles. Their beverage was named Scot, blended, or Greek whisky. As a result, the Scotch Whisky Association petitioned the Greek court of justice to prohibit the production of any beverage called Scots or blended. According to the Scotch Whisky Association appeal (2007), the company Kissamos G. Koutsourelis ABE "produced and distributed onto the Greek market an alcoholic drink bottled in such a way that confusion was created regarding the kind of drink and its country of origin. The word 'Scot' was written on the label of the bottle, there was a design depicting traditional Scottish dress, and under the design there was an English shield. Furthermore, most of the words were in English. Consequently, the consumers considered the above drink to be Scotch whisky."

Another company that was involved in the petition of the Scotch Whisky Association was the Greek firm Maria Katsarou–Alexandros Merzanakis OE, which produced an alcoholic drink on the label of which was the name "golden crown whisky." Also on the label was a picture of an English guardsman, at the bottom of which was written in Greek "Greek whisky." Another producer company and distributor of whisky was Apostolos Vamvounis. Vamvounis produced whisky in a bottle labeled with the words "Black Lion, finest blended whisky" along with a picture of a lion's head together with the words "Ailisburn, the finest whisky" and the design of a unicorn and a coat of arms. The Greek company A. and G. Georga OE also distributed a drink on the Greek market that bore no relationship to whisky. However, on the label of the bottle were written the words "Scotch Whisky" in Greek, and it was named "the golden horseshoe." There was also a design of a horse surrounded by a horseshoe. Consequently, the Scotch Whisky Association won the court case. Finally, the production of these companies was banned and no whisky was ever produced legally in Greece again.

Other companies that were engaged in the trade in whisky and other products in the food and beverages sector during the 1970s and 1980s included Nektar, Apka, and Perseus. Nektar was founded in 1976 as Kanelakis Bros. and imported Dewar's, Bell's, Dimple, Haig, and Classic Malts from 1985 to 1991. Nowadays, Nektar imports a variety of other products, such as ice tea, mineral water, and soft drinks. Another small importing company was Perseus, with whiskies such as Jack Daniel's and Usquaebach. Apka was also founded in 1985 and became the representative of the Russian vodka Stolichnaya.

After the 1970s, multinational corporations, including producers of whisky and other beverages, became more aware of the new markets that were emerging globally and therefore tried to take advantage of these new economic conditions. In addition, they were confronted with the rigidity of Fordist and Keynesian policies, and therefore new strategies had to be adopted to be able to deal with the global economy. As Harvey has pointed out, globalization entails the shrinking of time and space (1989). The capitalistic system has been through various phases, and its current phase began in the 1970s as a result of the crisis in the Fordist system of production (Harvey 1989).

The regime of flexible accumulation came after the crisis of overaccumulation of Western capitalism and more specifically after the 1970s. Until that time the Fordist system of mass production of standardized products was so efficient that it began to overproduce, resulting in massive unemployment and reduction of demand. The decline of consumer markets further influenced many sectors, corporations, and government revenues. Many states decided to print more money to solve the crisis, but this practice created further inflation. Consequently, the Fordist system of production was affected by the crisis to such a degree that it was abandoned. The overproduction of the standardized commodities of the system resulted in oversupply, which reduced demand. This decline of the Fordist system pushed capitalists to reexamine the value of mass production in the form of long-term contracts between the state, employees, and industries. Consumer markets declined, consumers could not buy the products that had been overproduced, and governments could not handle the escalating crisis.

Flexible accumulation became a strategic choice for many companies, especially after the oil crisis of 1973 (Harvey 1989: 145). Under these conditions, there was a shift to services, to more effective means of controlling and expanding commodity chains, to growing inequalities (such as the Nike factories in South East Asia), and to time and space compression, which makes commodities circulate faster and more easily around the globe. Especially after the 1970s, the goal became to speed up both production and consumption.

At the end of 1980s and the beginning of the 1990s, it was quite clear that the Greek whisky and alcohol market had grown large despite the small population of the country and the fact that tastes had for a long time been based on wine and ouzo. Furthermore, the low taxation policy for countries in the European Economic Community led to the development of larger corporations that could import and export their products in a much easier and more profitable way. The competition among small family companies that had been based on personal networking in distribution and in marketing was entering a new era.

Transnational Capitalism: The Multinationals Take Control of the Market

For the most part, the Greek economy was faced with many problems from 1980 until 1993. Average growth was among the lowest in Europe, with 1.3 GNP in 1980–1982 and 0.5 GNP in 1990–1993 (Close 2002: 168). Despite the fact that there was a large black market in Greece that was not represented in economic figures and therefore not captured in economic calculations, the EEC standards for convergence between the GDP per capita and the EEC average were far too high for the country. According to Close, these figures "indicate that Greece had somehow failed to benefit from a massive influx of EEC subsidies and loans, for which its government had bargained forcefully, and had become the community's seemingly incurable invalid—a despised one at that, given the flagrant way in which Community aid had been wasted in corruption and vote buying" (Close 2002: 169).

During the 1980s, the socialist PASOK party could not overcome the crisis, and as a result the GNP fell to 1.6 percent.[4] The second oil-price shock that caused international turbulence was moving the country into turmoil as the effects of inflation were found in all aspects of the economy. Despite the efforts of PASOK to support the welfare state and bring a more democratic social policy into practice, the country's economy did not become very competitive. In addition, "although EC membership revived foreign investment, the end of protectionism hit indigenous firms hard. High consumer demand had always outstripped domestic supply, increasing imports and inflation" (Koliopoulos and Veremis 2002). These conditions were far from ideal for negotiations between multinational companies and Greek distilleries or import companies.

A major problem within the imported beverages sector was the introduction by the Greek government of an import quota for alcoholic beverages, including whisky, during the 1980s. This import quota had a negative effect on the imports of Scotch whisky in Greece. Indeed, during 1983, a discussion began in the British parliament about the pressure of the government to Greece and to the EEC. The Hansard archive of the House of Commons provides an insight from this debate (Hansard Digitization Project):

> Mr. Roger Sims
> Asked the Minister for Trade whether, in view of the restrictions already imposed on Scotch whisky by Greece, he will make representations to the Greek Government concerning their proposed introduction of quotas for imported spirits.
>
> Mr. Sproat
> The Government made strong representations to the European Commission about the inclusion of whisky in the recent Greek request for quotas. But in

view of the doubling of Greek imports of whisky since 1980 and a substantial increase in imports of other spirituous beverages the Commission has now allowed Greece to introduce an import quota for spirituous beverages including whisky for 1983 at levels slightly below 1982 sendings. We shall continue to press the Commission for early action against a variety of Greek fiscal measures which illegally discriminate against whisky. (HC Deb 14 February 1983. Vol. 37 c59W 59W)

Despite this debate in the House of Commons the restricted system of commodity flow (of Scotch) continued to regulate demand, and by 1986 the import quota for spirituous beverages had increased several times (Stewart 1989). Particularly after 1985, Greek distilleries and import companies started discussions with the larger multinationals regarding cooperation or selling. According to one of the heads of a large import and production company in Greece, which came to be part of the Pernod Ricard Group,

> Many people in the importing industry realized in the 80s that a large quantity of imported beverages and whisky was flowing into the country. In that sense we could foresee that after some years we were going to cooperate with foreign and multinational institutions. After 1984, when PASOK was already in power, there was no option. And I don't put it politically but economically. The market in Greece was far too small in comparison to Europe and we couldn't compete with any foreign institutions. With this perspective, our company merged with the Pernod Ricard Group in 1990 and since then we have all the company's brands in our hands.[5]

Pernod Ricard was founded in France in 1975 and became the world's second-largest company dealing with the production and distribution of whisky and the first for aniseed drinks. The company trades in Scotch whiskies such as Chivas Regal and Ballantine's, malt whiskies such as Aberlour and The Glenlivet, Irish whisky such as Jameson, Canadian whisky, and Bourbon whisky as well. The company had already acquired the Campbell distilleries in Scotland in 1975, Austin Nichols in the United States in 1980, Irish distilleries in Ireland in 1988 and, in 1990, the EPOM distilleries in Greece, who were also importers of whisky. The biggest acquisition successes in recent years have been 38 percent of Seagram wines and spirits in 2001 and total control of Allied Domecq in partnership with Fortune Brands in 2005.

Similarly, in 1992 the multinational Berry Bros. and Rudd Ltd. took partial control of one of the biggest alcohol import companies in Greece, Karoulias. Karoulias had been a major importation and distribution company in the Greek market from the 1960s. However, in 1992, Berry Bros. (owners of Cutty Sark Scotch whisky) bought most of the shares in the company. Furthermore the company signed a deal with Brown Forman Co., the owners of Jack Daniel's and Southern Comfort, in 1994. In 1998, the company cooperated with Remy Hellas, part of the Maxxium Hellas group, and took control of their products, which included Famous Grouse, Plomariou Arvanitou ouzo, Cointreau, and Remy Martin. In 1999, the company managed to gain control of the distribution of Metaxa in Greece. In 2000, Berry Bros. acquired 100 percent of Karoulias. In recent years the company has been actively involved in the wine business by cooperating with Kir-Giannis distillery, Spyropoulos, Sigalas, and United Distilleries of Samos. Some of its most popular products are Cutty Sark, Jack Daniel's, and Famous Grouse.

The leading multinational in the alcohol industry in Greece is Diageo. The company's history in Greece (as Diageo Hellas) is related to the foundation of United Distilleries Boutari and the United Distilleries Greece. These companies merged in 1995 and acquired the business of United Distilleries Kanelakis. In 1997, when the global merger of Guinness and Grand Metropolitan created Diageo, the Greek subsidiaries of the two companies IDV Metaxa and United Distilleries Greece merged into UDV. In 2001, the company was renamed Guinness UDV Hellas, and in 2002 it adopted the name Diageo. Its products include the most popular whiskies on the Greek market, such as Johnnie Walker, Bell's, J & B, Haig, Vat 69, Black and White, White Horse, Dimple, Cardhu, and a variety of Scottish single malts. Furthermore, many brands that were traded by smaller companies such as Nektar from 1985 to 1991 finally passed on to Diageo. Today Diageo multinational has investments in more than 180 countries.

These three multinational companies have come to control the majority of the alcohol market not only in Greece but around the globe. In Greece alone, Diageo, Karoulias (Berry Bros.), Pernod Ricard (EPOM), Bacardi-Martini Hellas, AMVIX, and Mantis take almost 80 percent of the gross profit of the market, whereas there have been at least 285 companies competing to take a share.[6]

In conducting research relating to the above-mentioned companies, several themes became apparent that express their localized character over the past few years. Issues of nationality, for example, and the accumulated history of each company are expressed in the legal names attached to them. Pernod Ricard Hellas is followed by the abbreviation EPOM, the name of the Greek subsidiary that merged in 1990, and Karoulias still has the same name despite the fact that Berry Bros. & Rudd has taken total control of the Greek firm.

In terms of competition, the multinational corporations have fought to take as great a share in the market as they can by contracting with smaller importers and producers in Greece. According to the president of Pernod Ricard Greece, this has been achieved by a rationalization of distribution. The effectiveness of certain distribution strategies in recent years has resulted in easy and fast distribution to a variety of small communities. The multinational corporations have employees responsible for different areas of Greece who travel regularly to specific destinations to deal with the local distributors and take their orders. These employees usually work under the sales department. They offer detailed catalogues of all the products of each company, usually with photographs. The local distributor just fills out the order form, and within a short time the products are sent to him or her. The actual distribution is contracted with particular distribution companies that specialize in this sector. The main characteristic of this rationalization process, as Mr. Loutzakis put it, is that "in the past, production and distribution were pursued by the same means of operation, while now distribution employs different means such as experts on logistical operations."

Since the beginning of the 1990s, when the multinational firms took hold of the market, the amount of imported whisky has increased. That can be understood in terms of the effectiveness of the strategies used and the decreasing number of competitors. During this period the market for whisky in Greece has become the largest one in terms of imported drinks. This is illustrated in Table 1.1 where the dark section in the upper part corresponds to whisky in terms of quantity and the second one in value in comparison to other alcoholic drinks that include rum, gin, vodka, and liqueurs. The country of origin of these imports has mainly been the United Kingdom, with 70 percent of quantity and 78 percent of value of the total imports of alcoholic beverages (see table 1.1). Similarly, the consumption of alcohol in Greece in 1999 and 2000 was approximately 6.4 million boxes of twelve bottles totaling nine liters per person. This quantity corresponds to 40 percent of the total consumption of alcohol. Since then there have been small changes in these numbers, but still today Greece occupies seventh position in the total consumption of whisky globally, with 31 million bottles of 70 ml. (see table 1.2).

Despite the fact that in recent times new beverages (such as the ready-to-drink products) have been promoted, whisky still holds the biggest share of the market. The market for white drinks such as vodka, tequila, and rum has also been increasingly developed of late. However, this process is related to the establishment of the commodity chains of the multinational companies that are trading in a larger variety of drinks in a more efficient way and have larger marketing budgets for these products than in the past.

The promotion and marketing of whisky has been an important concern for the companies that have been trading in the drink over the last decade. It is worth stating that most of the multinational companies have recently developed marketing departments, taking into consideration local and national factors relating to consumption. Greece is the only country in Europe where the advertising of alcoholic drinks by almost every means is permitted. There are no legal constraints on the marketing of alcoholic beverages; restrictions on marketing rest solely in the hands of the companies themselves, and they are actually able to decide on their own so-called moral code. As a result, a large quantity of alcohol advertising exists in the mass media, in public spaces, and in other contexts.

Table 1.1. Imports of Alcoholic Beverages into Greece (Source: *Report on the Greek Alcohol Industry and the Sector of Beverages*, 1993. Foundation of Economic and Industrial Research of Greece (IOVE)).

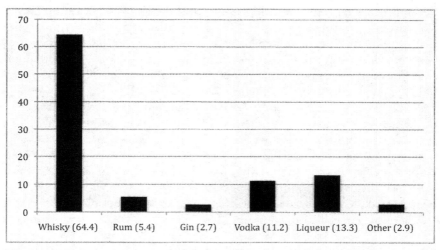

(quantity %)

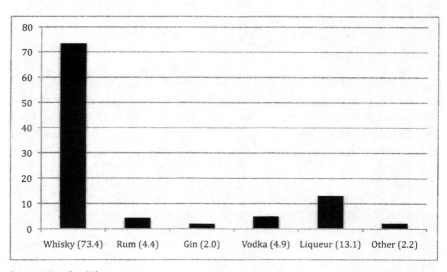

(economic value %)

Table 1.2. Scotch Whisky Global Export Markets in Terms of Value in British Sterling (Source: *Leaflet* published by the Scotch Whisky Association, U.K. 2007).

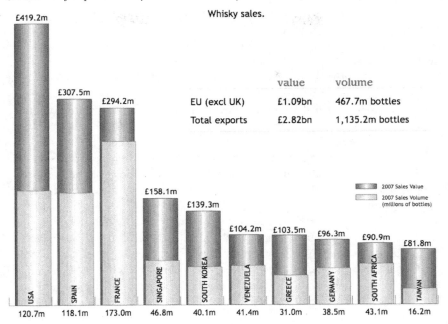

Whisky sales.

	value	volume
EU (excl UK)	£1.09bn	467.7m bottles
Total exports	£2.82bn	1,135.2m bottles

Table 1.3. Mergers and Cooperation in the Greek Beverages Sector 1988–1993 (Source: *Report on the Greek Alcohol Industry and the Sector of Beverages*, 1993. Foundation of Economic and Industrial Research of Greece (IOVE)).

Year	Investor	Target	Result
1988	METAXAS	KALOGIANNIS BROS OYZO 12	100% was bought
1989	GRAND METROPOLITAN	METAXAS	100% was bought and 35% of OYZO 12
1989	3 E, LEVENTIS GROUP	BOTRYS	
1989	ALLIED LYONS	GENKA	35% was bought; in 1993 90%
1990	PERNOD RICARD	LIZAS & LIZAS	90% was bought
1990	GRAND METROPOLITAN	OYZO 12	70% was bought
1991	BOUTARIS GROUP	KAMPAS	67% was bought
1992	BOUTARIS GROUP	HENNIGER HELLAS A.E. OF BSN GROUP	67% was bought
1992	BERRY BROS and RUDD Ltd. "Cutty Sark"	KAROULIAS AEBE	100% was bought
1992	BOUTARIS GROUP	UNITED DISTILLERIES BOUTARIS	50% was bought
1993	BOUTARIS GROUP	BOTRYS	100% assets were bought
1993	BOUTARIS GROUP	DISTILLERIE OF AEGEAN	100% was bought

From Local Trade to Transnational Capitalism

This short history of imported alcoholic beverages in Greece demonstrates the shift in ownership from local producers of alcohol and local importing companies to global corporations and multinational capital. This shift is nothing new; such processes are taking place in various forms everywhere and are entwined with globalization (Appadurai 2001). However, this story does not suggest that the shift is a unilinear process that can be found all over the globe. Various scholars have suggested that the opposite direction, that is, from global corporations to localized business operations, is also possible (Foster 2008: 71, Miller 1998). Coca-Cola, for example, is one such case of a localized network with its franchise system. It is therefore important to avoid generalizations in relation to economic globalization and be able to draw the different accountings of the competing supply of commodities as well as the interests that promote their production and consumption.

The transnational alcoholic beverage companies that appeared in Greece profited largely from their investments in the Greek market as the consumption of Scotch and other beverages rose considerably. Their decision to invest was based on the fact that the end of the 1980s signaled also the end of the *metapolitefsi* when transnational private capital investment was largely supported by the state and new private media such as television channels, radio stations, and newspapers were established for the first time in Greece. In addition, the new tax regulations of the European Union that came into power by 1990 harmonized the free movement of goods, the custom duties, and the taxation and as a result made the importation of alcoholic beverages a more profitable sector with much lower cost for the average consumer.

The speeding up of the processes of production and consumption during the 1990s resulted in the subcontracting and merging of Greek companies with the largest global competitors in the alcohol business, namely the Diageo, Pernod Ricard, and Berry Bros. companies. These companies in turn managed to gain control of almost 80 percent of the market within a few years, taking advantage of the local knowledge of their subcontractors and their associates in Greece. The companies used new technology and new production methods, but more importantly they established new distribution methods that made it possible to move the commodities faster from the production site and the import location to the retail store and the consumer.

As Appadurai has noted, "globalization from above" as defined by corporations, multinational agencies, policy experts, and national governments is a complex and powerful force of change (2001: 19). Within this context,

> Global capital in its contemporary form is characterized by strategies of predatory mobility (across both time and space) that have vastly compromised the

capacities of actors in single locations even to understand, much less to antici-
pate or resist, these strategies. (Appadurai 2001: 17)

However such statements might raise questions about the effectiveness of commercial strategies on consumers. One could argue that elite owners of the means
of production and distribution of alcoholic beverages as well as those who are
producers of cinema imagination and marketing do not leave consumers much
space for resistance. As Adorno has argued, the cultural industry creates a form
of mass deception, and as such consumers are disciplined to become modern
European emancipated persons, a form of instrumental rationality that makes
people submit to its authority as domination (1991: 98–106). This line of thinking will be critically reviewed in the coming ethnographic chapters that examine
the limitations and the weaknesses of such perspectives.

Furthermore, large-scale economic globalization is not necessarily a process
from above. Local businesses want to become part of global corporations and
actively search for these possibilities. In the words of Mr. Loutzakis, president of
Pernod Ricard Greece, who was the owner of the family alcohol business Lizas
and Lizas, "the big corporations were in search of us just as we were in search of
them, and that's how in 1990 our company got married to Pernod Ricard" (interview with C. Loutzakis, 22 February 2006). The "marriage" of local business
to global corporations continued in various other contexts of the market and
characterized many other businesses.

Notes

1. Scotch whisky possibly first arrived in Greece with the British communities that moved
   into the country to play an active role in the political and economic life of the country
   after the Greek independence war in 1821. The relationship between the two countries has
   been in one sense a long, romantic enterprise full of fictions and dreams and conversely a
   story of political, economic, and symbolic influence. Britain was instrumental in the creation of the modern Greek state, in large part due to its idealized notions of Greek culture
   and history. From the time of the creation of the Greek state, figures such as Alexandros
   Mavrokordatos actively supported British involvement in Greek affairs, and the British
   have had the opportunity to influence, participate, and promote their own interests in
   Greece.
2. An important role in the development of consumerism during the 1960s and 1970s was
   played by Spyros Markezinis, head of the Ministry of Economics under the Papagos Greek
   Rally (Clogg 1992: 168).
3. Interview with the president of Pernod Ricard Greece, C. Loutzakis, 22 February 2006.
4. The PASOK, or Pan-Hellenic Socialistic Party, first came to power in October 1981 and
   was reelected in 1985. During this period, the founder of the party, Andreas Papandreou,
   became the prime minister.
5. Interview with the president of Pernod Ricard Greece, C. Loutzakis, 22 February 2006.

6. These data are changing continuously due to new deals and mergers in the food and beverages sector. They are based on an economic report in the *Eleftherotypia* daily newspaper, Economy section, 25 May 2003 under the title "Anthektika ta kerdi."

CHAPTER 2

Dreams of Modernity

Imagining the Consumption of Whisky
during the Golden Age of Greek Cinema

Scenarios of the Future

The development of cinema and the film industry in Greece came long before marketing and television advertisements, which meant that new commodities were seen for the first time in scenarios that had usually been produced in Greece by the film industry. The refrigerator, the washing machine, the car, and the bottle of whisky were only a few of the many commodities projected in films. These fetish-like commodities would appear on the cinema screen similar to the way they would stand in a shop window: polished, new, and shiny. One could argue that they were presented with certain ambivalence: as entailing various forms of alienation or as investing consumers with a modern style.

During the period between the end of the civil war in 1949 and the end of the colonels' regime in 1974, Greece was transformed in various ways. External and internal migration, the massive urbanization and expansion of Athens, and the postwar liberal economic policies resulted in a new social landscape. Within this context, popular cinema consisted mainly of comedies and melodramas, with scenarios inspired by realistic social contexts. These scenarios represented social change and the consumption of modernness, along with various themes: migration from the countryside to Athens; the destruction of what were considered to be traditional houses and their replacement by apartment blocks; social inequality expressed in luxury goods (and specifically whisky); new American or British forms of entertainment and music; and the struggle between traditional and modern attitudes in social life. This symbolic conflict was a major preoccupation in most films, and the arrival of modernity was expressed in various ways: new and fashionable clothes, sexual freedom, consumerism, continuous night entertainment, and the consumption of imported alcohol. In that sense, the film scenarios recorded and expressed a sociocultural transformation, the transformation into a consumer society, a society of spectacle, and a society that was trying to get modernized.

However, such scenarios were and still are a "particular kind of performance" (Williams and Orrom 1954: 25) that does not ensure the consumption of the projected commodities by audiences simply because those audiences can absorb them. On the contrary, recent studies have challenged this view by arguing that "the meaning of texts or objects is enacted through practices of reception" (Ginsburg, Abu-Lughod, and Larkin 2002: 6). As various anthropologists have demonstrated, mass media (including cinema and soap opera) do not necessarily modernize, Americanize, or commoditize their audiences (Abu-Lughod 1995, Michaels 2002, Miller 1994) The scenarios of films and television series can be related to an active self-production and appropriation by the audiences who incorporate them into their life worlds.

In this historical part of the study, the aim is to illustrate the "structures of feeling" (Williams and Orrom 1954: 33) existent in the cinematic genre between the 1950s and 1960s and examine these film scenarios as potential material for imagining selves. The scenarios are stories about possible, alternative futures that integrate human diversity and uncertainty (Ginsburg, Abu-Lughgod, and Larkin 2002) but at the same time they constitute scripts/texts circulated by mass communication in the "public sphere" (Habermas 1989). Within this context, Scotch is presented as a beverage that is modern, urban, and local, a sort of modern Greek drink.

One of the main goals is to reveal the distinctiveness of the relationship between the Greek commercial cinema of the 1960s and the ethnographic perceptions about modernity as this is expressed in whisky. Whisky became a central symbol of a happy or a melancholic modernity; in many scenarios, Scotch is liked not because it tastes good but because it tastes modern. By elaborating on this relationship, I wish to suggest that the scenarios projected are rather different from their Western European counterparts because of the distinctive socioeconomic conditions under which they were produced. To understand the valuation and reevaluation process of whisky in Greece and the projections of the cultural industry in relation to the beverage, I will follow whisky in the scenarios of Greek cinema produced mainly between the end of the 1950s and the beginning of the 1970s, the golden era for the production and consumption of Greek cinema and the decade that preceded the emergence of Greek consumer society. This chapter is based on viewings of more than eighty films from the mentioned period; whisky is consumed or used in various ways in the vast majority of the films.

By examining these scenarios certain themes became apparent that incorporate various ideas about Scotch and modernity. The choice of these specific scenarios was based on the role of Scotch in each story. However, similar ideas and perceptions can be found in many other scenarios of the period. The chosen films were among the most popular of their time, and as such, they are representative of the mentioned themes.

The massive number of tickets sold during the decade of the 1960s is a reminder of the appeal and success that Greek films had for their audiences. From 1963 onward, annual cinema ticket sales were the highest in Europe, with 100 million tickets sold, whereas the population of the country at the time was less than 7 million (Sotiropoulou 1989: 44). Furthermore, the average number of film productions in the 1950s was fifty per year and in the 1960s almost a hundred (Soldatos 2002: 73). Consequently, the Greek film industry was a postwar miracle that expressed a specific structure of feeling of its modernist authors and directors.

This part of the study seeks to bridge cultural studies and social anthropology by borrowing theoretical insights from both disciplines. The work of Raymond Williams is particularly relevant to the aims of this chapter, and I have consciously employed his term *structures of feeling* to describe the culture that is exhibited in the scenarios of Greek films of the 1960s. Williams uses this term to refer to the culture of a specific historical moment and suggests a common set of perceptions and values that are shared by one generation and expressed in artistic forms and esthetic criteria and conventions. As Williams stated, with a large emphasis on cinema, "It is in art, primarily, that the effect of the totality, the dominant structure of feeling, is expressed and embodied" (Williams and Orrom 1954: 33).

Furthermore, the structure of feeling of the film industry seeks to describe the "cluster of dominant images, meanings and sentiments in a specific culture" and the "taken for granted aspects of social life" (Hughes 1998: 7). The structure of feeling in William's terms is "as firm and definite as structure," yet it "operates in the most delicate and least tangible parts of our activity" (1965: 64). It is "not feeling against thought, but thought as felt and feeling as thought: practical consciousness of a present kind, in a living and inter-relating continuity" (1997: 132). This is very evident in the film scenarios referred to above, as whisky emerges in the most subtle and unobtrusive forms. Bottles of whisky transformed into candleholders or actors surrounded by persons drinking whisky while they enjoy a night out are details that may go unnoticed, yet they encapsulate the core of feeling of the golden age of Greek cinema. In addition, Williams has noted that the structure of feeling is not possessed in the same way by different individuals, and it is not "not uniform throughout society" (1965: 80), but rather is constructed through power relations and expresses ideals that are most interrelated with norms and experiences of the most powerful social groups within society (Williams 1965: 80). The film industry in postwar Greece was one such powerful elite that influenced the social, economic, and political life in various ways.

Various historians have tried to approach cinema as a historical source under certain conditions (Ferro 1988). Ferro has argued that cinema represents various aspects of a given society, such as ideology, value system, and political establishment. However, the most important aspect of a film analysis is that the film industry can be viewed as a carrier and a producer of the culture of a specific time and place. This process might be on a conscious or unconscious level when the production takes place, as Williams has argued. In either case, the contexts produced are culturally influenced, especially when the themes projected are void and unimportant. For example the clothes, the food and beverages, and the music can be very interesting contexts of information regarding the social life of each period. In this sense, film scenarios can be viewed as generators of mentalities, expectations, dreams, and future alternatives.

Films on the screen also include commodified images that affect the perception of audiences/consumers by proliferating their desirable selves and daydreams and creating an imagined reality of a better life (Benjamin 2009). This imagined better life was a major preoccupation of many cinematic consumers in Greece who had experienced the depressing effects of World War II, the Civil War, migration (internal and external), unstable political life, and poverty.

Moreover, by borrowing from the anthropology of media (Ginsburg, Abu-Lughod, and Larkin 2002), the notion of the imaginary (Appadurai 1996), I seek to comprehend the values projected in the film scenarios and to demonstrate that whisky in Greece was not fetishized by marketing or multinational corporations but rather came to express certain imagined visions of future modernity in postwar Greece. In other words, Greek films became the means for the development of future scenarios of modernness and commodity fetishism. That process was a necessary requirement and condition for the localization of the beverage in Greece, especially because it provided the material for dreaming and imagining about the future.

The significance of imagination in the production of culture and social identity has been extensively noted by Appadurai (1996), who points to the role of mediascapes in influencing national and transnational processes. It is through mediascapes that imagined communities come together and reproduce their sense of identity, culture, and belonging. National imaginaries can be produced by the nation-state or by commercial agents and can have a wide impact as technologies of personhood (Ginsburg, Abu-Lughod, and Larkin 2002: 5).

The golden age of Greek cinema during the 1960s, and especially between 1960 and 1967 (precisely before the dictatorship in Greece), was a major source of consumer and modern imaginaries, and not only of whisky. These modern imaginaries have been materializing since at least 1970 with the end of the golden age of Greek cinema and the emergence of a Greek consumer society. In this sense, the film scenarios express a sociocultural transition that was actually taking place, but at the same time they express the visions and imaginaries of the film industry.

Urban middle- or higher-class authors who were well-educated and very much preoccupied with modernism and modernity wrote the scenarios of most films. Within this context, the subjects of tradition and modernity were represented in various forms and became central characteristics of the genre. More importantly, the constant opposition of these themes as expressed in traditional Greek beverages versus whisky illustrates that these cinematic scenarios were scenarios about the future and artistic dreams of modernity.

Greek Cinema

The invention of moving pictures at the end of the nineteenth century by Thomas Edison in the United States and the Lumiere brothers in Europe represented one of the most celebrated of modern technologies. Cinema was to be not only the offspring of modernity, however, but also the recording device of social and economic change, a tool of propaganda but also of interpretation, a vehicle of marketing but also of political and social critique.

Though cinema came into being in Greece very early, when the brothers Yannis and Miltos Manakia filmed in the area of Macedonia in 1906, the development of Greece's own cinematic industry came much later. The first cinema in Athens was established in 1908, and within a few years cinemas multiplied. The first Greek films were made during World War I, and they were limited to short news reports produced by well-known directors such as Georgios Prokopiou and Dimitris Gaziadis. *Golfo,* one of the first Greek feature films, was released in 1915 and presented a love story set in rural Greece. *Villar,* one of the first commercial successes, was shown to Athenians in 1920. The scenario of *Villar* was written and directed by the comedian Villar (Nikolas Sfakianakis) and was shown at the women's bath at Faliro. One of the first Greek film companies, known as Doug-Scenarios, was established between 1927 and 1928 and produced a number of well-known films such as *Love and Waves* (1928), directed by Gaziadis, and *Daphnis and Chloe* (1931), directed by Laskos. The first Greek-made picture with sound was *The Lover of the Shepherdess,* directed by Tsakiris. An early attempt with sound (played on a gramophone behind the screen) that proved successful was the *Apaches of Athens.*

During World War II, Filopemen Finos founded Finos Films (1942), which became one the most successful film companies in the industry within just a few years. The postwar period saw the activities of the production companies Finos Films, Anzervos Films, Novak Films, Spentzos Films, Karayiannis-Karatzopoulos, and Damaskinos-Mihailidis, all of which created an extraordinary number of films within just a few years.

However, the advent of television, the international economic crisis, the dictatorship, and the poor performance of the Greek economy were all causal factors in the general decline of Greek commercial cinema in the 1970s. However, the films produced during that time would continue to be rebroadcast in times to come on televisions in every household.

The postwar cinema of the period that came to be known as the golden age of Greek cinema has been criticized for being nonpolitical, especially because the films did not narrate the past (the civil war, the German occupation, postwar economic policies) and did not touch on troublesome issues such as the king's role in the political life of the country or the involvement of Britain and the United States in Greece's affairs. On the contrary, the scenarios of that period were mostly fixated on the present and the future, the arrival of modernity and its outcome. The films told stories of rapid urbanization, massive migration, family life, and—more importantly—social relationships. It is worth stating, though, that themes were necessarily limited because all films made between 1965 and 1975 were subject to censorship as a result of the dictatorship (Soldatos 2002: 53). Thus, many films were banned, whereas priority was given to light comedies and romantic dramas. For this reason, productions of this period have been characterized as "low quality" and "petit bourgeois" oriented, and they have been neglected by scholars until very recently (Delveroudi 2004: 19).

The distinction between artistic and commercial films has produced a rather partial understanding of the meanings and perception of these scenarios. As a result, the emphasis of various scholars on the artistic scenarios has reproduced an internal inequality existent in the cinematic genre that has not been put under question despite the fact that artistic taste has been demonstrated as a form of social differentiation (Bourdieu 1984). Moreover, the social and cultural analysis of scenarios is related to the cultural preference of scholars for specific artistic themes despite the fact that what is conceived as commercial cinema was viewed by the large majority of the population.

In many scenarios, the youth of the 1950s and 1960s were projected as the carriers of social change when faced with the crisis of adopting new modern values. This adoption led to conflict with their parents and their traditional surroundings. Young people were considered the social group that was influenced more than anybody else by the arrival of modernity. Though youth was the central theme in relation to modernity, it gradually became clear by the 1960s that many others would emulate their new lives. As Delveroudi has noted, whereas in the 1950s, middle-class families were trying to cover their basic needs such as food and clothing, in 1960 they were projected on screen as copying the elites, dressing in fashionable clothes, living in comfortable houses, and entertaining themselves in nightclubs (Delveroudi 2004: 68).

In these scenarios, commodities expressed social positioning, especially within the context of traditional and modern approaches toward life. However, Kapsomenos' observation that the posh Anglo-American lifestyle in Greek urban environments should not be regarded as a social norm because it belonged only to the world of on-screen scenarios and the world of the elites should be taken seriously into account (Kapsomenos 1990: 218). The commodity-object in the film scenarios emerged in a dream-like atmosphere, which could not necessarily be emulated by the viewer but could be consumed to the extent that the viewer identified with the protagonists. Despite the serious questions that such a critique poses, the consumption patterns projected in the film scenarios of this period should have influenced the consumer imaginary. In the films of that period, the modern commodity-object became fetishized to the extent that its use-value was overshadowed by the conspicuous projection of the commodity. The refrigerator was placed in the living room as part of the furniture, as was the television; imported beverages were regularly seen on the tables of *bouzoukia* (music halls with live popular Greek music)[1] whether they were consumed or not; American cigarettes were smoked by the protagonists, and ballet dancers performed with whisky bottles in their hands. Shots of the city were usually of people walking at a fast and agitated pace, and there was constant traffic noise and the sound of construction work in the background. The countryside was set in diametrical opposition to the urban contexts and projected as a nostalgic setting untouched by the advent of modernity. Films set in the countryside presented villagers as pure and unspoiled by liberal ideas of profit and individualism, and they showed them becoming alienated when they visited or were touched by the city. The urban and cosmopolitan styles shown in most scenarios would stand as polar opposites of the rural ones, and the difference would be expressed through language use (Georgakopoulou 2000: 119–133), profession (Kartalou 2000: 105–118), clothing, and consumption habits. The styles projected can further explicate the structure of feeling of modernity performed by the actors. Georgakopoulou has argued that many Finos Films are about four basic characters, all caricatures that express age, gender, and class: the newly rich, professionals, blue-collar workers, and nightlife types or small-time delinquents (2000: 122). These types can be further divided according to gender and age; the newly rich are usually young men or middle-aged women; professional types are middle-aged men; blue-collar workers can be men or women; and nightlife types and petty criminals are usually men. These characters express various symbolic struggles: between foreign and Greek culture, between modernization and tradition, between conservative and progressive, between high and low classes, between educated and uneducated, and between marginal and mainstream. I would further argue that whisky is used as a major marker of these oppositions. Whisky usually stands as a symbol of foreign influence, of modernization, of the progressive, of the educated, and of both the marginal and the mainstream. Other characters might include Greek migrants or students from the United States or the U.K. who usually drink whisky and might be young or middle-aged men and women; villagers who express ignorance in relation to consumer goods when compared with urbanites; and industrialists who are usually middle-aged or older males who drink whisky.

The cinema industry producing such a massive number of films during that period resulted in low-budget productions with similar plots. The main characters also included various female types ranging from women who would fall in love and be seduced by evil men to women who lost their virginity and ended up as prostitutes, and also fathers who tried to preserve their daughter's moral values in changing urban contexts. In general, the films showed a struggle for honesty, honor, and values with the advent of modernity. However, despite the fact that most films either tried to be very modern or made fun of a new modernity, the plots remained within the context of Greek values; the ultimate success or the happy ending was usually a wedding, honesty would always prevail and be rewarded in the end, the main context of socialization was kinship relationships, and the norms of the majority of the characters were based on traditional Greek practices (dowry, extended kinship, masculine domination, patronage, and hierarchical relationships). As a result, the plots tended to be either very comic or very tragic—melodramas or music-centered films that reproduced cultural patterns in an imaginative modernity.

Even though the films did not receive very positive comments in the media of the time because of their low artistic quality and the repetition of similar scripts, the industry proliferated and generated a star system (Soldatos 2002). Certain actors repeatedly performed almost the same roles, and these became crystallized in the popular imagination. Kostantaras, for example, would play the humorous father and Iliopoulos the low-income public servant or the poor junior clerk; Hatzihristos was the amusing and pure peasant who left his village to visit Athens, Voutsas the amusing youth and victim of beautiful women, Kourkoulos the serious young womanizer. Fotopoulos was always the masculine, macho figure. Female actors likewise had their own distinct roles: Vougiouklaki was the carefree young woman in love, Karayanni took the party animal and funny woman roles, Mavropoulou and Zilia were usually good-hearted prostitutes or badly treated housewives, Karezi was the melodramatic heroine suffering difficult relationships, and Laskari played the dangerous woman or the young, fun-loving wealthy daughter.

Within this context, whisky emerged as a symbol of modernity that was consumed by young characters on the move, by alienated individuals, and by successful wealthy Athenians. In addition, the fetishism of the product exercised a certain alienating quality in relation to several characters in the plots to the extent that Scotch was projected as an evil drink of the underground world and of the alienated foreigners or Greek Americans. In this manner Scotch became the symbol of either a celebratory or a melancholic modernity. To use gadgets and live in modern houses, to dress and talk foreign was not enough; the ultimate change was to embody modernity and its tastes. The expression *you have taste* (*ehis gousto*), for example, refers to the habitual refinement of a person and reminds us that taste as a sense is socially and culturally influenced.

The "Evil" Drink: Trespassing and Destroying Ourselves

Greek cinema reached its peak in the 1950s and 1960s. The rapid modernization, urbanization, and socioeconomic change are depicted in the cinema of the period in various ways, and the new city life inspired the various scenarios. During this period, various films were shown to Greek audiences and became extremely popular. In many scenarios, whisky and imported beverages are depicted as part of a modern way of life; sometimes they are projected as forces of alienation or as drinks with a criminal association. In that sense, commodity fetishism is clearly expressed in whisky, leading to alienation. As a result, this form of alienation is presented as a rupture with the traditional values, the moral cosmos of the protagonists, and the world around them. However, these scenarios do not necessarily imply that alienation is a result of commodity fetishism. On the contrary, whisky is personified by the modern urbanite and, in certain scenarios, the underground world and the prostitutes.

The structure of feeling expressed in several scenarios is loss, alienation, and seduction. Plots present divided persons as a result of modernity rather than individuals in possession of themselves, a scenario found in various forms of screen technologies (Pels 2002: 91–119). As Pels has argued, one distinct modern form of alienation identifies modernity itself as an alienating instance (Pels 2002: 111). This alienation has been conceptualized as a form of division between people who are not alienated and those who are imagined as self-possessed. Scenarios range from villagers who lose themselves and identify with the influence of urbanites, to Greeks who are seduced by foreign habits and commodities, to moral and rational male individuals who become immoral, irrational, feminized, and divided, and finally to women who turn to prostitution and seduce honest male individuals.

A characteristic scenario, which demonizes whisky and objectifies it as a destructive force that alienates and threatens the moral values of the middle-aged rational male individual under certain circumstances is *Ena votsalo stin limni* (*A Pebble in the Lake*), by Millas Film in 1952. The penny-pinching, hard-working, and conservative Manolis is married and lives a moral life. His wife asks for certain gifts that Manolis is not willing to offer her, as he is very stingy. However, the course of events will transform him into a generous man who is happy to buy and consume. One day a cousin of his wife's arrives who lives in the United States. Manolis has never met her and so does not know what she looks like. The following morning, Manolis's colleague tells him that he has met an American woman (who, ironically enough, turns out to be a friend of Manolis's wife's cousin). The colleague sets up a date with the two women and invites Manolis to come along. On the evening of the date, the two women arrive at Manolis's office to go out and have a few drinks. Manolis meets his wife's cousin but has no idea who she really is. He calls his wife and pretends he is busy working, and then spends the time with the Greek-American woman who—unbeknown to him—is his wife's cousin. The colleague offers the women whisky to drink, but there is not enough whisky, so he and the other woman leave to buy some more. During their absence, Manolis drinks whisky with the Greek-American woman while she does her best to seduce him. However, Manolis is not used to the drink. The woman downs her whisky in one gulp, and when Manolis imitates her, he chokes and exclaims, "What is this thing? What burning sensation is that? Is it produced on Vesuvius?" Manolis and his colleague take the women to various *bouzoukia* for entertainment and much whisky is consumed. The drunker Manolis becomes, the more bottles he orders, and he spends a huge amount of money in an irrational manner. The end result of this frenzied night is that Manolis is left by his friend completely drunk at the entrance of his apartment, where the neighbors find him and carry him to his flat. The next day, Manolis pretends that he remembers almost nothing, thanks to the devilish beverage. Then the American cousin arrives at the house and, to her surprise, encounters Manolis. The cousin understands the tragic coincidence that has occurred, but she decides not to reveal her date with Manolis to his wife.

The main character in *Kalpiki Lira* (*The Counterfeit Coin*), by Anzervos in 1955, is Anargiros, an honest engraver of metal who has his shop in the center of Athens. A man working in the investment agency where Anargiros puts his earnings tries to persuade him to collaborate in producing counterfeit money. To this end, he arranges for Anargiros to meet up with a woman who is to play a Trojan-horse role to break into his honest life and persuade him to become a counterfeiter. In this context, the woman uses whisky to relax Anargiros and create an intimate atmosphere. In other words, whisky is a tool for creating a false consciousness and a dishonest life. The woman is shown as an immoral agent who aspires to a modern way of life and seduces innocent men. Anargiros, who is conservative and traditional, is inexperienced with women. As a result, he is finally seduced by the woman and is later caught by the police. The connection of whisky with a modernity that consists of fake money and false consciousness suggests that there should be an authentic self that is not alienated and divided. The nonalienated self uses authentic money earned by nonalienated labor and cannot afford to be seduced. The seduction of traditional subjects by modern ones is a scenario that is repeated in many films and expresses an ambiguity about the outcome of modernity as well as a fear of being fundamentally changed by modern objects and subjects.

A similar plot is narrated in the comedy *To Prosopo tis Imeras* (*The Man of the Day*), by Afoi Roussopouloi in 1965 with Kostas Voutsas. Grigoris, the main protagonist, lives in a small village in rural Greece. In a radio competition he wins a fifteen-day trip to Athens to stay in one of the best hotels. He leaves his village with his suitcase, which happens to resemble a suitcase belonging to a smuggler of Greek antiquities. When he arrives in Athens, members of a criminal ring confuse Grigoris with the smuggler, and he ends up drinking whisky in the house of a female partner who tries to seduce him and persuade him to cooperate. Members of the criminal ring are also seen drinking whisky with dancers in a jazz club. Grigoris tries to escape the ring in a frantic chase, with all the gangsters believing that he is carrying an ancient Greek statue in his suitcase. Along with the central opposition of city/consumerism and country/moderation, another opposition is added in this scenario, that between tradition and modernity. Tradition is clearly rural and is related to Greek beverages, while modernity is urban and is expressed through whisky. Whisky is again placed on the side of the nonauthentic self, which is deeply divided by a modern coincidence. Consumer modernity not only alienates the self here but also alienates the inalienable Greek heritage (which is linked to the Greek tradition) by commoditizing it. These opposite poles of alienable consumerism and inalienable Greek heritage are central to any understanding of contemporary Greek culture (Yalouri 2001: 101–137).

Whisky is also portrayed as a decadent beverage in the film *Kalos Irthe to Dollario* (*Dollar Welcome*), by Anzervos in 1967 starring Giorgos Kostantinou and Niki Linardou. The Blue Black bar is situated close to the harbor of Piraeus in the bad neighborhood of Trouba in Athens, where prostitution, strip shows, and the consumption of alcohol are all to be found. The main protagonist is an honest teacher of English. The prostitutes of the bar want to employ him to teach them to speak English, as the sixth fleet of the United States Navy is approaching the harbor. The teacher accepts the offer, even though he does not like it, as he is short of money. The American soldiers finally arrive and visit the bar to drink whisky and have sex. One of the women working as a prostitute falls in love with the teacher and tries to seduce him with whisky. The teacher has no idea about the beverage, however, and when it is served he drinks it at a gulp, his face clearly expressing his negative reaction to the taste. His sensation of taste is clearly one of uneasiness, surprise, and disgust because he is innocent and not cosmopolitan enough to know about and appreciate whisky. The woman, surprised at his ignorant way of consuming the drink, states, "Whisky needs to be consumed slowly," and she orders (in local) dialect two cups, or detonators (*skagia*). With the help of the beverage, the woman seduces the honest man and they both fall in love. This scenario clearly connects whisky with a decadent and supposedly Americanized way of life that commoditizes sex and human relationships.[2] This feeling of a loss of innocence through modernity is related to certain historical circumstances. Trouba was indeed an area characterized by prostitution and cabarets where whisky was served during the 1950s. Furthermore, this area, which was visited by other foreign seamen as well as the United States Navy, is very likely one of the first places where whisky was regularly drunk and became localized. In that sense, part of the cultural biography of whisky is clearly connected with the decadence of prostitution and the commoditization of women. Similarly, several underground *bouzoukia* after the 1980s were also connected to prostitution and consummation, the practice of buying the company of women in exchange for alcoholic beverages. As chapter four demonstrates, this commoditization of *bouzoukia* during the 1980s was in parallel development with the commercialization of contemporary Greek popular music and the establishment of Scotch as a celebratory beverage.

Whisky has also been projected in various scenarios as a decadent beverage consumed by the spoiled young people of wealthy families. Gender is extremely important in this context, as women would rarely play a decadent role despite the fact they were portrayed as drinking or even getting drunk. In most films, the alienated persons were young or middle-aged men who enjoyed partying and seducing women. Women were not portrayed as independent persons who were able to be in control of their lives and, more significantly, live in a bohemian cosmopolitan style. An exception to this was Vlahopoulou's role in *Mia Treli Sarantara* (*A Crazy Forty-Year-Old Woman*), by Finos Films in 1970. The protagonist is a bohemian woman in her forties who challenges the conservative attitudes of her family by spending her money on nightlife and drinking whisky. Within this context, whisky is presented as the modern beverage that disrupts conservative family values and the traditional practice of matchmaking. She falls in love with a violin player in a nightclub while her brother is trying to arrange a marriage for her with an old wealthy Greek man who lives in London. One night she returns home drunk with her boyfriend and upsets her family, who happen to visit her that same night. The next morning, the couple leaves the house to get married. The importance of marriage and family life was central even in scenarios that purported to criticize the conventions of conservative or traditional social life. In this context, whisky is shown threatening family values by projecting an alternative bohemian modern lifestyle. The importance of marriage and the family in modern Greece has been noted by many ethnographers who have specifically outlined how personhood is shaped by these values. Even today, Greece has one of the lowest divorce rates in Europe, and the rite of passage of marriage is seen as transforming young people into adults and social persons.

A male figure representative of the spoiled young man is Kostantinou in *O Anthropos Gia Oles tis Doulies* (*The Man for All Kind of Jobs*), by Afoi Roussopouloi in 1966. Whisky dominates the entire film. The story begins with the main protagonist waking up next to a bottle of whisky (VAT 69) and an unknown woman. His father, a wealthy ship owner, is deeply disappointed in him because he is not able to run the family business on account of his drinking and constant craving for entertainment. The young man decides to give up his old lifestyle, make his own living, and quit drinking and partying. He leaves his father's house and moves to a new place, where he starts working in a hotel as a waiter, but unfortunately he is pushed again to drink whisky by a Greek-American customer with whom he has developed a good relationship. While drinking, the Greek American talks about the problems in his life. When the waiter finally manages to leave the room of the Greek American, who has persistently tried to make him drink more and more whisky, he is faced with a customer who has ordered whisky in the hotel lounge but cannot pay for it. The waiter lets this young man go after berating him: "What do you want with whisky and a luxurious life?" (*Ti tis thelis tis ouiskares sou kai tin megali tin zoi?*). This expression is intended to be a lesson to the young man who cannot afford to pay for the Scotch and who should focus on constructive activities instead of drinking whisky.

The connection of Greek Americans with whisky is evident in various other scenarios, and it is repeated throughout the films of the golden age of Greek cinema. Greek Americans are shown as alienated from their own Greek culture and traditions; they might be presented drinking alone, even sometimes to the extent of alcoholism, and in the case of women they might be shown enjoying an overt expression of sexuality. Both of these scenarios can be deeply condemned in a conservative Greek context, as drinking alone is a stigmatized activity. The moderation (in alcohol and sexuality) that is the ideal for women in Greece is also shown in opposition to the expressive sexuality and hard drinking of the Greek Americans.

The structure of feeling of commercial Greek cinema is therefore intertwined with the processes of modernization and, more specifically, urbanization of Greek society during the 1960s. Within this context, alienation is felt as a form of disruption of the traditional values of Greek society, a feeling of loss of community values, and a corruption of morality. Indeed, the social changes taking place in urban and rural Greece during this period are clearly portrayed in the films of commercial Greek cinema. In the films under discussion, this form of objectification takes place with whisky, which is fetishized and comes to reify relationships of symbolic domination between the modern Western world and the margins of Europe. However, such forms of objectification are not necessarily viewed as relationships between objects. There is also a process of personification at play. Those who are at the margins of the society, the petty criminals, the frequenters of parties, and those who violate traditional Greek values (like the Greek-American immigrant characters), are personified with Scotch whisky. However, this objectification is not necessarily an alienated instance; as will be demonstrated, the objectification of Scotch in the scenarios of commercial Greek cinema is also related to a celebration of modernity.

Modernity in a Bottle

In various films, the alienation entailed in whisky drinking is replaced by a feeling of modernness. This modernness is not necessarily negative; in many cases it can in fact be presented as very constructive. The cosmopolitan styles found among those main characters who are emigrant Greeks returning from their new lives in America, the newly rich or industrialists, and middle- or upper-class Athenians are demonstrated in foreign accents, foreign words, and the conspicuous consumption of American or British products: cigarettes, cars, whisky, and expensive clothes. However, the foreign accents and the use of foreign words and language in many films are not surprising given that in the literature of the time, heteroglossia was reemerging after a long period of "monological linguistic representations and enforced unifications" (Georgakopoulou 2000: 127). That suppression was a result of a long effort by the state to suppress local dialects and introduce the clean language, the *katharevusa*. In this context, whisky as shown in the scenarios of the film industry came to represent the future and the consequences of modernity at large. These included the rapid urbanization of Greece, the individualization or commoditization of the self, migration to the United States or other European countries, class inequalities in postwar liberal Greece, and the marginalities that were emerging in a highly commodified world.

In 1960, the Thessalonica Film Festival was established with the aim of presenting a panorama of European and Greek cinema and honoring the best directors and actors. The Festival had long-standing effects on the production of cinema and would, in time, become one of the best known in Europe. In the same year, Greece participated in the Cannes Film festival with the film *Never on Sunday,* directed by Jules Dassen. The film was a great success, and its main star, Melina Mercouri, shared the award for best actress with Jeanne Moreau. The following year the same film received five Oscars, including best director for Dassen and best music for Manos Hatzidakis with the song "Children of Piraeus."

Never on Sunday was a landmark in modern Greek cinema. It narrates the journey of an American writer into what is presented as a true and authentic Greekness that finds material expression in *ouzo* and dancing. It is possible that Melina Mercouri, Dassen's wife, the star of the film and later the Minister of Culture in the 1980s and 1990s, influenced her husband's representation of this Greekness, tradition, and Greek heritage, which is the main preoccupation of the film (Tsitsopoulou 2000: 80). An American classical scholar called Homer (not by accident), who has a stereotypical image of Greece, travels in the country and is charmed by a beautiful Greek woman who expresses her sexuality freely and is in the service of men as a prostitute. Homer falls in love with the Greek woman while he is preaching at her according to his ancient Greek standards and ideas taken from history and philosophy books, lecturing her on the proper Greek moral values and what the Greeks are and should be. This colonial-type attitude is presented ironically, as Homer does not speak modern Greek and is shown as unable to understand Greek modernity. Amid the film's energetic atmosphere, he is alienated because he does not understand that dancing and drinking are not so much entertainment for the Greek characters as important emotional values. Therefore

> Music does not bring the two main characters of *Never on Sunday* together, on the contrary it emphasizes the distance that separates them. Only at the very end of the scenario after imbibing a considerable amount of ouzo, is Homer finally able to join the dance in the Taverna. (Tsistopoulou 2000: 83)

This scenario, intended for an international audience, stands in sharp contradiction to the films of Greek directors of the same period who projected whisky as a symbol of a particular modernity for their Greek audiences and totally neglected *ouzo*.

I Thia Apo to Chicago (*The Aunt from Chicago*), by Finos Films in 1957, is a comedy that became extremely popular during its release. A retired brigadier has four daughters who are of an age to get married. However, his military discipline and strict manners do not leave his daughters any chance to meet anyone to marry. The arrival of an aunt from Chicago, a refugee from the family who is living abroad, shakes the brigadier to his traditional and conservative foundations, as he has to follow her eccentric wishes. This modern aunt's first wish is for a bottle of whisky, which the brigadier buys to the surprise of the owner of the neighboring shop; "You don't take this kind of beverage in your house, sir" says the grocer. The brigadier replies, "Just wrap it well so people can't see the bottle." The aunt with the progressive modern ideas smokes and drinks whisky while she tries to transform the house into a modern place. She replaces the old cupboard with a mini-bar and dances to jazz music with her nieces. Throughout the film, the father is preoccupied with marrying off his daughters, but the daughters cannot meet anyone, as they stay at home most of the time and their father is very strict. The aunt therefore comes up with a tactic to lure potential bridegrooms into the house: by pouring jugs of water from the balcony as if by accident, she manages to bring prospective husbands into the family's home. Each time, the prospective husband is served whisky while he waits for his coat to be ironed and the prospective wife dances to jazz music to entertain him. In this way, the aunt manages to find husbands for all four daughters within just a few weeks. Whisky in this context is projected as a symbol of modernity and change. Though the brigadier criticizes the modern techniques of the aunt at the beginning of the film, the aunt, with the help of whisky and jugs of water, succeeds in marrying off all of her nieces.

In 1960, Iliopoulos played the leading role in the film *Tris Koukles kai Ego* (*Three Babes and Me*), by Afi Roussopouloi in 1960. The main protagonist is a clothing salesman who travels with three models around the islands of the Aegean during summer to promote his products. During their trip they meet a wealthy Athenian disguised as a middle-class person who invites them to stay in one of the two rooms he has booked in a hotel. The salesman and the three girls all accept, and a new acquaintance is established. During the time they spend on the island, the disguised wealthy Athenian gradually falls in love with one of the models. The Athenian likes to drink whisky and introduces the drink to the salesman, who thoroughly dislikes the taste of this strange new beverage he has never tried before. But he accepts the offer of something he does not like because he would rather "be disgusted in a wealthy way than suffer in a poor way" (*Kalitera na ipofero plousia, para na aidiazo ftoha.*). The taste of the beverage is therefore disgusting especially when someone is poor. The disgusting taste of something foreign to Greek palates is embodied in whisky, and it is accepted by the protagonist especially because it is expensive; it is for the rich and tastes modern. In other words, whisky is accepted as such—not because it tastes good (as the film demonstrates) but because it is a sign of a successful life, an expensive modernity in a bottle. As the film progresses, both men become involved in affairs with the models, and the wealthy Athenian gets engaged to one of them. It is only at the end of the film that the wealthy Athenian reveals his real identity, to the surprise of his fiancée and his new friends. By disguising himself, he has made sure that his social relationships throughout the film are untainted by financial interest and that people do not want to be with him just because he is wealthy.

Whisky is also the predominant alcoholic beverage in the film *Isaia Mi Horevis* (*Isaias Do Not Dance*), by Karayannis-Karantzopoulos in 1969. The niece of the owner of a matchmaking agency (a conspicuously modern form of socializing for people interested in getting married) in Athens is in love with a young man, and they want to get married. Her uncle, however, a very austere individual, believes he will find the right husband for his niece through his agency. The couple therefore creates a plan so that they can get married. For the plan to be realized, the boyfriend comes to the uncle's matchmaking agency to find the right bride. The boyfriend pretends to be a very successful young professional and also pretends that he does not know the owner's niece. The owner thinks this is just the right man for his niece and decides to marry her to him. He therefore arranges an evening out in a jazz club, where whisky is the predominant drink, and orders whisky for himself and his niece. The whisky comes in long glasses for the uncle and the niece, but the prospective husband orders only lemonade and the uncle praises him for his abstention. Obviously, the owner of a very modern type of agency will drink whisky, but the young man pretends not to drink the beverage—or any alcohol at all, for that matter. This performance by the prospective bridegroom is intended to persuade the uncle that he is honest, hard-working, and traditionally oriented, at least in relation to the values of marriage. In this context, whisky stands in opposition to the values of productivity, honesty, and tradition, and that is the reason the young man does not order it. The owner of the agency, on the other hand, can afford to drink whisky, as he is already an old and respectable successful businessman in the privileged position of deciding who is the right man for his niece. The couple's plan finally succeeds, and the two marry at the end of the film.

Modern Aristocrats Drink Whisky and Poor Men Drink Wine

Class in the Cinematic Cosmos

The imagination of hierarchy and social class in most of the films discussed here was deeply influenced by the social conditions of the production of these scenarios in postwar Greece. As already noted in the introduction, the decades of the 1950s and 1960s in Greece were focused on rebuilding the country after World War II. That period saw a positive economic performance and very successful economic development despite the deep social and political crisis. The liberal ideas that were successfully pursued by the postwar governments did not solve the social problems of poverty and social inequality. On the contrary, access to the means of production remained in the hands of a few, a characteristic example being the figure of the successful Greek ship owner and industrialist, such as Aristotle Onassis. These inequalities would influence the film scenarios of the formation of social class. It is no accident that in the majority of films the rich are not upper middle class but instead wealthy capitalists who own villas and have servants. Class conflicts would be symbolized by the consumption habits of the wealthy and the poor. Such differences were imagined to be the future of modernity in many films that feature the consumption of whisky and the final outcome of the postwar reconstruction. In this context, whisky incorporated distinction and an expectation of a class-oriented society. Feelings of success or disappointment as a result of upward or downward social mobility are evident in a number of films in this period.

The film *Ftohadakia ke Leftades* (*Modern Aristocrats*), by Afoi Roussopouli in 1961 with Nikos Stavridis and Mimis Fotopoulos, clearly shows the different consumption habits of rich and poor. More importantly, as the title of the film makes clear, the aristocrats are modern, expressing the expectations of a class-oriented modernity. The wealthy bourgeoisie of Athens is placed in opposition to the working class of Piraeus. The expression of this differentiation is embodied in the roles of the two main characters, who are both poor (one is from the poor neighborhood of Piraeus) and are competing to marry a young, beautiful, and wealthy woman. The two prospective bridegrooms visit the bride's family to establish their interest. As soon as they arrive, they are offered whisky by her wealthy mother; "What do you think—shall we stay inside, or shall we take our whisky on the patio?" The amusingly competitive relationship between the two men arouses the young woman's sympathy. The two men are ready to fight over her, and, indeed, a conflict erupts. The woman finally manages to reconcile the two men and reestablish their relationship by persuading them to accompany her to a *bouzoukia* to enjoy the live music of the singers Linta and Hiotis. Their celebratory beverage is clearly whisky (Johnnie Walker, see figure 2.1), accompanied by fruit. As chapter four demonstrates, the social realism exhibited in such scenarios is in accordance with the commercialization of night entertainment and music that took place during this period in *bouzoukia*. In this context, Scotch became a major celebratory beverage of live popular Greek music and entertainment.

Certain actors were filmed drinking whisky precisely because the roles they embodied were of wealthy men. One particular example is the actor Kostantaras, who usually played the role of the father, as in *O Mpampas Mou kai Ego* (*Me*

Figure 2.1. *Ftohadakia kai Leftades* 1961 (Source: The film).

and My Father), by Vedouras in 1963. The actor was filmed drinking whisky at home while playing cards, in nightclubs accompanied by beautiful women, or in hotels on holiday. The masculine character of Kostantaras was combined with a womanizing charisma in various films, always in bourgeois contexts. In his films, Kostantaras usually had housemaids, a large office, fashionable clothes, and a car, but he also had also moral values and a good sense of humor. Consequently, his taste in whisky expressed his social status and urban background, as was characteristic of many other characters in Greek cinema in the 1960s.

The consumption and entertainment practices of wealthy Athenians is also a central theme in the film *Otan Llipi i Gata* (*When the Cat is Away*), by Afoi Roussopouli in 1962, starring Avlonitis and Vlahopoulou. The ship owner Zeberis goes on a cruise with his family and various guests. This is an ideal opportunity for the three people who work in the service of his household to wear their boss's clothes, take his car, and go out to a *bouzoukia*. In the *bouzoukia*, whisky and champagne are the main drinks. The servants' preferences, clothing, and car confuse the owner of the *bouzoukia*, who thinks that the servants are the ship owner's actual family. Another level of deception is introduced when the unknown singer who is performing there pretends he is a famous singer (while the real singer has in fact left on the cruise with the ship owner and his family). The poor and un-known singer tries to seduce the supposed daughter of the ship owner. The result is total confusion, which ends when the deception is exposed by the ship owner and the real singer. The unknown singer and the housemaid who pretended to be the daughter of the ship owner get married anyway after a romantic interlude.

Upward social mobility is expressed through the consumption of whisky in the context of *bouzoukia* in various other films. One example is *O Ahortagos* (*The Voracious One*), by AK Films in 1967, with Gionakis as the main protagonist. A man who has been unemployed and extremely hungry all his life is hit by a rich factory owner's daughter in her car. The factory owner offers him a position in his company as compensation for the accident. The factory owner's other daughter falls in love with the poor man and soon they get married. Their marriage is an opportunity for the couple to spend some of the rich family's money, especially when the daughter pretends she is pregnant. The couple spends money on whisky in the *bouzoukia,* which clearly expresses their economic mobility. The story ends in conflict between the main protagonist and the factory owner as a result of the former's greed.

The distinction of the wealthy is also expressed in the film *Mia Kiria sta Bou-zoukia* (*A Lady in Bouzoukia*), by Finos Films in 1968. A poor footballer has a sister who has a secret romantic relationship with another member of his team. However, this relationship has no future; the brother informs his team mate that he has already arranged that his sister should marry a friend of his uncle who is living in the United States. One night a rich woman comes to a poor local *bouzoukia* with a friend. She orders whisky, whereas the poor company of foot-ballers at the next table is drinking wine. In the course of events, the rich woman develops a relationship with the disappointed team mate. The woman he had loved (the other footballer's sister) is deeply hurt and decides to participate in a beauty contest. That same night the team mate arrives at the beauty contest and they reestablish their relationship. At the end of the film, both footballers marry the women they love.

The taste for whisky is clearly developed by education, as various scenarios suggest, and their preference for the beverage expresses the social position of the actors in each case. This form of distinction is intertwined with the structure of feeling of the generation of the 1960s that transformed gradually into urbanites, salaried workers, and capitalists who distinguish themselves with the modern taste for Scotch whisky.

Materiality, Consumption, and Imagination

The earliest trajectory of Scotch whisky within the context of mediascapes began with the commercial Greek cinema during the 1950s. From that period until the dictatorship (the beginning of the 1970s), the scenarios of commercial Greek cinema constituted the material for imagining selves and became stories about possible alternative futures that integrated human diversity and uncertainty. In addition, commercial Greek cinema expressed the structure of feeling of modernization and change in the Greek society of the 1960s, which was viewed as an inevitable stage of Greece toward progress and urbanization as well as a moment of rupture. A major preoccupation in all these scenarios was the consequences or the potentialities of modernity for the self. In many cases, modernity was expressed through imported commodities such as automobile, fridge, television, Scotch whisky, fancy clothing, and interior design. The consumption of such commodities lent the actors a modern style and reproduced social inequalities such as rural/urban, poor/wealthy, or traditional/modern. Furthermore, the consumption of imported commodities could be portrayed as an alienating force that might corrupt the morality of the person and as such might realize fears about modernity. Consequently, their consumption in the films of commercial Greek cinema expressed an uncertainty about the outcomes of modernity and a plurality of future potentialities.

The imaginary that was expressed in the scenarios of the golden age of Greek cinema appropriated whisky in various ways. Whisky was projected into the public sphere through mass communication (cinema and television) but at the same time expressed the structure of feeling of modernity. The structure of feeling expressed through whisky is highly ambivalent and can be described as alienation, consumerism, and a loss of innocence, whereas conversely the beverage is full of the taste of modernity, of optimism expressed in upward social mobility, and of celebratory companionship. Within this context, Scotch whisky becomes a fetish capable of making and unmaking humans.

As Pels has argued, the fetish indicates the crossing of categorical boundaries, "a border zone where one cannot expect the stability of meaning that is routine in everyday life" (1998: 13). This relationship dissolves the Saussurian relationship of signifier and signified that a large body of the modern discourse of representation has built on. It is this discourse that has maintained the dichotomy between a material signifier and an ideal signified and has understood the one as a result of the other.

For example, when Manolis spends a fortune in an evening in the film *Ena Votsalo stin Limni,* Scotch is blamed for unmaking his moral values. By contrast, Scotch whisky is imagined as a constructive and optimistic modernity in a bottle in the film *I Thia Apo to Chicago.* Within this context, Scotch is a positive force of change for traditional and backward values. It replaces tradition with an aura of cosmopolitanism, upward social and economic mobility, successful migration to the United States, and respectability. Moreover, the theme of upward social and economic mobility is repeated several times and establishes the distinction between modern aristocrats who drink whisky and poor men who usually drink wine.

Such contradictory scenarios did not claim to represent the future but to imagine it, as most forms of artistic expression did. However, at the same time they encapsulated the structure of the feelings and dreams of the period, which constructed the views of modernity shared by commercial cinema in Greece. These views preceded what can be described as a consumer society in postwar Greece and influenced the way in which Greeks felt this deep socioeconomic transition.

The cinematic perceptions of Scotch were further influenced by imported American, British, or other films that became very popular in postwar Greece. Especially American Westerns and spaghetti Westerns included elaborate scenes of whisky consumption that would be broadcasted over and over again as television viewership expanded in the 1970s and 1980s. The connection in various scenarios between machismo, aggressive masculinity, and whisky is certainly another important realm of the appropriation and imagined value of the alcoholic beverage among various audiences.

By 1967, the deep political crisis, the king, the involvement of the British and American partnership in the political life of Greece, and the politically active army together brought an end to the unstable democracy of postwar Greece. The democracy collapsed in 1967 when the colonels' regime took over. Their dictatorship tore the country apart and brought a deep political crisis that remained until 1974. In this period, Greek commercial cinema would come to an end, as one production company after another closed down. The emergence of television during the dictatorship, the censorship that films had to undergo, the limited state support, the difficulties of filming under a dictatorship—all of these factors marginalized Greek commercial cinema and finally led to its decline.

By contrast, a different mediascape—that of marketing—started developing. Marketing companies and professionals proliferated. In 1966, the Association of Advertising Companies called EDEE (ΕΔΕΕ-Ένωση Διαφημιστικών Εταιριών Ελλάδος) was founded and played a major role in promoting advertising in Greece, creating a legal and structural context for its development. In the following years, marketing agencies multiplied and created a professional context for the promotion of imported beverages and whisky. Consequently, the career of Scotch whisky in Greece would come into a new era, the era of promotion and marketing in postauthoritarian Greek society.

Notes

1. The term *bouzoukia* usually referred to music halls with live Greek popular music where night entertainment took place. However the term *bouzoukia* has very diverse meanings and depends on different periods, lifestyles, and social groups in Greece.

2. It is very possible that whisky was the main drink of consumption in cabarets and so-called sex bars in various areas of Athens and more particular in the area of Trouba before and after World War II. The sex bars are spaces where the company of women is exchanged for the offering of alcoholic beverages by the customers. According to Ampatzi, the bottle of whisky was found in various sex bars also before the dictatorship (2010).

CHAPTER 3

"Keep Walking"

Whisky Marketing and the Imaginaries of Scale Making in Advertising

"Keep walking."

>—Political statement in English by G. Papandreou (MP and president of PASOK) in the mass media (*Eleftherotypia* daily newspaper, 7 March 2008), adopting the slogan of Johnnie Walker advertising campaign into the national political discourse.

"Keep walking Greece."

>—Advertising slogan in English for Johnnie Walker Greece in support of Greece during the economic recession. The Greek television advertisement used the slogan in an optimistic way to provide hope for the future and was broadcasted in the television news (Mega Channel on 16 February 2012).

Imagining the Global and the Local

While commercial Greek cinema was busy with the nationalization and translation of modernity and tradition, marketing and advertising were more inspired and excited by the global and the local. Moreover, the marketing industry would influence to a large extent the consumption patterns in contemporary Greece; for example, products that did not exist before the 1950s or 1960s, such as frappé and Scotch, were entirely invented or reinvented as national. In this project, the role of television and the proliferation of printed material, such as magazines and newspapers, is undeniable. The role of mediascapes in this process was pervasive and impossible to assess fully. As Appadurai has argued that "mediascapes, whether produced by private or state interests, tend to be image-centered, narrative-based accounts of strips of reality, and what they offer to those who experience and transform them is a series of elements (such as characters, plots and textual forms) out of which scripts can be formed of imagined lives, their own as well as those of others living in other places" (1996: 27–47).

Generally speaking, the mediascape is the full panoply of distributive mechanisms, institutions, media technologies, and the images they carry. Both mediascapes (cinema and marketing) have focused on the image of Scotch whisky in their own ways; they have used narrative to tell their stories to their audiences, and they have offered character types such as the cosmopolitan, the urbanite, or the successful male as food for imagination. In addition, these mediascapes have circulated widely imagined modernized and globalized lives and have based their techniques on the seduction of acquisition and consumption. Their distinct difference lies in their use of ideology, which is also time specific. From the end of the 1950s to the period of the dictatorship, commercial Greek cinema produced narratives of modernization as that was the period when several major social transformations were taking place. Urbanization, economic development, capitalistic commoditization, youth movements, migration, and a consciousness of rupture with tradition emerged in various forms. Marketing and advertising, on the other hand, was established as a professional career in 1966 and capitalized on various forms of scale making.

Recent scholarship has argued that an emphasis on the terms *global* and *local* or *national* and *foreign* can be understood as a form of scale making (Tsing 2000: 327–360). The ideology of scale, that is, "cultural claims about locality, regionality, and globality," "stasis and circulation," and "networks and strategies of proliferation," has been apparent in marketing and advertising projections (Tsing 2000: 327–360). Scale making is "a key issue in assuming a critical perspective on global claims and processes in the making of scales—not just the global but also local and regional scales of all sorts" (Tsing 2000: 327–360). Such scale making is manifested in the mediascapes of Scotch whisky and, more specifically, in the project of marketing and advertising in the last decades.

Now that mass media have become a part of people's daily lives, the efficacy of marketing and advertising cannot be underestimated. The quantities of images and discourses relating to products, commodities, ideas, and (more recently) services are growing ever larger with the arrival of new forms of communication and information, such as the Internet and mobile technologies. This is a period in which almost nothing is excluded from the sphere of marketing and advertising. Moreover, mediascapes have become increasingly influential as they refer to a large production and distribution of information through various mechanisms in which "the world of commodities and the world of news and politics are profoundly mixed" (Appadurai 1996: 104).

Such images can directly impact social landscapes that have become filled with neon advertisements and large wall posters, and they are able to influence the way audiences perceive reality (Baudrillard 1994: 166–184) and live in their "imagined worlds" (Appadurai 1996: 103). These landscapes are multiple worlds constructed by the historically situated imaginations of groups and persons around the globe. These imagined worlds can in some cases influence and even challenge official and widely held views. However, although the project of marketing is very powerful, we cannot presuppose its ability to remake the social world according to its ideas.

Marketing agents are among the producers of such images that constitute mediascape formations of imagined worlds. It follows that their major products, that is, advertisements, express their imagination and the values that they want to project to consumers. More importantly, advertisements express their ideology of scale, which is historically and culturally specific. Any effort to understand it and situate it outside of the social conditions in which it was produced is bound to collapse (Tsing 2000: 85). The social life of whisky in advertisements should therefore be understood as a continuous process of evaluation and reevaluation from the side of the marketing agents.

Moreover, the development of marketing in Greece is based on a globalized paradigm of "consumerism as an inclusive formal system that strives to appropriate—and thereby also produce—local cultural difference as content" (Mazzarella 2003: 4). Locality, nationality, and globality have been invested with various meanings and have been intertwined with a marketing ideology of consumerism.

In his well-known work about the history of sugar in the Caribbean, Mintz makes an important distinction between inside and outside meanings (1985: 167). Inside meanings are the multiple meanings that consumers give to a product. These are placed in opposition to outside meanings, which have to do with the significance of a product for colonies, political institutions, commerce, and law. Similarly, de Certeau has argued that the powerful strategies of commercial institutions such as the cultural industry aim at projecting such outside meanings, in Mintz's terms, to the consumers (1984). However, consumers give their own inside meanings to the products they consume, and within this context they practice a tactic against the strategies of the powerful industry. Although both sets of meanings are important for an understanding of globalized commodities, this chapter of my study examines the outside meanings, or the strategies of projecting whisky in marketing and advertising and how they have become an ideology of scale and a concrete project (Tsing 2000: 85). More specifically, by analyzing the materiality and discourse of whisky advertising in Greece, I seek to illustrate how whisky has been imagined and valued by marketers and by the marketing agencies involved in creating their advertisements. I argue that these advertisements are exercises of imagination on the part of corporate officials and marketing agents to imagine the consumers they are seeking (Foster 2008: 72) and constitute mediascapes that express and form "imagined worlds" (Appadurai 1996: 103). However, these exercises of imagination not only express the cultural industry's imagined conceptualizations of a product but also tend to construct and give legitimacy to a "discourse of authenticity" and cultural knowledge (Mazzarella 2003). This discourse of authenticity can be expressed in the making of global, local, or even national scales (Tsing 2000: 86).

Anthropological approaches to marketing have shifted from understanding it as a rhetoric of persuasion to more complicated models where the overall result is affected by a number of different agents and practices (Lien 1997, Miller 1998, Foster 2002, Moeran 1996). Some anthropologists have tried to understand the production of the culture of marketing as expressed by marketers and other agents who cooperate in marketing agencies and projects. Their work has indicated that decision making at this level is not necessarily based on rational choices and reasoning but is influenced by the value systems and social codes within such contexts.[1] Miller, for example, has examined marketing in an ethnographic perspective to conclude that "it is the actions of rival companies rather than the actions of the consumers that is the key to understanding what companies choose to do" (1998). Furthermore, O'Hanlon's research in New Guinea demonstrates how foreign advertisements or products are used to express issues of particular local character (1993).

Rather than focusing on this continuum (of production), marketing and advertising can be examined as ideologies of scale (Tsing 2000: 85). By examining marketing and advertising discourse in Greece on a large body of advertising in print media and on television from the end of the 1960s (when professional marketing was established in Greece) to the present, I argue that the product (whisky) was caught up in a project deeply intertwined with the concepts of the national, the local, and the modern. These meanings are based on the globalist fantasies of marketers (articulated in their products) and their abilities in scale making, and they are socially and culturally specific. However, this is not to say that they do not follow international trends in the discipline of marketing. Despite these trends, the case of marketing and advertising alcoholic beverages in Greece is quite unique in comparison with other European countries, as Greece has no state regulations in relation to the advertisements of alcohol. Massive amounts of whisky advertisements follow the broadcasting of evening television news in the private-owned channels, and the first impression a visitor to Greece gets upon arrival to the airport of Athens is a 100-meter Johnnie Walker "keep walking" corridor-bridge connecting the airport to the metro of Athens. Furthermore, Greek advertising companies export Scotch whisky advertisements to other Mediterranean countries, and Greece is known to be a sort of experimental no-regulations zone for those in the business.

As Lien has argued, marketing is both a practice and a discipline (1997: 11). Marketing as a practice has to do with the production process, which is the context where actual actors engage in practicing this profession with their own cultural notions. Marketing practice and products can be localized, always depending on the circumstances of their production. The discipline of marketing, on the other hand, is an expert system, a discourse of strategies that aim to commoditize and sell a product (de Certeau 1984). As such, marketing is a Western liberal discourse that operates within capitalism and has deeply influenced the formation of contemporary multinational capitalism internationally.

However as the coming ethnographic chapters will be demonstrating, the inside meanings of the consumers vary significantly in relation to the projected views of marketers and advertisements. Depending on the context, Scotch transforms into a powerful critique of the projected and emancipated modernity of advertisements and mediascapes. Consumers subvert the established meanings of the cultural industry into a complex expression of freedom from modernity, which involves the acknowledgment of friendship, love, and independence instead of the projected values of success, distinction, and Greekness. It is therefore worth noting that images of *bouzoukia,* which involve the highest amount of consumption of Scotch in Greece, do not appear in any Greek whisky advertisements.

From Making Brands to Advertising

Brands of whisky have been in existence for a long time. The oldest distillery dates back to 1608 in Ireland, and its product is still known as Bushmills (Jackson 1998: 9). Brands such as Johnnie Walker, Jameson, Bell's, and many more have been exported and widely distributed for more than 150 years. These brands were based on the family names and history of ownership of the distillery of production. However, some brands, such as Cutty Sark, were inspired by historical circumstances.

Brands first appeared in the food industry in mass-produced standardized commodities like Heinz pickles, Campbell's soup and Quaker Oats cereal "in an effort to counteract the new and unsettling anonymity of packaged goods" (Klein 2000: 6). Familiar, everyday personalities and attributes were projected through brands that replaced the anonymous food products of small neighborhood shops. In the same manner, the moment that whisky was exported and widely distributed in other countries in a standardized form, the brand had to be part of the package. Within a few decades most anonymous standardized products had been transformed into brands.

Nowadays there are few standardized products that are not branded. Even small production units try to brand their own commodities and present them to their consumers in a friendly way. Brands are now necessarily bound to commodities, but they can also include services, means of transport, and even international institutions or nongovernmental organizations. It is therefore instructive to see how brands, which emerged as signs of particular products, have evolved into a world of symbolism.

More particularly, the power of branding has become more pervasive through the commercialization of fashion clothing. Before the 1970s, the logos on clothes were placed on the label inside the garment and were not visible. Gradually this trend changed, with Lacoste's crocodile and Ralph Lauren's Polo horseman taking the lead (Klein 2000: 28). Logos were placed visibly on the outside, and this placement made clear the price that the consumer had to pay to obtain these products. This practice was the beginning of the brand mania that has extended to most commercial standardized clothes all over the globe. The trend is so powerful that within a few years so-called fake brands appeared on the market, copying the logos of the original brands and making seemingly brand-name clothing accessible to people of any social stratum.

Whisky brands are imagined by marketers as global brands, or megabrands. That means they are available in most countries in the world; they share the same structure and administration principles as well as similar marketing and advertising choices, and they carry the same logo everywhere (de Moij 2005: 14). They are also regarded as single-product brands, or monobrands, because they represent one particular product and nothing more. However, this trend has been changing in the alcohol sector with ready-to-drink (RTD) beverages such as the products of Smirnoff and Bacardi. The basic characteristic of any brand is the deep symbolism that it carries. The meanings that are attached to a brand involve a lengthy marketing endeavor that requires both time and money. The effect of this process is always ambiguous, and the success of any product is a combination of social, historical, and economic factors.

At the end of the 1980s and the beginning of the 1990s, individual brands in the beverage sector moved a step further to become actively engaged in cultural branding. Through marketing and advertising, brands of whisky in Greece became associated with high culture and art (as in the case of Haig), with sophistication (Johnnie Walker), with spaces and sponsoring, and even with particular personalities. Thus, the brand began to occupy various aspects of social life. Typical examples are the branded whisky ashtrays found in coffeehouses and bars all over Greece, along with cigarette lighters and playing cards, bar towels, glasses, and various other objects.

The branding of whisky as a strategy began in Greece with the expansion and popularity of bars in Athens and other areas. On Skyros most bars opened in the 1980s, though the first bar had appeared at the beginning of the 1970s. This expansion coincided with the development of tourism and the pursuance of state policies and construction plans for several areas of Greece both during and after the dictatorship. Under these conditions, the bars became standardized products for the mass consumption of alcoholic beverages, where the importers would invest in branding. Through the bar, the first branded objects appeared that were given to the owners by the retailers. Still today, the towels bartenders use, the ashtrays on the bar, and mirrors in the bar are all branded products. On Skyros as well as in Athens, only a few bars do not display products branded with whisky logos. More surprisingly, coffeehouses that traditionally did not serve any imported beverages (and especially not whisky) nowadays serve whisky in branded whisky glasses. Nightclubs are also extensively branded, with small logos added next to their advertisements or with advertisements for whisky on their façades.

Despite the strategies noted above, advertisements of whisky brands in recent years have also been based on abstract ideas, and, in some cases, the commodity as such has gradually disappeared to be replaced by landscapes, people, other objects, slogans, or information about the product. The commodity yields its position to images in a virtual form and usually moves into the background or to the side or even disappears completely.

The creation of a brand by a corporation is intertwined with marketing and advertising so that the brand becomes recognizable and associated with specific values that can influence consumers and relate to their lifestyles. To understand how specific brands have been projected in Greece and how marketing agents have imagined the values projected through these images, I will now trace the social history of the different styles of advertising.

Advertising in Greece

The cultural industry in Greece was expanded when the professional discipline of the advertiser and marketing agent appeared on the public scene in the 1960s. The development of the marketing profession in Greece coincided with the decline of commercial cinema and the emergence of a consumer society. Especially at the end of postauthoritarianism, the gradual development of private media and television massively spawned marketing and advertising. One of the main reasons for the expansion of marketing and advertising was the foundation of Greek national television (EPT) and the establishment of the two private channels ANT1 and MEGA in 1989.[2] It was not until the 1970s that the national television broadcaster became widely available to the Greek public. The first public television broadcast was in 1968. It took the form of a journalistic interview of the two of the most popular Greek cinema actors of the time, Aliki Vougiouklaki and Dimitris Papamihail. During the interview, the guests were offered Scotch whisky, which they drank with the journalist while discussing their careers and relationships. The offering of alcohol in this context was intended to create a more intimate and relaxed atmosphere, whereas the choice of whisky represented the particular view of the director and the journalist regarding the modern beverage that should be offered to these movie stars. No doubt this instance of localization of marketing was unintended; it had not been designed by marketing directors, and no import company had sponsored the program and supplied the drinks. The style of the first television interlocutors and the journalist as modern Athenians, the very first to be broadcast on Greek television, encompassed whisky as the appropriate beverage to consume.

Marketing agents, like their associates in the film industry, used mediascapes to express their imagination and to deal with the emerging concepts of imported commodities, style, and consumption. However, there is a clear difference be-tween them and their predecessors in the film industry: the marketing agents did not project whisky as an alienating force. On the contrary, the project of market-ing and advertising invests Scotch with a positive modernity, a national character, a global aura, and a local meaning.

The marketing and advertising of imported alcohol and whisky in Greece has been a long endeavor by various importers and, more recently, multinational corporations. This project of communicating consumption patterns and com-modities to the Greek public has been more successful since the establishment and development of television and new technologies of communication after the 1970s. The fact that alcohol is the glue of Greek society, in combination with the absence of any legal prohibition on marketing and advertising alcohol in mass media and television, has given rise to a certain impunity in marketing. This impunity can easily be observed nowadays when watching evening films or soaps on any private television channel where the programs are interrupted for advertisements. It is no coincidence that a large number of these advertisements are for whisky brands and a few other imported alcoholic beverages.

Furthermore, the strategies of marketing can be experienced in various other ways in the Greek capital: in an outing to an Athens jazz club in which the spon-sor is Scotch whisky, in a Greek music club that has been transformed into an advertisement for whisky (see figure 3.1), on advertisements in boulevards, on ashtrays in coffeehouses and bars, in magazines, at public events, in the streets, and finally within Greek households with the glasses, ashtrays, and lighters used there. The extent to which whisky brands are projected and promoted in daily life is striking. However, even more striking is the fact that most people take this for granted—especially because this phenomenon has been part of their lives for quite some time now.

According to one of the major brand managers of whisky in Greece, whisky has the highest consumption rates because "it was one of the first spirits im-ported into the country and the one with the biggest advertising budgets over the years."[3] As a result, the marketing of whisky has major significance for the importers as the special issue of Sihroni Diafimisi magazine (17–23, 1992, v. 528) demonstrates The fact that Greece is the only country in the European Union where there are no restrictions on alcohol marketing has resulted in a mas-sive number of campaigns by various companies. The field is so diverse that new ideas and concepts are constantly being put into practice and more local Greek advertising companies are taking the lead. In recent years, whisky advertisements made in Greece by Greek advertising companies have been exported to Portugal, Spain, and other countries.[4] Although there are no restrictions and no state regu-lation, the industry has created a self-regulatory code, which is based on the idea of moderate and safe drinking.[5] As a result, many advertisements include slogans such as "drink with responsibility" (*apolavste ipevthina*).

Figure 3.1. Stavros tou Notou. Entrance to a club with live Greek quality music known as *stavros tu notu*. The club represents modern Greek arty (*entehni*) music. The façade of the club has been completely transformed into a whisky advertisement (Photo by the author).

This development in Greek marketing in recent years can be understood as a result of the arrival of multinational companies. These companies have been focused on their corporate citizenship and their own marketing strategies, and some have been eager to create their own marketing departments. Within this context, local national symbols, familiar places, and aspects of cultural heritage have repeatedly been used in marketing in recent years (Foster 2002, Yalouri 2001). In Greece, as elsewhere, the national and the local are concepts that are strategically used, reused, and recycled, whereas also comprising important ideological categories in daily life (Appadurai 2001: 6).

In recent decades, and more particularly since the 1990s, the belief that advertising should be localized has been prominent among many marketers and multinationals all over the world (de Moij 2005: 26). In that sense, a new trend has been emerging, which can be described as strategic localization (Coe and Lee 2006), a form of localism. Despite the fact that many whisky advertisements and campaigns are still standardized for global markets, it is no surprise that new strategies have been used in different countries, taking the supposed local into consideration. More specifically in Greece, various Greek and international marketing agencies have been producing an extraordinary number of Scotch whisky advertisements, not only for Greece but also for other Mediterranean countries.

One of the few ethnographies that has paid special attention to the issue of marketing in Greece has been the study by Petridou, *Milk Ties, A Commodity Chain Approach to Greek Culture* (2001). In this rather experimental work, Petridou examines the way commodity chains such as the milk and cheese industry in Greece construct and reproduce social relationships. By approaching marketing departments as cultural contexts with certain values and principles, she elaborates on perceptions of tradition and modernity from the side of the industry and that of the actual consumers. Marketing in this context is the means for expressing certain socioeconomic processes; for that reason, her analysis illustrates how conceptions of modernity and tradition have been invested with particular meanings throughout different decades. In fact, the projections of industrial progress and computerized technology in television advertisements after the 1980s were associated with the modern despite the fact that during the first half of the twentieth century, milk and cheese were advertised as traditional subjects. The main reason for this change has been the fact that the industry conceived itself as the torchbearer of modernization because it had to struggle to establish itself in political and economic structures that did not favor the industry's development or its neoliberal values.

Similarly, Greek marketing of whisky has invested in the meanings of modernity as well as in globality and locality during different periods. Modernity and globality came first during the 1960s, to be followed by locality much later.

Distinction: The Emergence of the Main Advertising Themes in Greece in the 1960s and the 1970s

This part of the study examines the way in which local and global advertising in Greece has been projecting whisky since 1970, the period when the drink became widely promoted and distributed. After World War II, a number of Greek advertising companies were founded and engaged actively in the Greek market. Some of the most famous are Adel (1946), which came to be connected in 1987 with Saatchi & Saatchi advertising, Alector (1947), Olympic (1958), Delta (1965), and Ikon (1974). However, most advertising companies were founded after the 1960s and particularly in the 1970s. The Association of Advertising Companies, called EDEE (*Enosi Diafimistikon Eterion Ellados*), was founded in 1966 and played a major role in the promotion of advertising in Greece, creating a legal and structural context for its development.

During the 1960s, the marketing of whisky was mainly based on advertising in magazines, newspapers, and posters, and it was concerned with the clear projection of the commodity (in contrast to the gradual disappearance of the commodity from advertising images nowadays). Advertisements at that time had very limited space in which to circulate their meanings, and most of them were very simple and small. Promotion was limited to the printed media and radio, and slogans were not widely used. The emphasis would be on the cosmopolitan global nature of the drink, the beverage's prestigious connotations to the King of Greece and the global preference (see figure 3.2), or its global appreciation, as in the White Horse campaign of the 1960s (see figure 3.3). More importantly, Scotch is projected as a beverage of class distinction in various occasions.

Many whisky advertisements in the 1970s and the 1980s were adapted to Greek standards. In this adaptation process, the marketing agents would take

Figure 3.2. Haig and King George IV Whisky Advertisements. *Kathimerini* daily newspaper in 1963. The bottles are clearly depicted. The first caption reads "Superior whisky all over the globe," and the second, "Supplier to His Majesty the King of the Greeks." This latter phrase symbolically corresponds to the British phrase "by royal appointment" found on various products (Source: *Kathimerini* 13 November 1963).

the main advertising theme (that is, the photograph or the style of the portrait), which had usually been created for the British and American market, and change the text to adapt it for a Greek audience. The meaning of the advertisement would change as a result. Marketing agents in other countries also followed this process of localization of the text.

One of the first advertisements actually made for the Greek market, by the advertising company Alector, was for White Horse whisky (see figure 3.3). In this simple sketch, there is a horse at the top; further down, one hand holds a whisky bottle while the other holds the proper whisky glass. The hands are masculine and well groomed, and thus there is a clear representation of a certain class and gender. The whisky glass is made of crystal, short and old-fashioned but also quite luxurious. In this way, the knowledge of how and in which glass the drink should be served emerges. The old-fashioned glass also has the connotation of something classic and durable. The advertisement is one of the few that presents the name of the whisky translated into Greek. However, the translation is probably there because the whisky was not yet popular or well known. The advertisement reads, "Scotch whisky of global preference since 1742." Scale making is again used to invest the global with a cosmopolitan and high-status aura. Similar global themes also emerged in a variety of advertisements for other brands, such as Johnnie Walker, and not only during the 1960s.

Figure 3.3. Scotch whisky of global preference since 1742. Advertisement for White Horse 1960s (Source: Institouto Epikinonias).

Advertising for whisky was based on an initiative of the importers in cooperation with the company that owned the whisky label or was associated with the importer. The design of the advertisements usually focused on an image of the bottle, the name of the whisky, and a comment about how famous, superior, cosmopolitan, global, and popular this whisky was. Most of the advertisements for Johnnie Walker from this period, which were reproduced in various forms, are typical examples (see figure 3.4). Usually they place Mr. Walker in the center, and under the name of the whisky is written the following: "The whisky of absolute superiority"

(1960s) (*To ouisky tis apolitou ipero-his*). This phrase characterized the whisky for a long time, establishing the brand and creating a distinctive placement for the product: whisky was projected as a distinctive drink for superior people. The word *superiority* also expresses the superior character of the whisky in relationship to other beverages.

Since that period, various other whisky brands (including Haig, Chivas Regal, Dimple, Special Malts, and others) have also projected an image of whisky as superior (*iperohi*) and distinctive (*anoterotita*). It was no accident that a similar trend was projected in Greek cinema in the 1960s. In several films, whisky was projected as the drink of the wealthy, whereas wine and *ouzo* were the drinks of the poor. Economic and social differences were thus expressed through consumption habits and, more particularly, alcoholic beverages. The word *superior* is thus bound to the economically superior person who is able to spend more money on alcohol.

Τὸ οὐΐσκυ
τῆς ἀπολύτου
ὑπεροχῆς

IOHNNIE WALKER

Ἔχει τὸ προβάδισμα ἀπὸ τὸ 1820

Figure 3.4. Johnnie Walker, the whisky of absolute superiority, 1960s (Source: Institouto Epikinonias).

During this same period in Greece, the right accent often appeared at the threshold of perception (see figure 3.5). At the bottom of the advertisement, below the name of the whisky (which was always written in English), the pronunciation of the name would be given in Greek script. The focus on the right pronunciation of the whisky presented was an important characteristic of these advertisements. Even though people who would not be able to read the name of the whisky in English did not speak English, there was an effort to pronounce it correctly even by non-English speakers. The importance of this advertising technique lies in the transfer of actual knowledge to the consumer, which can be valued when it is practiced as a form of distinction of consumption. The knowledge of how to pronounce the name with the right accent in English (and in foreign languages in general) carries a heavy ideological significance in Greece that is associated with the status and distinction of the actor. Even more importantly, standard Greek phonology does not contain a *w* or an initial *w*, so ordinary people would not be able to pronounce the word in its English form unless they were bilingual or multilingual cosmopolitans. Therefore, to speak a

Figure 3.5a,b. Pronunciation at the threshold of perception. In both advertisements the right pronunciation is given in Greek at the bottom of the page. The first one is a Dimple (1987) and the second a J&B (1980) (Source: Institouto Epikinonias).

foreign language is a sign of education and therefore a form of distinction. Nowadays, Greek education has included the promotion of foreign languages; in recent decades courses in French, German, or English have been obligatory in public schools. In addition, the preference for international-cosmopolitan education is expressed in the variety of French, German, British, and American schools in the Greek capital as possible educational choices for the children of middle- and higher-class Athenians.

This technique should be understood in general within the context of the use of foreign languages in Greek-made advertisements, where phrases, words, or dialogs appear entirely in English. In recent decades almost half of the slogans for whisky have been in English, thus pursuing a form of distinction (Papanikolaou 1996: 34). This awkward trend of Greek-made advertisements that insist on the use of English indicates an effort on the part of marketers to identify whisky with a certain notion of something foreign and distinctive. Moreover, the use of foreign languages, including the English accent seen in the advertisements above, appeared during a period in which Greece was emerging from linguistic homogenization and enforced unification of the state. As such, the linguistic style of these advertisements (with a specific focus on English) was not strange to the literary production of the time, which expressed a heteroglossia (Tziovas 1994). Similarly, Greek films produced during this time of the golden age of cinema included an extraordinary linguistic spectrum that incorporated English, French,

Italian, and even Turkish expressions, depending on the occasion and the characters (Georgakopoulou 2000).

The use of foreign words and phrases can be seen in many contexts within social life in Greece. Apart from placing the social actor within the social stratum of the middle or upper class, it is connected to a certain notion of being modern, progressive, and knowledgeable. Already from the 1960s in Greek cinema words such as *daddy* and *bye* were widely used in many films to satirize the adoption of these words by high-class Athenians. Furthermore, the number of non-Greek names of clothing shops in many areas of Athens, such as the shopping areas of Kolonaki and Patision, is striking. Names are usually in English or French, or Greek names may be written in Latin script. Even more surprisingly, shops that sell Greek commodities might transform their names into English or Latin versions to connote cosmopolitanism, Europeanness, and modernity.

Since the 1970s, when advertising became the norm with the advent of television in Greek households, television advertisements have been based on a particular set of economic and legal relationships involving three agents. The first is the client, which is usually the importer of the alcohol and has a set of expectations for the marketing of the product. The client is also aware of the different strategies that can be used, but the design of the overall project is within the control of the contractor, that is, the advertising company. The advertising company has as its responsibility the actual creation of the scripts for the television advertisements and the design of the other means of marketing, in collaboration with the client. However, advertising companies in Greece do not usually have the means to direct and film television advertisements. Therefore, the third agent takes over, namely, the production company. The production company contracts with the advertising company to film and produce the script. Usually the client supervises the process of filming, but the completion and success of the advertisement is the responsibility of the production side. When the project is completed, it is handed over to the advertising company to be presented to the client. The client inspects it and suggests possible changes that should be made or accepts the advertisement as is.

The creation of the advertisement is thus a continuous collaboration among director, client, and advertising company and is characterized by different aesthetic, cultural, and consumption criteria. According to a director of television advertisements who was interviewed during my research (and whose identity is kept anonymous), "the advertising company supervises the filming. Therefore the director is always restricted and often in disagreement with the supervisors. However, there has to be some kind of consent between the parties. Personally I have had many problems directing advertisements, but in the end it has to be filmed according to the client's wishes."

Although many of the television advertisements made for the Greek market before the 1990s were designed elsewhere and adapted for Greece, in recent years more and more companies have decided to create their own television advertising in Greece.

Along with the language theme, a second theme that emerged in various advertisements for whisky during the 1970s and later is that of female emancipation. More particularly, women were projected as stylish persons through the consumption of alcohol, as well as modern and independent beings. A classic example from this period is the advertising campaign for Teacher's in 1973 (see figure 3.6) with a text adapted for the Greek market. The idea of a woman in the position of a male academic teacher was used in various countries, but the text was changed for the Greek audience. In the center of the poster is a woman dressed in British academic dress, just like the man pictured on the brand's logo. The advertisers preferred to replace the old man with this glamorous woman, who is projected as British-educated and a teacher; she is blonde and charming but at the same time very sophisticated, and above all she has quality. The slogan invented for the Greek market was "It is drunk by those who are thirsty for quality," thus distinguishing the female consumers of the beverage who are presented as having elevated taste.

Figure 3.6. Teacher's 1973. "It is drunk by those who are thirsty for quality" (Source: Institouto Epikinonias).

It should also be noted that Britishness is associated with quality, a tendency that is observable in Greek social life. The connection of Britishness with whisky is apparent also in the actual consumption of whisky in Greece, expressed in the total control of the market by Scotch. The idea that women who are thirsty for quality and who are modern and independent can consume Teacher's whisky as an expression of their identity is obvious. Such themes emerged in many advertisements, especially in the 1970s and 1980s when feminism was at the center of public discussion. However, since the 1990s, whisky advertisements have focused more on a projection of masculinity rather than femininity. Whisky has been presented as a masculine drink in various other countries as well as Greece, and most advertisements around the globe express this perspective. This globalized and standardized projection of masculinity is concerned with images of economic success, maturity, and leisure, whereas other themes are combined in different cases. Views similar to those of marketers elsewhere are also evident in Greece and are articulated clearly in the fourth theme that emerged after 1990s, namely, lifestyle and sexuality.

The third theme, sexuality through drinking, was already appearing in a variety of advertisements from the 1970s. A 1976 Ballantine's poster (see figure 3.7), for

Figure 3.7. Ballantine's (1976) "Carefree life—good whisky necessary" (Source: Institouto Epikinonias).

example, presents several heterosexual couples dancing close together while at the center of the poster a happy, smiling female face emerges. The slogan is "Carefree life—good whisky necessary." The carefree life refers to a life without problems, a life young people know how to enjoy and that brings them together—and whisky is a necessary ingredient. The possibility of meeting a partner through drinking at a party or out dancing has been projected by various other whisky brands, including Johnnie Walker, Haig, and Cutty Sark. Indeed, alcohol, including whisky, has been a means for meeting sexual partners or engaging in relationships throughout Greece as elsewhere. Bars and clubs are spaces in which alcohol consumption is encouraged, and they provide possible socializing spaces for both genders. These modern spaces, in which men and women can easily mix, stand in opposition to the traditional male spaces, such as coffeehouses, in which access by women is restricted in most parts of Greece, including Athens. In that sense, whisky, like other imported beverages such as vermouth, has been presented since the 1970s as part of a lifestyle in which people socialize in modern places with modern drinks and meet possible partners. This trend emerged after World War II with the popularization and standardization of night entertainment, but became even more apparent during the 1960s and 1970s.

A fourth theme evident since the 1970s is related to the production of the product. In magazine advertising, the focus was on the way in which whisky is produced. This standardized form of advertising has been used in global campaigns in various ways, though it has not always been very successful. Knowing how the whisky is made, and with what processes it is preserved and aged, has also been a consideration for marketers in the Greek market, especially in recent decades when single malt whiskies have become more popular and distinctive. A variety of whiskies (such as Jack Daniel's, Glenfiddich, Grant's, Dewar's aged whisky, and Jameson) have used their own production heritages as symbols. More specifically, issues of tradition, time spent maturing, knowledge of the family of producers, and issues of love and care for the spirit are articulated. Kinship is also a major subject in this type of advertisements. Usually the story begins with the founder of the whisky brand and the continuation of the tradition by the family—despite the fact that most distilleries are owned by multinational companies.

The final theme, lifestyle, emerged during the 1990s. This involved an effort to relate the product to a certain social identity. For example, at the beginning of the 1990s, J&B presented a campaign with an interesting use of language. One magazine advertisement read (see figure 3.8): "Modern men, dynamic ones, those who know how to live fully and enjoy every moment of their lives, have their own whisky, J&B. Rare moments do not just come. Create them." The concept of lifestyle can be articulated as a set of concepts and practices, a way of doing and being in the world, which has been clearly projected in various advertisements of the 1990s and 2000s. Brands like Johnnie Walker and Cutty Sark project

Figure 3.8. J&B
(Source: Institouto
Epikinonias).

leisure as a distinctive paradise for a certain class of people who know how to live their lives and engage in yachting and skiing. Whisky is thus connected with successful people, usually men who are aged between thirty and sixty and have a modern image. The modern is presented as upper class and close to what could be considered distinctive forms of leisure. Furthermore, certain localizations are expressed in these advertisements—such as the appearance of the whisky-cola cocktail, which is very popular in Greece, especially among women.

The economic prosperity and the modernity expressed by the characters in such advertisements are also intertwined with the theme of success. Success is a target fulfilled by modern men—whisky consumers—who have a distinctive style. Whisky is indeed a symbol of success to the extent that consumers can afford it. Success is also presented as a masculine attribute in most advertisements of the 1990s.

A similar case can be found in advertising for Haig, which since that period has been projecting an identity closer to art, thus distinguishing the consumers of the beverage. One of the first advertisements to set this trend had the caption "Famous friends of art at openings, in company with John Haig." The poster presents a man and a woman in their thirties who are visiting a gallery and drinking whisky. Since then, Haig has maintained this same attitude by supporting cultural events, cooperating with jazz clubs and publishing jazz news leaflets. "ART IS REAL" is a monthly leaflet covering jazz news, concerts in Greece, and new jazz releases. The whisky logo is dominant in most parts of the leaflet, and the front cover always features the most recent advertisement for the brand. Furthermore, at the first jazz club of Athens (called Half Note), Haig is a major sponsor of many ethnic and international events, thus claiming a global and cosmopolitan identity. Similar techniques have been used by Jameson, which sponsors jazz events in the other jazz club in Athens, Bar Guru Bar.

Since the 1990s, single malt and special brands have also begun to be circulated in the Greek market by the various multinational corporations that nowadays own these distilleries. Single malts have been booming internationally, especially since the 1980s, as a result of the purchase of the distilleries by multinational corporations. It was during that period that many forgotten distilleries were reopened and single malt whisky was reinvented. Diageo owns, for example, Caol Ila from the Island of Islay, Cardhu from the Highlands, Clynelish from the Highlands, Cragganmore from the Highlands, Lagavulin from Islay, Talisker from the Isle of Skye, Oban from the Highlands, and many more distilleries all over Scotland.[6] Pernod Ricard owns Laphroaig on Islay, Aberlour in Speyside, Glenallachie in Speyside, and many more. Single malts have been promoted in Greece in various ways in recent years. These whiskies appeal to connoisseurs who have already been drinking whisky for a long time and are interested in expanding their taste; they are presented as top-quality Scotch whiskies, targeting consumers who will continue to drink whisky but who want to be distinctive, especially in a country in which blended whisky is highly popular.

Localisms

As noted in the first part of this chapter, the Greek market for imported drinks grew larger during the 1990s as a result of the arrival of huge multinational corporations. The corporations tried to expand their own products, including whisky, through various strategies. Marketing departments became part of these companies, and advertising (especially on television) was increased. In this context advertising became more competitive. Despite the fact that the consumption of whisky was already high during that period and individual brands were well known and very popular, advertising became more intense as a result of the competition.

In recent years, and more particularly at the first conference on alcohol marketing in Greece in 2001, a number of issues have been articulated from the perspective of the marketers.[7] These have included conceptions of masculinity, success, maturity, modernity, and the values of tradition, friendship, honesty, and devotion. These themes still appear in a number of advertisements made in Greece or adopted from abroad, and in that sense their localized character is ambiguous. However, according to the brand manager of Johnnie Walker in Greece, the issues of modernness, success, and masculinity have emerged as central concepts in Greece. According to her, whisky expresses masculinity in Greece, and the beverage "is promoted as a sophisticated drink for modern people who know what they want in their life and succeed in achieving their goals" (interview in Athens, D. K. 17 January 2006).

Though these themes appear continuously in a variety of advertisements, in recent years, and more particularly after the 1990s, the theme of lifestyle has been emerging. Furthermore, during this period localism has become part of marketing, which has extended to nationalization in several advertisements.

Until the beginning of the 1990s, several companies tried to advertise their own products all over the world with a single advertisement or similar advertisements. Characteristic of this period were the advertisements for Jack Daniel's, Cutty Sark, and Johnnie Walker that were also adapted for the Greek market. Despite their wish to minimize advertising costs by using the same idea everywhere in the world, some companies decided that marketing should be adapted to local circumstances and that local advertising companies within the importing countries should produce the advertisements for their own markets. Coca-Cola, for example, has tried to adapt in numerous cases, as Miller has demonstrated (1998). This trend emerged in a period when companies were becoming more concerned about the local and were trying to suit their strategies to the specific case in each country. In Greece, advertisers for the beers Heineken and Amstel, for example, had already been trying since the 1980s to associate their products with an authentic Greek life in their television advertising and had paid close attention to their ideology of scale (Tsing 2000: 85). At the end of the 1980s, the plot of an Amstel advertisement was as follows:

> A shepherd is sitting in a cafe in a mountain village square drinking beer.
> The square fills up with his flock of sheep.
> The shepherd continues to drink his beer, relaxed, while the villagers complain.
> The shepherd praises Amstel beer.

In contrast to beer, whisky emerges in advertisements as the ideal gift (*doro*). This is accurate enough, as whisky has been in recent decades an appropriate and prestigious gift for birthdays and name-day celebrations. Alcohol is a very common gift in Greek social life. More recently, at Christmas time, baskets of champagnes and special whisky have become common gifts between professionals in companies. The Greek shipping companies in particular, which own one of the largest fleets in the world, send baskets of whisky and champagne to the families of their employees. In addition, whisky gifts regularly appear in a number of magazines, such as *Epsilon* (in the Sunday newspaper *Eleftherotypia*) and *Athinorama* magazine, during Christmas (*Eleftherotypia* 18 December 2005, *Athinorama* 8 December 2005). The same theme also appeared on television in 1991 in an advertisement for Chivas Regal (Source: Institouto Epikinonias):

> Focus on the bottle of Chivas Regal
> Voiceover: "Expensive gift? Of course! But when you give someone this gift, they will always remember you."

The same technique has also been used for more than a decade in magazines and on posters, a characteristic example being the advertisements for Johnnie Walker Black Label. The text of the advertisement is "Give the most personal gift with just a phone call" (see figure 3.9). On the advertisement, there is a phone number that people can call to specify the name and the message that they would

Figure 3.9. Johnnie Walker Black Label (2005). "Give the most personal gift with just a phone call" (Source: Institouto Epikinonias).

like printed on the whisky label and have the gift sent to the recipient's address. Also on the label in the advertisement is written "Long live John," a wish that is articulated at name-day celebrations and on birthdays. On the actual bottle are dozens of Greek names, making it clear just how personal this gift is. According to the brand manager for Johnnie Walker, this advertisement has not been used in any other country because in Greece whisky is characteristically local. The Greek Christian Orthodox name-day celebration is also conceived as being local due to the cultural particularity of this form of celebration.

Another popular localizing strategy has been the use of particular places that carry cultural or national significance, another form of scale making (Tsing 2000: 86). Several imaginaries have employed the national scale in an effort to address patriotic feelings and follow the local ideology of marketing. A characteristic example is the television advertisement for J&B (2003) that was filmed in the Athens metro a few years after its opening in March 2000. The Athens metro opened at about the time that Greece gained official entry into the European Monetary Union, and that relationship added prestige to the new transport system and its opening. Consequently, the metro system was projected by the Greek government as one of the biggest achievements in postauthoritarian Greece, and it was used as a persuasive argument for the city's capacity to host the Olympic Games in 2004. The metro system gained public approval, and it became the most recent symbol of Greek modernity and modernization (Calotychos 2003: 7). The metro advertisement was filmed in English and shown with Greek subtitles despite the fact that it was made for the Greek market.

The use of recognizable spaces and its strategic projection can be found in a number of other magazine advertisements for whisky. In 2006, the Lowe Athens company created a campaign for Grant's whisky. Among its advertisements was one that presented a structure designed by the famous architect Calatrava for the Olympic stadium in Athens in the context of the Olympic Games of 2004, which was intended to be a landmark of modern Greece (see figure 3.10). More specifically, the stadium was celebrated as the trademark of the Greek Olympics and came to rep-

Figure 3.10. Grant's 2006. "When everybody could see only bones, somebody could see architecture" (Source: Lowe Athens).

resent meanings of Greekness, Europeanization, and cosmopolitanism (Traganou 2008: 185). The advertisement reads, "When everybody could see only bones, somebody could see architecture." The connotation is that some people look back to bones or the kinds of things that hold up progress, whereas others look into the future. In the same way, consumers are encouraged to try a different angle, look into the future, and view a different reality with the new angle of Grant's. Within this context, localism embraces a landmark of the nation, a symbol of Greekness, to invest Grant's with a local aura.

More recently, the theme of national scale making has been projected by several brands, a characteristic example being the Famous Grouse advertisement shown while the European Football championship was taking place in 2004. Nationalization as a strategy aims at the association of the product with certain national characteristics. It can appropriate certain key symbols such as flags, national colors, or cultural heritage. The famous Grouse was presented in this way for the Greek audience (see figure 3.11):

Grouse with its head bent behind a football.

Slowly straightens up while turning its face to the front.

Its face is painted with the national colors of Greece, blue and white, and the characteristic cross that forms part of the Greek flag.

Walks slowly.

Slogan states, "Think different … think Greece."

The advertisement was greatly appreciated as an expression of the popularity of whisky in Greece and as a tribute to the Greek team in the European championship. Again, localism and an ideology of scale had tried to appropriate and materialize Greekness and nationality in a clear case of scale making (Tsing 2000: 86).

Lately, and more specifically during the Greek crisis, Johnnie Walker made another campaign named "Keep walking Greece." According to the public announcements of the company, the campaign was made as a gesture of solidarity and support for the Greek nation in crisis. One of its television advertisements filmed in Greece shows various scenes of everyday life in Athens and other Greek cities accompanied by the famous song "You Will Never Walk Alone." Various people are filmed walking together in large groups in the city and the advertisement ends with the slogan "We inspire each other." The advertisement was also broadcasted in the television news of Mega Channel on 16 February 2012 and was discussed as a positive publicity for Greece.

However, this has not always been the case with national scale making attempts in advertisements. In 1992, an advertisement produced by Coca-Cola depicted Coca-Cola bottles replacing the columns of the Parthenon. This generated

Figure 3.11. Famous Grouse campaign, 2004 (Source: Institouto Epikinonias).

widespread dissatisfaction, expressed in the mass media and political discourse, because one of the sacred symbols of Greece had been compromised by a symbol of Americanization and U.S hegemony. Yalouri (2001: 110) describes how issues of the distortion of the actual form of the Acropolis, of commodification, Americanization, and the dislocation in Greece of power over the Greek past are associated with such unsuccessful practices.

Marketing, Advertising, and Scale Making

An understanding of marketing and advertising requires an already established knowledge of the cultural and economic processes that initiated and reproduced this initial trajectory of Scotch whisky within the context of the strategies of the cultural industry. The mediascapes of commercial Greek cinema and of marketing and advertising are filled with exercises of imagination about various themes such as modernity and tradition, the local, the global, and the national. More specifically, the imaginaries of marketing and advertising have shifted from the ambiguous identity of Scotch whisky evident in the cinematic genre to clear techniques of scale making (Tsing 2000: 85).

Moreover, marketing and advertising influenced to a large extent the consumption patterns in contemporary Greece as various new commodities appeared for the first time on television, in newspapers, and in magazines. Although marketing and advertising were also present in various ways at the end of the nineteenth and the beginning of the twentieth century, they became a concrete project and a professional discipline from the 1960s onward. Scotch whisky, Nescafé frappé, American cigarettes, and blue jeans are just a few of the widely marketed and highly consumed products in Greece since the end of World War II.

Of course it would be an oversimplification to argue that marketing and advertising were the sole forces that propelled a modernizing consumerist ethos in contemporary Greece. As the introductory parts already demonstrated, these processes were accompanied by a distinct structure of feeling already existent in postwar Greece, which was preoccupied with modernity in various ways. The cultural industry developed further its dreams about the future through specific marketing imaginaries that capitalized a number of themes such as globality and nationality.

This chapter discussed the cultural claims of locality and nationality as forms of scale making (Tsing 2000: 85). By shifting away from approaches of marketing and advertising production, this part examined the concepts of scale making in marketing and advertising discourse to conclude that the terms *national* and *local* have excited and inspired the imagination of marketers. Moreover, Scotch is projected as a superior distinctive beverage for high-class people who have taste. Following Bourdieu, it is argued that distinction in advertising is a way of concealing and reproducing social hierarchies and inequalities (1984). The distinction is reproduced by education, which is expressed in the use of the English language and in the accent at the threshold of perception. Scotch whisky advertisements produced in Greece for the Greek market for example are always in English. Generally speaking, the use of the English language in the marketing of Scotch has been a long-lasting pattern that claims a higher status in Greek society and expresses cosmopolitanism and distinction. Within this context, it has been appropriated by public discourse and has even been used in politics.

Moreover, distinction in the marketing and advertising of Scotch is evident in terms of art and lifestyle. These two features became entangled with an upper-class style and were expanded to the themes of culture and arts. Haig, for example, has become the arty, jazz, and ethnic drink, Johnnie Walker the scientific and serious beverage (sponsoring talks by scientists and intellectuals such as the astronaut Neil Armstrong), and Cutty Sark the sporty and dynamic beverage.

Distinction is followed by scale making with a specific focus on the categories of local versus foreign and national versus Scotch (Tsing 2000: 85). The local is expressed by transforming name-day or Christmas celebrations into occasions for gifts of Scotch whisky. More specifically, names and name days (*giortes*) can be engraved on the bottle of Scotch (Johnnie Walker), thus personalizing the impersonal realm of the commodity.

In addition, the national can be seen in the use of various landmarks that are deployed strategically as symbols of the Greek nation. The metro system, for example, a recent symbol of Greek modernity and modernization that was projected by the Greek government as one of the biggest achievements in post-authoritarian Greece and became a persuasive argument for the city's capacity to host the Olympic Games in 2004, has been used in a strategic localist manner. The 2004 Olympic stadium, which was celebrated as the trademark of the Greek Olympics and came to represent meanings of Greekness, Europeanization, and cosmopolitanism, has been incorporated in a Scotch whisky advertisement (see figure 3.10). Finally, the Greek flag adorned the body of the grouse of Famous Grouse Scotch whisky during the European football competition in 2004.

Surprisingly enough, Scotch has not been advertised in relation to *bouzoukia* and contemporary Greek popular music, where a large majority of Scotch is consumed and a distinct whisky subculture has emerged. Neither has the beverage been projected as being part of the coffeehouse (*kafenio*) culture or other public spaces that might be imagined as being traditional. The aim of the coming ethnographic chapters is precisely the examination of whisky trajectories in locations and networks that the cultural industry would not choose to imagine. As such, the following chapters transcend the limits of an imagined modernity projected by the cultural industry and examine the practices and perspectives of people in relation to Scotch whisky in urban and island Greece.

Notes

1. The relationship between audiences and media is much more complicated. Ethnographies have presented a world in which the messages of the industries are not always circulated and internalized according to their strategies and in which advertisements have come to signify more diverse meanings than sociologists and anthropologists had claimed (O'Hanlon 1993, Miller 1998).
2. Greek radio broadcasting began in 1938, leading to the foundation of EIR (*Elliniko Institouto Radiofonias*). In 1965, the first experimental television program was broadcast from Zappio; in 1966 came the first news report; and in 1968 the first journalistic program was presented to the Greek public. In 1970, EIR was renamed EIRT, and in 1987, under law 1730, the radio and television stations merged to create ERT (*Elliniki Radiofonia* kai *Tileorasi*), the national broadcaster of Greece.
3. Interview with the brand manger of Johnnie Walker, D.K. Athens, 17 January 2006.
4. One characteristic example is the campaign for Grant's Scotch whisky designed by Lowe Athens in 2006.
5. Personal communication with the general secretary of the Greek Alcoholic Beverages Association, Mr. Kardaras (interview in Athens, 22 December 2005).

6. Most of the single malt whisky distilleries in Scotland are owned nowadays by Diageo and Pernod Ricard. For more information on ownership and distillers of single malt whisky, see Michael Jackson's *Malt Whisky Companion* (published by Dorling Kindersley Limited).
7. Report on the first marketing conference in Greece 2001.

CHAPTER 4

The Social Life of Whisky in Athens

Popular Style, Night Entertainment, and Bouzoukia with Live Greek Popular Music

Δεν κοιμάμαι τώρα πια τα βράδια,
Σβήνω στο ουίσκι τα δικά σου τα
Σημάδια.

I can no more sleep at nights,
I get rid of signs of you with whisky.

Popular song by Makis Christodoulopoulos

Introduction

Leisure in Greece is interconnected with the consumption of alcohol. This is visible in most leisure spaces such as *kafenion,* taverns, restaurants, bars and clubs, as well as on social occasions such as gatherings of family and friends, celebrations, public festivals, weddings, and funerals. In each location and on each social occasion certain types of alcohol are consumed. This part of the study deals with the locations in which the consumption of whisky has become institutionalized, especially during and after the period of post authoritarianism in Athens. More specifically, it examines the *bouzoukia* and *skiladika* where live Greek popular music is performed and certain cultural styles are negotiated.

The *bouzoukia* is a music hall where Greek live popular (*laiki*) music is performed. As a term, it is highly problematic as it might refer to various types of music halls, different types of music, diverse periods, and many styles of entertainment. Therefore, the term is used in two different ways in this chapter. In the introductory historical part, it is used as an analytical term to refer to a very diverse and largely undocumented space and form of leisure in postwar Greece, whereas in the second ethnographic part is used in reference to specific places in which my interlocutors entertained themselves. Similarly, the term *skyladika* is used in the first section of the chapter in relation to the history of popular music and entertainment and refers to a type of music hall that has been conceived as second class or not authentic. The second part of the chapter has more ethnographic references about the term. Both types of music halls are distinct, as they play live Greek popular music. However, the term *Greek postwar popular music* is impossible to define as it encompasses a variety of music styles. The term *popular music* is a rendering of the Greek *laiki mousiki.* It is related to *bouzouki* music, a style of music widely adapted and adopted especially by the lower social strata in postwar Greece (Oikonomou 2005: 363). A major characteristic of these diverse styles of popular music is a reference to an Eastern connection (Oikonomou 2012) or heritage. Although there are various other styles of popular music that do not necessarily relate to an Eastern heritage, this chapter focuses specifically on these styles with the mentioned association.

Although this chapter of the study focuses on the history and ethnography of whisky consumption, it is a continuation of the first introductory parts that dealt with the macro processes of localization in the spheres of the alcohol industry, commercial Greek cinema, and marketing. As already noted, these processes of the establishment of multinational capitalism and the development of the cultural industry laid the foundation for the consumption of whisky and its localization.

Even though many scholars have viewed localization as a process from above, it is argued that the appropriation of whisky and finally its localization is a complicated process that is intertwined with various political, cultural, and historical patterns. As such, it is not entirely influenced by multinational capitalism, the cultural industry, marketing, and advertising. The localization of whisky from above, as in the case of the cultural industry of marketing and advertising, has not invested in the Eastern associations with Greek popular culture and music. On the contrary, the media projections of Scotch are usually Greek visions of Europeaness, nationality, and locality, identified as strategies of scale making.

Therefore, this part of the study examines a second trajectory of Scotch whisky, different from the strategies of the cultural industry investigated in the preceding chapters. The following ethnographic investigation focuses on the tactics of the consumers in relation to Scotch whisky consumption in de Certeau's sense of the term (1984: 29–42). Scotch has emerged from a music scene and a form of entertainment from below, which was popularized in postauthoritarian Greece. It is argued that within the context of the commercialization of entertainment in *bouzoukia,* Scotch whisky was institutionalized and became associated with a representation of a popular style of entertainment in Athens. In many cases, style is related to a process of self-identification and self-presentation within the context of consumption (Ferguson 1999). Such processes are characteristic of urban landscapes in which social identities are constructed or negotiated on the basis of mass consumption (Miller 1987). However, the appeal of the beverage has been much wider, and as a result it has also been widely consumed in bars, clubs, and households. Within this chapter the focus is mainly on the consumption of the beverage in the spaces of *bouzoukia* and *skyladika* to elaborate on the localization processes and the cultural meanings that the beverage has among my informants in the center of Athens (Kypseli), where my research took place. In addition, this chapter seeks to identify the cultural specificity of the consumption of the beverage in these locations and thus to elaborate on the distinctiveness (or not) of such consumer practices. The practices of the groups identified are examined ethnographically in various contexts through participant observation. To understand the position of whisky in relation to the consumption of night entertainment in Athens, an anti-domestic discourse is traced, which has been reproduced in the context of popular music and entertainment. The social history of Greek popular culture, music, and leisure in Athens is linked with the scene of *rebetiko* that became nationalized, essentialized and profoundly influenced postwar popular Greek music and entertainment. Within this context the Eastern anti-domestic discourse that was an integral part of *rebetiko* influenced at large contemporary Greek popular music and leisure in *bouzoukia*. This discourse is interpreted historically and accompanies various practices that have been related to whisky consumption and night entertainment in modern Athens.

The emergence of postwar contemporary popular Greek music is interconnected with a commercialization of music and entertainment in general. The commercialization of night entertainment in the capital of Greece should be understood in the wider context of consumer society that emerged especially in postauthoritarian Greece. As noted in the introduction to the study, it was at the beginning of the 1970s that the first supermarkets appeared in the urban landscape and consumer goods, including whisky, began to circulate widely. Within this context, the emergence of the popular singers of *bouzoukia*, known as *firmes* (literally, brands, metaphorically the big, well-known singers), coincided with the proliferation of branded clothes, commodities, and beverages in general, including Scotch. It is the aim of this part of the study to investigate the relationship between the emergent consumer society in Greece and the excessive practices accompanying the above-mentioned forms of entertainment without moralizing the term commercial.

The emergence of the Greek consumer society in postauthoritarian Greece reproduced the social and economic inequalities that were already existent in Greek society. However, the consumption of commodities and services was accessed by larger parts of the population who had not had this opportunity previously. Despite the significant class/socioeconomic differences, consumption and Greek contemporary popular music influenced the category of a style of modernness as a form of social identification and signification that cuts across the poles of class as well as other poles in society. Therefore, in this part of the study, the micro practice of an urban popular style based on contemporary Greek music and night entertainment is examined with the aim of elaborating on the distinct trajectory of consumer practices in such contexts and their relationship to social differentiation and entertainment in general.

The Changing Face of Night Entertainment in Athens: From *Rebetadika* to *Skiladika* and *Bouzoukia* with Contemporary Popular Live Greek Music

Athens was already booming from the beginning of the twentieth century, centered on music venues that served champagne, brandy, and imported wines and that offered live music, dance, and occasionally food. These were the clubs of the Athenian elite, standing in opposition to the lower-class taverns and smoky basements, the *rebetadika,* the places where marginal, underground, and popular music known as *rebetiko* was forming. *Rebetiko* music was a result of migration of Christian Orthodox, Greek-speaking refugees who came to Greece from Asia Minor and other areas of the Ottoman Empire due to Turkish nationalism and the consequences of World War I. In addition, *rebetiko* expressed a deep melancholia that was related to the changing and uncertain conditions of the social life of immigrants, and this structure of feeling profoundly influenced the popular music of Greece.

The development of the genre of *rebetiko* was also influenced by the rapid urbanization in the early twentieth century and as such was an urban culture (Kotaridis 1996: 21).[1] Ironically enough, this music that was stigmatized and characterized as the music of the underground world and of hashish users (*hasiklides*) was to become essentialized, nationalized, and even part of Greek heritage (Andriakena 1996: 225–257). As Andriakena has demonstrated, the process of the popularization of *rebetiko* was first pursued by Greek intellectuals who were in search of new forms of Greekness and postwar fantasies (Andriakena 1996: 225–257). Within this context, live Greek popular music as entertainment culture was gradually developed. Taverns were slowly transformed into successful music scenes or marginal music halls, and the music from the East was appropriated to express particular urban styles.

The processes of popularization and essentialization of the genre of *rebetiko* profoundly influenced postwar popular music. However, the Eastern sounds as well as the style of entertainment had to become as Europeanized as possible in various contexts—especially because *rebetiko* and *bouzouki* music was associated with Turkey and the Ottoman occupation, concepts that were related to the dark ages of the Greek nation.[2] As a result, the meanings of modernness in urban entertainment coincided with a Europeanization of the consumption practices and of the spaces where music was performed. Within this context, music transformed, the style of nightclubs was refined, wine was replaced with champagne and whisky in various cases, food practices gradually disappeared from *bouzoukia* or other types of music halls, and the marginal style of popular music was slowly appropriated by various new musicians and clubs. As a result, modernness was materialized in Europeanized, European-like, or American symbols that were (like Scotch whisky) adopted and adapted and became widely consumed with the emergence of consumer society. This modernization did not necessarily Europeanize the music or the style of entertainment, as it will be demonstrated. The conceptualization of an Eastern-oriented musical tradition and entrainment was able to encompass and tactically subvert the dominant visions of modernity.

As demonstrated in the first chapters of the study, a process of localization had already started after World War II and, more specifically, during the 1950s and 1960s as a result of the first wave of importation, commercial Greek cinema, and advertising. Within this context, Scotch was projected as a symbol of modernness (sometimes ambiguous), which represented postwar consumer dreams and fantasies.

To understand the second trajectory of localization of Scotch whisky in *bouzoukia* and *skiladika*, I should first mention how these clubs were influenced by popular music and under what conditions an anti-domestic and excessive mentality became representative of such nightclubs. *Rebetiko* began forming at the end of the nineteenth and the beginning of the twentieth century when the first migrants from Turkey arrived in Greece (Damianakos 2003: 142). Immigrants moved to the harbors of Greece and stayed there, either seeking employment or lacking the resources to move to other areas. The music that first formed in these harbor cities (such as Smyrna, Syros, and Piraeus) was influenced by the populations of Anatolia and was based on a mixture of many styles and sounds, just like the mosaic of the Ottoman Empire that included a vast number of cultural groups. The music was simple, based on a *bouzouki* (stringed instrument) and a *baglama* (small stringed instrument), with slow and sometimes sad rhythms. The lyrics were also simple, expressed in the colloquial language of the immigrants that was based on a mixture of Ottoman Turkish and Greek. Major points of knowledge transmission for these migrants in Greece were neighborhoods, prisons, and *tekedes*.[3] The music in many cases was self-taught; the composers were mainly anonymous; transmission was oral; and written notation was rarely used. Groups that identified with this music were at the beginning the marginal and stigmatized networks of the society, including drug addicts, pimps, petty criminals, prisoners, and in general people who were discriminated against and lived in poverty. Family women, wives, or any kind of woman who was not a prostitute or a singer was rarely allowed to enter the male-dominated spaces of the *rebetadika* (Petropoulos 1987: 132). Gradually, *rebetiko* became a part of the urban subcultures and by the time of World War II could be found in small taverns (Damianakos 2003: 146). However, a family man or families in general would avoid entering these spaces until the 1930s, as they were considered dangerous and the lowest form of entertainment for those on the margins (Damianakos 2003: 146). In addition, most songs expressed an anti-domestic discourse and were highly critical of social conventions and appearances.

Rebetiko was deeply criticized as a decadent and marginal music during the Metaxas regime in the 1930s. It was conceived as a popular music that corrupts people, a leftover of the Ottoman occupation, a Turkish and Eastern style that did not relate to the national music of Greece and that was deeply censored and stigmatized (Oikonomou 2012). The marginalization of the music and the large debates surrounding its existence resulted in a gradual nationalization, essentialization, indigenization, and later authentication of this genre. As a result, the term was constructed in postwar Greece by intellectuals, scholars, and even politicians as the real Greek popular music.

According to Oikonomou, *rebetiko* should be conceived as a social construction that entails various different types of music, diverse periods, and social groups (2012). As a term, it has represented an entire urban music from 1850 to 1950, produced in the cities of the Ottoman Empire, the Greek Diaspora in the United States, and the harbor cities of Greece. It was a hybrid music that encompassed various different styles and musical traditions. It was a product of many well-known and unknown artists who were not necessarily marginal but were portrayed as such (Oikonomou 2012). Moreover, it was produced in music studios and performed in public music halls that affected to a large extent the development of postwar popular music.

After World War II, in Athens a variety of places, such as Stelakis in Haidari and Vlahou in Aigaleo, offered live music and food along with wine and beer (Perpiniadis 2001). The music in these places would vary from *rebetiko* and folk to more popular songs, and the role of the band/orchestra was very important in shaping the identity of each music tavern. Even more important was the artist's name, a major investment for the success of a business. The patrons of these establishments were usually middle- and lower-income working-class Athenians, and the geography of this kind of entertainment also reflected the poor and working-class neighborhoods of Athens. Kokinia, Haidari, Trouba, and Kalithea were only a few of the neighborhoods where music taverns offered alcohol, food, and music.

This period (the 1950s) coincided with the restructuring of Greece under the Marshall Plan and the slow development of the night entertainment industry. Taverns and restaurants that used to be stigmatized by the presence of underground working-class musicians, or *rebetes*, gradually became trendy and transformed their programs to attract a wider audience. The music of the *bouzouki* that had been a monopoly of *rebetiko* slowly colonized the high-class entertainment clubs that became known as *bouzoukia* (*bouzoukia* is the plural of *bouzouki*), and a new postwar popular music began to form. Names such as Tsitsanis, Perpiniadis, and

Zambetas emerged in this period, which was vividly represented in the golden age of Greek cinema in the 1960s.

It was after World War II that entertainment in Athens became increasingly influenced by the visions of modernity employed by the night industry and the performers. This new modernity brought an upmarket shift and a Europeanization of the entertainment and music produced at that time. This was a slow but effective process that affected music, food, clothing, language, and alcohol. The sound of orchestras became electrified, and sound systems were installed in various *bouzoukia* (Varouhaki 2005: 24). The Western major scale replaced the Eastern tonalities, and the music became softer and more European-sounding, especially in the genres of *elafrolaiko* and *arhontorebetiko*. A characteristic figure of this period was Tsitsanis, who adopted a European style of playing and abandoned the traditional Turkish scales that had been central to popular *rebetiko* music before the war. As he stated in one of his interviews in 1976, a shift toward Europeanization of music began in 1937 when the Greek state decided to censor the lyrics and the rhythms of the music produced in Greece.[4] More specifically, lyrics that were about drugs, sexuality, or shocking subjects were cut from the songs, and any rhythms that sounded Eastern had to be removed. In postwar Greece, the music of Tsitsanis and his songs dominated the night entertainment scene, and his popularity grew greater as a result of the refinement of his sound. Whereas this type of music was taking shape and growing in popularity, the musicians who had remained faithful to the old styles and tonalities did not enjoy success. Musicians such as Marcos Vamvakaris played music in poor taverns for a living when the jukebox replaced the expensive orchestras that small restaurants could not afford.

Rather surprisingly, the commercialization of night entertainment gave a boost to Greek music, which had not been very popular among the upper strata of Athens until that time. The *bouzouki* gradually came to represent Greekness and was projected in films for international audiences (*Never on Sunday*, *Stella*). Popular music expanded into soft (*elafri*) and heavy (*vary*) popular categorizations and was represented by star singers such as Kazantizidis. Within this context, Greek song gained larger audiences and music became a stylistic marker.

The amalgamation of the heritage of *rebetiko* with other musical traditions, the formation of various branches of new popular music, and the domination of the *bouzouki* led to the well-known debate about the value of the *bouzouki* in Greek music during the 1960s (Oikonomou 2005). The fact that the *bouzouki* was associated with the underground *rebetiko* music that was played by marginal groups of immigrants who had adopted Turkish and Eastern sounds attracted harsh criticism from various intellectuals. This debate was similar to the language debate (*glosikon zitima*) at the beginning of the century, which Herzfeld (1989) has described, in which certain intellectuals argued for a pure or purified use of the Greek language, whereas others argued for the use of the demotic language that the majority spoke and wrote. Accordingly, *bouzouki* was viewed as a polluted vessel of Turkishness in contemporary Greek culture that was brought in the country by immigrants and should not have been related to any aspect of Greek music. Especially the association of the musical instrument with hashish (mainly because there were *rebetes* who had produced music with lyrics that praised hashish) produced considerable unease among the Athenians who imagined the hashish users as outcasts and criminals. Although this marginalization of the musical instrument lasted only until the 1960s, the connotations of music played with *bouzouki* in the popular imagination of the European-oriented Greeks persisted. This created a tension with the contemporary popular music that internalized *bouzouki,* a symbol of the East (variations of *bouzouki* are known to be of Turkish Ottoman origin).

In general, during the first decade after World War II, the simple style of the taverns was transformed; stages and electric sound systems were added, and previously unknown artists grew rich. Popular music was emerging and was deeply associated with *bouzoukia,* many recordings were made by American companies (His Master's Voice and Columbia were two of the big record companies), and artists such as Hiotis, Bithikotsis, and Mery Linta appeared on the scene. Such artists would perform at music restaurants where food, wine, and whisky could be ordered and the clientele were entertained with music and other performances.

By contrast, in the same period high-class Athenian clubs in the center of Athens with a Western aesthetic and music included bands, singers, and performers from abroad in their entertainment programs (Kerofilas 1997). These clubs would also sometimes include stripper performances, and the main alcoholic drinks consumed there were whisky, vermouth, champagne, and other imported beverages. Such clubs, which had emerged in Athens at the beginning of the century (Kerofilas 1997), expressed a refined aesthetic. The style of the customers was clearly elitist and European; their clothes would follow the trendiest fashions, the music was always foreign, and the performers either were from abroad or had foreign names (usually nicknames).[5] Taverns or *bouzoukia* did not have this kind of clientele and did not serve imported beverages. According to one Greek historian, already during the carnival of 1965 several changes had taken place in the night entertainment of *bouzoukia*—such as the replacement of retsina with whisky in many places (Kerofilas 1997: 310). The consumption of whisky was already popularized among high-class Athenians who spent time at parties in the King George Hotel or nightclubs. In addition, the *bouzoukia* where the popular singers of the time performed institutionalized the breaking of plates. A historian who witnessed this transformation states,

New Year's day in 1966 was celebrated by Athenians in taverns and nightclubs and that was an opportunity to notice the social transformation that was taking place. Entertainment had changed. The parties (*glentia*) of high and low-class

Athenians had changed. ... The plates that people were breaking for entertainment ran to tens or hundreds. There was also a technique. Customers would
ask the waiter to bring the plates, then he could place them on the table or on
a chair and then somebody among the company of people would throw them
on the floor. Immediately after the event another waiter would come to clean
up the mess so this kind entertainment could go on [...] This kind of entertainment was popularized not only in popular clubs (*laika kentra*) but also in expensive places where the ship-owners and the 'new rich' could entertain themselves
and show off their wealth. (Kerofilas 1997: 349)

Though these habits were becoming a mainstream phenomenon, the practices outlined above were still characteristic of a genre with its roots in underground sectors of society. The breaking of plates, the assertive masculine dance
of *zeibekiko*, the assertive feminine dance of *tsifteteli*, the burning of money, and
the performative destruction of wealth were all characteristic of the underground
clubs that were situated on the working-class neighborhoods of the city. The
practices taking place in these clubs were not widely accepted and indeed carried
a stigma. These styles of dance, for example, were popularized with the commercialization of *bouzoukia*.

Zeibekiko is a male solo dance that has its immediate origins among the Zey-
bek warriors of Anatolia. It came to Greece along with the post-1923 population
exchanges following the Treaty of Lausanne. In the past the dance was associated
only with *rebetes*, but gradually the commercialization of music brought wide
popularity to the dance. This highly performative and individualist dance, which
is performed with the arms held horizontally at shoulder level in an almost cross-
like figure, has been described as an anti-domestic and anti-family-discourse
(Cowan 1990: 185). *Tsifteteli* is considered a typically female dance with its origins in various areas of the Ottoman Empire. *Tsifteteli* is a very common dance
in *bouzoukia* and is danced by women in a seductive manner. The arms are held
wide open, expressing the eroticism of the subject, and mostly stay in a vertical
pose while the palms move in circular motions. One very performative act is the
ability to move the hips with a twist of the bottom. These movements are done at
a fast tempo, following the music, and are considered highly arousing.

Doubtless the breaking of plates was also a characteristic *rebetiko* practice that
symbolically opposed the household, the feminine sphere of food, and the family
values. According to Petropoulos, the breaking of plates was practiced among *rebetes* in taverns where small groups of musicians would perform at the beginning
of the century in Athens (1987: 132). They would smash either glasses or plates
that were used for food. On a symbolic level, this practice can be associated with
the plate as a symbol of the household and family values; breaking plates can
be understood as a way of breaking out of this system of obligations and social
restrictions. Still today the expression "Let's break them" (*na ta spasoume*) means

"Let's entertain ourselves." A similar phrase is "Let's burn it" (*na to kaspoume*). According to the *rebetes,* the fans of the genre of *rebetiko,* there were particular ways of breaking plates. Petropoulos states that among the *rebetes* the rituals of breaking glasses and plates were different (1987: 131). The glasses that were to be broken were short tavern wine glasses and water glasses. Other glasses, such as beer glasses or short *ouzo* glasses, were not to be broken because the base of the glass was thick and such glasses would not break easily. Older *rebetes* broke glasses with the blade of a knife, and the younger generation started breaking them with their palms on the table. Throwing glasses on the floor was highly inappropriate, as this could be dangerous for others. Plates were broken by being thrown onto the stage where the musicians were situated. Each time there would be no more than a single plate thrown. However, the plates had to be thrown in horizontal position so that when they touched the floor they would break evenly and without creating danger.

The popularization of these marginal practices of *rebetiko* could be related with the essentialization and indigenization of the genre in postwar Greece. The legitimation of this type of music in the postwar period incorporated various practices that became fashionable and authentic, especially in music halls with popular music.

From 1965 to the end of the 1970s, for example, whisky became a major drink in various *bouzoukia*, the consumption of flowers to throw on the singers and the breaking of plates became institutionalized (although it was forbidden from the dictatorship and onward, the practice continued in *skyladika*), and the focus shifted gradually to the singers so that the orchestra was placed at the back of the stage. The music varied from light popular songs (*elafra laika*) to heavy popular songs (*varia laika*). The audience became much broader-based and more numerous than in the past. The night entertainment was accordingly divided among large clubs situated at the city center, where famous artists performed, and underground clubs situated at the periphery of the town, where unknown singers made their appearances.

Bouzoukia slowly became popular, replacing the music taverns and the high-class Athenian clubs (*kosmika kentra*) that remained in the center of the city. Sometimes famous artists would perform in the music taverns in the outskirts (for example, Tsitsanis and Bellou in the well-known *bouzouki* venue Harama). Customers in *bouzouki* halls would vary from laborers to people in middle-strata jobs such as sailors (Kerofilas 1997: 349). The clubs situated in the center of the city, conversely, kept their Western character and appealed more to middle- and upper-strata Athenians.

Particularly during the 1970s, the commercialization of entertainment into a more mass phenomenon resulted in several changes in the capital. A well-known popular singer coming from a family of *rebetes* who worked into this sector from the 1950s described the situation in 1971 as follows:

The "night" and entertainment in general were already changing. The singers did not sit for eight hours on the stage like in the old times. Five or ten songs at the beginning, the same in the middle of the program, and the night would finish with all the performers together. The breaking of plates that had already started in 1964 was institutionalized almost everywhere. One time my shoes were cut through because there were so many broken plates on the stage. Another night they hit my legs. They apologized of course, it was not on purpose. What can you say, and how can you stop it—especially if the shop owner is waiting to make money out of this? Likewise nowadays the same happens with flowers. ... Along with the fashion of breaking plates around 1964–1965, there was no kitchen and no food served and we passed to whisky with ice and dried nuts. I have never understood how you can enjoy only drinks and no food. (Perpiniadis 2001)

Within this context, a new form of consumption emerged in various music halls. Hard spirits and more specifically whisky replaced wine and food; the breaking of plates and the excessive aspect of entertainment were institutionalized; and the anti-domestic discourse of *rebetiko*, which was represented in the dances, the breaking of plates, and the lyrics of the music, was reproduced.[6]

The establishment and commercialization of *bouzoukia*, especially during the dictatorship in Greece (1967–1973), was accompanied by the emergence of a consumer society. Consumption and mass commodities became central in the social lives of Athenians. These included television, cars, apartments, tourism, and hygiene products. Traditional professions such as shoemaking and tailoring became almost extinct, and the salaried worker emerged. The average salaried worker and the middle social strata would be interested in spending their salaries on homogenized mass commodities that were for the first time available in massive quantities.

According to Oikonomou, it was at the end of the 1970s that much of the music of the 1950s and 1960s was rediscovered by intellectuals and wider audiences (2005: 361–398). The music that had been neglected after World War II was classified as *kapsourotragouda* (meaning songs of the *kapsura,* or love songs; for information on *kapsura* see the last part of the chapter) or heavy popular songs in opposition to *elafrolaiko* or *arhotnorebetiko*, the light version (Oikonomou 2005: 378). The fact that *rebetiko* had become legitimized and indigenized made the other types of music less authentic and marginal (Oikonomou 2012). Despite the fact that all these musical styles were inspired by Eastern sounds, *rebetiko* remained a marker of distinction and anything not resembling it was considered as low quality.

A shift in entertainment and music from a European-oriented style of music to an Eastern one after the dictatorship has been addressed by various scholars, writing about this period. Papazahariou argues that the Eastern shift in music and entertainment should be understood as a reaction to the Westernization and Americanization of Greek society (1980: 249). More importantly, this trend emerged in postauthoritarian Greece in the context of strong anti-American feelings that developed as a result of the American legitimation of the dictatorship. Within this context, the middle and lower social strata reacted to a trend that characterized Greece throughout the twentieth century and adopted a new style or a new aesthetic that could be personified in singers such as Glykeria, Lefteris Pantazis, Stratos Dionisiou, and Antypas.

The shift toward the commercialization of the *bouzoukia* where contemporary popular music was played during the 1980s coincided with the gradual disappearance of the practice of breaking plates and their replacement with flowers. The breaking of plates had been abolished in *bouzoukia* during the dictatorship, but it had carried on secretly and illegally. The breaking of plates, as a potentially threatening act of freedom and a practice that represented anti-domesticity, was against the fascist and family values that the dictatorship had promoted.

The modern *bouzoukia* dominated Athens after the 1970s and the less popular *skiladika* appeared on the scene. The term *dog clubs* (*skiladika*) has come to refer to a number of *bouzoukia* with popular Greek music on their programs and as a neologism is widely used in popular discourse to refer to the lesser-known *bouzoukia*. Though the term is used nowadays to refer to a broad category of music, there are several theories regarding how the word first appeared and what it means. The popular myth about the origin of the term *skiladika* relates to the low quality of the singers and the music in the *bouzoukia*. For example, in an article about Athens in the *New York Times,* we read: "Today, Iera Odos is packed with dance-until-dawn live-music clubs devoted to *skiladika*—the Greek bouzouki-backed music, both reviled and beloved, that, because of its singers' tendency to howl agony-filled lyrics of set-me-on-fire love, literally translates as 'the place of dogs'" (21 January 2007 by I. Kakkisis).

This simplistic view of *skiladiko* as referring to a low-quality expressive form and leisure spaces were singers "howl" is widely used by those who differentiate themselves in relation to the term and do not identify with this style of entertainment. Those who prefer opera or the *entehno* (artistic) Greek music, for example, might deny that there is any quality or artistic value in contemporary popular music.

According to Oikonomou, the word *skyladiko* was used widely after the 1970s in reference to commercial popular music in Greece and the underground, second-class *bouzoukia* that became popular during the dictatorship (2005: 360–398). However, the author stresses that the term is much older than that. According to various sources, it was used after World War II to refer to small, hidden taverns that offered a bit of food, wine, and a single *bouzouki* performer and occasionally had connections with prostitution and the smoking of illegal substances (a sort of music tavern). These places were called dog clubs because dogs (*skili*), meaning street urchins (*magas*), were regularly to be found there.[7] According to other sources, the word *dog* might have referred to a man who danced only *zeibekiko*. Other sources claim that these places appeared after the 1950s in Trouba, a neighborhood with a bad reputation close to the harbor of Piraeus. This area was full of cabarets and prostitutes who were called dogs (*skiles*). No matter when and how the term came to be invented, dog clubs were *bouzoukia* for a working-class or low-class audience. One of my informants from Aigaleo who was a regular customer in *skiladika* since the 1950s stated, "I still remember several dog clubs here in Aegaleo after the World War when I was a child. There were people coming from Athens to entertain themselves. The 'dog clubs' were mainly halls with live music but they were called 'dog clubs' because anybody with any kind of clothes could get in. You could see people with their working clothes on, with their dirty boots. It wasn't neat men that came there; there were men who were like dogs (*skilia*), *skiladika*."

Skyladiko was widely popularized as a genre during the end of the 1970s and the 1980s for various reasons. Firstly, artists who had been representative of the genre, such as Lefteris Pantazis, Rita Sakellariou, Antzela Dimitriou, and Katerina Stanisi, would be invited to perform in the commercial and widely accepted *bouzoukia* of Paraliaki (Oikonomou 2010). Within this context, artists who were thought as second class or low quality would start to dominate the mainstream music halls, such as Asteria. Similarly, their songs with the themes of unfulfilled love, crazy love, nightlife, or money would influence to a large extent the production of mainstream popular music (Oikonomou 2010). *Skyladiko* also incorporated certain practices and consumption habits that were widely popularized in postauthoritarian Greece and can now be found in many *bouzoukia* in which contemporary Greek music is played. Scotch whisky became a major symbol of entrainment of the genre, an important beverage in the lives of the interlocutors and patrons of such music halls and a drink praised in songs and narratives of *skyladiko*. Dance on the tables and on the *pista* (stage) was a practice popularized by Lefteris Pantazis (Oikonomou 2010), and the throwing of flowers was also a practice that was widely used in *skyladiko* and has now become synonymous to popular music and entertainment.

During the 1980s, more artists who had been performing on the outskirts of the city moved into the central *bouzoukia* of Athens (Varouhaki 2005). The music that had been characterized as *bouzouki*-hall music gradually became commercial, despite the stigma that had been attached to it and especially to the practices associated with it. The performances and music of artists who were part of this scene became mainstream and a new style of modernness emerged. There was an increasing number of *bouzoukia* where popular music could be heard. The debate relating to *skiladika*, *emporika*, and *laika* in relation the quality and the taste of the practices associated with the new popular Greek music arose during this period.

In Greece, a number of newspapers, magazines, and intellectuals referred to the phenomenon of *bouzoukia* and *skiladika* with disgust by criticizing the so-called meaningless character of the excessive consumption practiced there. For example, a 1988 article in *Oikonomikos Tahidromos* (see figure 4.1), a weekly magazine that circulated widely in Greece in the 1980s and 1990s, blamed the *bouzoukia* mentality (meaning expensive whisky and hundreds of broken plates for entertainment) for the decline of modern Greece and the Greek economy. The article concludes by stating that the underdeveloped Greek economy would not prosper as long as such phenomena of waste and irrational economic behavior are practiced in Greece.

It was during this period that the Omonia sound (*o ihos tis omonias*) was created. This musical scene was so named because most of the tapes of such artists were sold in Omonia, in the center of Athens. The advent of the CD and the development of the music industry in Greece after the 1980s further developed the Greek contemporary popular music scene. More and more recordings were made, CDs could be easily recorded, and more music stores were established.

A major form of legitimation of popular music was its use by PASOK (the postauthoritarian political party known as *Panelinio Sosialistiko Kinima*). The PASOK political party, which came to power in 1981, adopted popular music

Figure 4.1. Our economic development is calculated in plates. The photograph shows a pile of broken plates from *bouzoukia*. Empty whisky bottles are placed purposefully on the top of the pile in reference to this style of entertainment. The article refers to the decadent practice of Greeks breaking plates and drinking whisky (Source: *Oikonomikos Tahidromos* magazine, 14 Απριλίου 1988).

in public appearances by Andreas Papandreou, who was himself a fan of *vari laiko* music. This adoption of popular Greek music signaled the political turn of PASOK toward the lower-income strata of Greek society. Papandreou as well as other PASOK members of parliament entertained themselves regularly with popular Greek music in *bouzoukia*, drank whisky, and listened to artists such as Stratos Dionisiou. The political slogan that PASOK and Papandreou adopted during this period was "Greece belongs to the Greeks"—in opposition to the slogan "Greece belongs to the West" that Karamanlis had used after the dictatorship. PASOK realized the disadvantage of always basing Greek identity upon a European and Western reference point and stressed instead an inner Greek identity. The denial of the dependency of Greece on Europe was actively promoted on various political and ideological levels, as in the collaborations and exchanges of Papandreou with Libya and Palestine during the 1980s. Within this context Papandreou and PASOK gave an alternative to European-oriented postauthoritarian politics and took advantage of the growing popular music and culture that was very appealing to lower and middle-class strata. Thus a major differentiation between cultural styles that identify with European, Western, or Europeanized music and cultural styles that identify with Greek music was reproduced.

With political legitimation, *bouzoukia* gradually grew more popular, and along with them the habit of consuming whisky. Members of parliament made public announcements in *bouzoukia* and threw flowers to their favorite singers. Vagelis Giannopoulos was one of the many members of parliament who regularly patronized *bouzoukia* to enjoy live popular Greek music.

Despite the large economic and social inequalities in postauthoritarian Greece, the income of the lower middle class rose considerably during the 1980s (Varouhaki 2005: 18). More public servants were employed by the state in Athens in an effort to rebuild the public sector. Rising salaries in 1982 increased the average consumption of salaried workers and led to more spending on leisure and evening entertainment (Karapostolis 1984).

The fact that *bouzoukia* proliferated and gained public acceptance during the 1980s and the 1990s (Varouhaki 2005: 26) is also associated with the growing influence of the cultural industry. The invention of CD technology and the proliferation production companies affected to a large extent the music industry. Moreover the private television channels that have been sponsors of various social events have massively promoted whisky and have taken an active role in shaping certain music halls and Greek popular music. Shows like *MEGA-star* on private television have been promoting popular singers for almost a decade now. Other television channels, such as ANT1, have taken promotion a step further by cooperating with—or even co-owning—*bouzoukia* in Iera Odos. One of their most popular television programs, *The X Factor,* has created some new careers in *bouzoukia* with its music and singing competition. The winners are awarded a contract with a music company and nightclubs where they can sing live.

Under these circumstances, this form of entertainment has entered the mainstream of popular culture, and popular music can even be imagined as a representation of contemporary Greekness, as the closing ceremony of the Olympic Games in August 2004 demonstrated with its performances by the big names of this genre.

Generally speaking, the mainstream culture of *bouzoukia* reproduced the consumption of Scotch. More particularly, whisky has become entangled with the culture of contemporary Greek popular music (Oikonomou 2005). Whisky has come to symbolize the out-of-control party atmosphere in *bouzoukia* and *skyladika*. Furthermore, the domination of whisky has excluded the category of food; the beverage is consumed with just a few fruits and dried nuts. In the context of the developments outlined above, the widely shared perception of the high value of Greek contemporary popular music, the consumption dreams embodied in the singers or the fans of this genre, the excessive consumption in the outings of such networks, and the signification of Scotch by the patrons of *bouzoukia* with this style of entertainment will be discussed in the following sections.

The Consumption of Whisky in Relation to Cultural Style

While researching the meaning of imported beverages among the *parea* (company) of my school friends in the center of Athens in Kypseli, I participated in several outings and gatherings in *bouzoukia* centered on popular Greek music. My interlocutors were mainly men between their late twenties and early thirties. Most of them lived in Kypseli in the center of Athens, some working in small family businesses and others in private companies or the public sector. My methodology was based on qualitative social research, including open interviews and participant observation, for six months in total during 2006. My primary questions were associated with the cultural practices in night entertainment, the position and symbolism of imported beverages in the lifestyles of my interlocutors, and the establishment of whisky as a celebratory drink in popular music and discourse.

A major problem in urban research is the diversity of the urban population—the multiplicity of the neighborhoods people live in, the differences in economic and educational backgrounds, and their diverse professions. The anthropological parameters of age, gender, and nationality further complicate our understanding of urban processes, especially within the context of increased migration, an early age of drinking alcohol, and the multiple femininities and masculinities to be found in urban landscapes. Despite the fact that clear spatial divisions exist in Athens (such as central, northern, and southern) that might correspond to middle, upper, and lower classes, these divisions are totally subjective and do not correspond to any clear-cut social groups.

The use of the terms *subculture* or *social group* could not be anything other than problematic in a city like Athens, which has a population of over 4 million people, flows of hundreds of thousands of migrants on the move who bring their villages and islands into the city, diasporic Greeks and expatriates, new cosmopolitans, and illegal workers. In addition, the process of mapping quarters or neighborhoods might be highly deceptive given the diversity of urban landscapes where people walk, eat, sleep, work, and entertain themselves in totally different areas. One has only to walk in the city, as de Certeau argued, to realize the diversity and plurality of human trajectories (1984: 91–110). If we could follow the monthly trajectory of just one person who lives in Athens, that would be enough to give an impression of the complexities of space, place, and social networks.

To discuss the socioeconomic differences that are embodied within my informants who entertain themselves in *bouzoukia, skiladika,* and *ellinadika,* I employ the term *style* as an analytical tool to cross-cut the poles of social class and social group.[8] Cultural style refers to practices that signify social differences among social categories and, as such, style as a term does not refer to "total modes of behavior but rather poles of social signification, cross-cutting and cross-cut by other such poles" such as class and gender (Ferguson 1999: 95). In Athens, for example, masculinity and femininity constitute opposed poles of style, but this does not imply any unitary masculine or feminine pattern of behavior. The style of masculinity exhibited in *bouzoukia* might derive from a lower, working-class style that is learned, acquired, and performed. This style of masculinity is different from the masculine style performed in the gay clubs of Athens or in the jazz clubs in which upper middle-class styles are usually the case. As a result, an upper middle-class masculine style might be completely different from a working-class style. Therefore, cultural style emphasizes the performative aspects of the practices of the person and is related to his or her performative competence.

Furthermore, to conceive of cultural style as a performative competence and a practical signifying activity that positions the actor in relation to social categories implies being cautious about questions of identities, commonalities of values, shared world views, or cognitive orientation in taste. As Ferguson has argued "that members of culturally-stylistically distinctive subgroups of a society share such commonalities is an unexamined assumption of a great deal of subculture theory in anthropology and sociology. Such groups *may* of course have such commonalities. But the assumption that they *must,* or that shared experiences and values are logically or temporally prior to stylistic practice, is unwarranted and has caused an enormous amount of confusion" (Ferguson 1999: 97).

Likewise, my interlocutors might be united by a shared style of entertainment, but the meanings in their lives, their values, and their everyday practices might differ radically. In addition, large socioeconomic differences might exist among my informants, but an Eastern style of entertainment that is based on *bouzoukia* unites these differences in a similar way. This mainstream style cross-cuts the class and gender differences and, more importantly, conceals the large economic inequalities in contemporary Athens. As will further be demonstrated, those who adopt the same inner popular mainstream style of *bouzoukia* are divided by large spatial (the neighborhoods where they live) and economic (the salaries they receive or the amount of money they earn) gaps. It is therefore important to state that "those participating in common stylistic practices are united in sending similar stylistic messages, but they may at the same time have very diverse motives, values, or views of the world" (Ferguson 1999: 97). Describing an inner style of entertainment, therefore, does not mean defining a set of values or a subculture; it is a mode of signification.

A major way of socializing in Athens is going out (*pame ekso, vgenume*) with a group of friends. Going out is not synonymous with the actual action of going out from one's home, which might include such activities as going for a coffee, visiting friends, or going to the supermarket. Going out refers to a night outing to a restaurant, bar, club, or music venue. Night outings are related to a person's lifestyle, which usually corresponds to one or more music scenes. Techno, house, or electronic music is played in large and small neighborhood clubs; jazz, soul, funk, rock, Latin, and ethnic music are part of the programs of bars; and Greek popular music is found in live-music *bouzoukia skiladika* or certain other clubs. A person's style, including clothing, bodily gestures, and consumption habits, is very different depending on the occasion. For example, one of my interlocutors (Christos) would call and specifically ask the other friends of his group before going out what kind of club, party, or *bouzoukia* they would be attending so that he could adapt his clothes to each occasion. When I asked him what kind of clothes fit each occasion, he stated that the house people (*housades*) dress in fancy trendy clothes, wearing colorful shirts or sweaters and trainers and sometimes wearing sunglasses at night. The rockers, on the other hand, do not usually wear name brands and have an unkempt appearance. Old jeans, worn-out shirts, or military trousers are a few of the choices one might have in a rockers' outing. Christos and Antonis (who were both part of the group that I regularly went out with) insisted that outings to *bouzoukia* require neat clothes. Surprisingly enough, on several occasions, some people of the group who wanted to go to *bouzoukia* avoided the outing because someone among them was not dressed well. Being dressed well, I discovered, included a long-sleeved formal shirt, a pair of good-quality trousers or sometimes blue jeans, and a formal single-breasted jacket.

Hence, the persons who use style as a mode of signification present themselves in specific ways, consume in specific ways, and—perhaps more importantly—claim a relationship with specific music scenes. It would be no exaggeration to say that style in Athens is identified with the type of night entertainment a person frequents and the kind of music he or she identifies with. However, it should be made clear that a person who identifies with a Greek style of entertainment (Greek music) and goes out to *bouzoukia* is not necessarily excluded from a nightclub with techno or Latin jazz music. A particular style serves as a mode of sig-nification by the actors and does not foreclose shifts in style as far as these actors are competent to perform on each occasion. As Herzfeld has noted, one major polarity within contemporary Greek identity exists in relation to the polarity of outside/inside Greece (1989). Greeks identify with a European or Western heritage and perform this identity in the outside world as *ellines,* whereas inside Greece, Greeks feel closer to the East and view themselves as *romious.* As Argyrou has stressed, these polarities are also found in Greece and Cyprus on an everyday level among social groups and express a symbolic domination by larger powerful schemas (Argyrou 2005: 111–137). Therefore, an inside aspect of Greek cul-ture that does not identify with Europeanness is asserted in performances that identify with Greek popular music. Christos, for example, narrated a story in relation to *bouzoukia* and inside Greekness and Europeanness. When his Scottish brother-in-law arrived from Scotland (a foreigner, *xenos*) Christos suggested that he should see how Greeks entertain themselves in a *bouzoukia,* because Europe-ans are not familiar with this style of entertainment. He said, "The foreigners who come to Greece only know souvlaki and the Acropolis and are not aware of how Greeks entertain themselves." In addition, by visiting such a location, his brother-in-law would be able to better understand contemporary Greek culture and Greekness. The venue in this case was viewed as an inside part of Greece that only Greeks identify with. More importantly, Christos considered the style of entertainment in *bouzoukia* (including dancing, music, and partying) to be in-ner and authentically Greek. After visiting a *bouzoukia,* Christos's brother-in-law was surprised because most of the people there were consuming Scotch whisky. Christos explained to him that Scotch has been adopted by this music scene and has become entangled with partying in *bouzoukia.*

The style of those who entertain themselves in *bouzoukia* is constructed in relation to their musical taste, and whisky is also a major symbol of entertain-ment and celebration among those who identify with this style. The patrons of *bouzoukia* believe, for example, that excessive spending within the context of their preferred entertainment is a necessary requirement for fun and for keep-ing spirits high (even if patrons are divided by large socioeconomic differences). In that context, there are various ways to spend excessively (including paying a high price for the bottle of Scotch) and various emotional states that accompany such actions. Therefore, the excessive consumption in *bouzoukia* is not necessarily related only to a nouveau riche group of people who appeared in Athens during the 1980s as a result of urbanization and state contracts, as some authors have argued (Karapostolis 1984) or to high-income salaried workers and businessmen. Low-income networks from the center of Athens also engage in excessive con-sumption, which can be partly understood from the point of view of Ferguson's analysis of style. It is this style of entertainment that my interlocutors identify with and through which they feel part of a wider imagined community. For example Varouhaki (2005), after examining many publications on the lifestyles of artists in *bouzoukia,* concluded that most are focused on spending conspicuously and excessively and projecting their selves as consumers.

As Bourdieu has argued, taste is used as a reference among social classes to legitimate and reproduce their inequality (1984). The education of taste is a process that is embodied and performed with time and constitutes a major arena of objectification of social relationships. Whereas taste as a sense is socially and culturally influenced, the actual expression *you have taste (ehis gusto)* refers to the habitual refinement of a person. As a consequence, taste as a sense and as a metaphor is a major context of the reproduction of social inequality and an arena in which social relationships are expressed and negotiated. However, taste preferences do not necessarily define the style of a person, and they can be very diverse. Even those who share a liking for contemporary Greek music might have very different preferences in relation to the singers they like, the Greek television series they watch, the Greek football teams they relate to, the clothes they choose to wear, the cars or motorcycles they drive, and the beverages they drink. Whisky, for example, will be consumed regularly in house parties or in *bouzoukia,* but the brands one person prefers can be completely different from the brands another person likes to consume.

Consequently, drinking Scotch whisky in Athens is a common practice among many different people. However, consuming Scotch and claiming a preference for a specific type of entertainment within the context of *bouzoukia* is a mode of signification that connects the beverage to a certain cultural style.

Modes of Signification

In recent years, various scholars have researched the night entertainment of Athens. More particularly, Souliotis has examined the role of urban landscapes as the means of constructing collective identities (2001: 211–238). This process is based on collective practices and discourses in relation to the areas of Kolonaki and Exarhia in central Athens. Both areas are characterized by an enormous number of cafes and bars and constitute busy spaces for Athenians to socialize in. The people interviewed by Souliotis stressed their social identity in relation to the consumption of leisure and symbolic goods in both areas and were included or excluded accordingly. Kolonaki is considered a place with so-called quality people, and therefore various bars have face control at the entrance of the club in an effort to exclude those who are not wearing quality clothes. On the other hand, Exarhia is considered an alternative and uncommercialized place. The rock bars and the leftist history of this place are major concerns among people who identify themselves in opposition to Kolonaki. Therefore, leisure in relation to the social life of bars and cafes emerges as a primary source of self-identification within the context of imagined urban identities.

Likewise, social identities and, more particularly, lifestyles are constructed on the basis of entertainment among the subjects of Ioannou's research in Kastela (Ioannou 2001: 239–262). In Ioannou's study, people identified themselves in opposition to the people they call dogs (*skili*) even though they themselves also went to dog clubs (*skiladika*), that is, down-market, lower-class clubs. The concept of dog identifies those who do not have quality, do not know how to behave, and, more importantly, do not know how to consume properly in the context of *bouzoukia* popular music venues and nightclubs.

Papagaroufali has also investigated the role of alcohol in the construction of gender identity among feminist groups in Athens. According to her, drinking practices can be media for gender redefinition and negotiation (1992). She states that women use drinking as "a violation, or resistance, or reversal, or transformation of the 'Establishment' and the legitimation of these women's actual and dreamed of interest: to become culturally visible the way they 'wished'" (1992: 66). It is within the context of alcohol that women articulate an alternative discourse, going against the dominant view of men to pursue their own tactics. It is therefore the use of alcoholic beverages that cross-cuts the social and economic differences of women and expresses an alternative femininity.

Further research in relation to gender identity has demonstrated how imported alcoholic beverages are divided into male and female drinks in the context of sex bars (*bars me consommation*) (Abatzi 2004: 152). Male drinks are further divided into special and regular, with whisky as the central symbol this categorization. According to Abatzi, the majority of male customers drink whisky and only rarely vodka or gin. Customers are able to distinguish themselves through the brand of whisky they drink, which will usually be known to the bartender, and the way in which they drink it. People will insist on using a long or short old-fashioned glass and having a particular number of ice cubes in their drinks.[9] It is the context of this classification that reproduces gender identity and makes clear how objects and particular alcoholic beverages objectify social relationships.

Furthermore, according to Stewart, the consumption of whisky in Greece has exhibited an ongoing pattern of claiming higher and higher status. He states that

> The recent increase in the quantity of whisky imported into Greece (124.000 liters in 1971 to more than four million liters in 1982) could not possibly be interpreted as an indication of increased consumption by this elite. … Rather, these statistics suggest that the drink has been adopted everywhere … evidence of the degree to which elite style has penetrated the society at large. … Such changes in "taste" elicit responses from the elite who may alter their own style in order to retain distinct identity. One elderly Athenian woman, whose fluency in several European languages signaled her high degree of cultivation, took evident glee in parodying the pronunciation of the masses clamouring for whisky. "What do they want with gouiski?" she mocked. Granted that whisky is no

longer an effective marker of elite style, those who would claim elite status are opting for new patterns of consumption. (1989: 86–87)

Nowadays, the number of brands has proliferated, giving more choice to those who want to distinguish themselves. Among my interlocutors there are individuals who claim to be more knowledgeable than others in relation to whisky. One of these is Kostas, who was educated in England and works as a broker. Kostas stated, "Special whiskies are not good. People drink without knowing; everybody drinks whisky nowadays. The best whiskies are single malts. I have a collection of single malts with some representative pieces." The category of single malt whiskies has emerged in the last decade as a popular category of whisky among the elite who want to distinguish themselves in opposition to popular consumption patterns. The prices of these whiskies range from 50 to several hundred euros. Though they can be purchased in a few places in Athens, some people buy them from abroad and more especially from the United Kingdom, where there is a large variety. The fact that the bottle was purchased abroad and could not be found in Greece adds more to its symbolic value and the cosmopolitan nature of the consumer.

Single malts have been advertised massively in recent years. The fact that most Scottish distilleries have passed into the hands of multinationals that trade a variety of beverages all over the globe has resulted in a reinvention of single malts. Many distilleries that produced single malt were closed (being nonproductive) and have only recently reopened after being acquired by large multinational corporations. Their popularity in Greece has been growing, but they are still very expensive beverages drunk by the few. In a bar on the island of Skyros, for example, a wealthy company of Athenians came in to order their drinks. As I was sitting at the bar I heard this dialogue:

Man 1: What shall we drink?

Man 2: Let's see. He has single malts [with surprise]! I would never expect to find these on Skyros.

Man 1: You've got Oban and Lagavulin.

[Barman passes the bottles to them.]

Barman: Some people order them; that's why I've got them?

Man 1: Yes, but you know there's a ritual of how these should be drunk. In a short glass and with no ice, of course. First you have to smell it and then taste it slowly. There are even special glasses for this. This is really good whisky … I know how to drink it because I've read about it, and there was even a presentation about it in the company where I work.

Man 2: OK. Give us two of the Lagavulin.

The single malt has emerged in recent years as a positional good that is clearly related to the elite and high-income groups who claim that they know how to drink, who travel to find their cosmopolitan bottles, and who are willing to pay large amounts of money to consume this type of whisky in bars or in their homes. People also express their consumption knowledge in terms of bodily techniques. The way a person drinks the beverage—the way of smelling it, looking at it, and ordering it—is also a means of reproducing the taste of refinement (see figure 4.2).

Figure 4.2. Single malt experts. A cartoon about the popularity of whisky in Greece and the emergence of so-called experts on single malts. The shepherd is wearing traditional clothes, while the expert on the right is wearing a Scottish kilt and is carrying a cask of twelve-year-old whisky. The expert is exclaiming in a local accent, "If you don't know, don't speak. How can you put ice in pure malts?" (Source: Magazine *Sinhroni Diafimisi*, 572, 1993).

However, most of my interlocutors are not necessarily single malt drinkers. They might describe themselves as whisky men (*ouiskakias*) or drinkers (*potes*). As such, they are expected to appreciate good whisky and consume it on occasions that include an outing in *bouzoukia* or a nightclub, a good company, in a *parea* (drinking company), or on an exceptional occasion that should be celebrated. Name-day celebrations, birthdays, meetings among friends at home, or in bars are occasions on which whisky will be consumed. Whisky is considered ideal drink for men and is going to be used in the right moments. In most cases, alcohol is a masculine symbol (Papataxiarchis 1991: 238). It is not to be consumed every day because it is strong, but it is ideal for social occasions that are meaningful for people. Women who associate with the mainstream inner style of entertainment will also drink the beverage, usually mixed with Coca-Cola.

Usually Scotch whisky will be consumed in *bouzoukia* or *ellinadika*, contextualizing the location and the entertainment. As such, Greek popular music should be accompanied by whisky consumption, even at parties in homes or on other private occasions. However, whisky consumption in general is not confined to spaces and groups who identify with Greek popular music; various lifestyles can include whisky.

Those who are fond of whisky, such as the low-income group (*parea*, drinking company) from Kypseli with whom I went out to *bouzoukia*, display their favorite whisky brands in their homes. Antonis, for example, has placed next to his desk a metallic Johnnie Walker statue that was part of a marketing campaign. It sits in a prominent position next to his CDs, and it matches his style criteria. Kostas, who is a collector of single malts, places his empty bottles in a visible place in his house, on top of his bookcase, to keep track of what he has tasted. While these examples demonstrate that whisky is an object of their lifestyles for those who go regularly to *bouzoukia*, whisky might also represent a stylistic value for others. Another Kostas, the thirty-five-year-old owner of a *pro-po* (lottery shop), drinks only whisky and has hung a large Cutty Sark poster in his bedroom. Style in these cases is increasingly related to mass-produced commodities and, specifically, whisky brands.

Assertive styles of femininity and masculinity are also expressed through beverages. Maria, for example, is a high-income logistics expert in her mid-thirties who lives in the northern part of Athens (which is considered to be in a wealthy part of the capital) and drinks only whisky. As she explained to me, she likes the beverage because it has been considered a masculine drink. But she is also as assertive, dynamic, decisive, and independent as a man, and in that sense she likes to drink whisky. It fits her style and her independent character. Since she started working as a professional, her income has risen considerably. She owns a new car, she chooses her clothes carefully, she smokes, and she identifies with Greek popular music despite the fact that she also likes rock and ethnic music. She remarked, "Most men are very surprised when they notice that I drink whisky on the rocks. I am also tough, I should say—but most people realize that when they see me drinking."

Similarly, Kostantina is a high-income woman in her early thirties who drinks only whisky. I explained to her my subject of study and she said: "Well, I should say that whisky is certainly my drink because I identify with *bouzoukia* and popular Greek music. This is my music, my kind of entertainment, and that's the reason I like whisky. Almost every week my company and I go out to a *skyladiko* or to a *megali pista* [music venue where well-known artists play]."

Kostantina, who is also a young professional, can afford this style of entertainment regularly because her father is a broker and has been very successful with his business. More recently, her father has been investing in paintings and art; he is a new cosmopolitan who travels internationally on business on a regular basis. Kostantina can afford to spend a lot, as she receives a regular allowance from her father. In addition, she works in her father's business and receives a salary. Her consumerist style is also expressed in her Tod shoes and her branded clothes in general.

Thus, from the perspective of my interlocutors, whisky is related a specific style of entertainment. Regardless of their income, men and women professionals and salaried workers identify with excessive consumption, conspicuous consumerism, and—perhaps more importantly—with popular Greek music and entertainment in *bouzoukia*. Although the beverage clearly expresses masculinity, alternative femininities are also expressed through its consumption. More specifically, women who are assertive, view themselves as modern, and identify with a particular mass popular culture can be consumers of whisky and view whisky as a symbol of their own negotiation of femininity. Those who want to differentiate themselves from the rest of the Greek population and from those who drink blended whisky use single malts as a new form of distinction, thus situating themselves at the pinnacle of whisky connoisseurship.

It follows that a preference for contemporary Greek popular music and the style of entertainment in *bouzoukia* usually signifies the category of alcoholic beverages consumed by my interlocutors. It is this mode of signification and this claim of a cultural style that has localized the beverage in the spaces of *bouzoukia*.

The Unification of Differences

During my fieldwork in Athens, I spent most of my time in Kypseli in the center of Athens. Kypseli is the most overpopulated area of Athens. The population increased even more in the 1990s because of the legal and illegal immigration from Albania and various African countries such as Egypt, Ethiopia, and Senegal. The small streets of Kypseli are usually crowded with cars, and most of the time cars are also parked on the pavement. As a result, pedestrians find it very difficult to walk in this area. Despite the noise and the little public space left for the inhabitants, Kypseli is the most multinational area of Athens. The Ethiopian restaurants, Egyptian coffeehouses, African mini markets, Nigerian video clubs, and Senegalese boutiques make Kypseli a unique area.

I have long been familiar with this area, as I lived there during my school years, and I had several acquaintances from school there. During my long absence from Athens and Greece, I had been in contact (mainly through email) only with a schoolmate from primary school called Antonis, a young professional from a low-income background. Through him, I was gradually introduced to several other people he went out with as well as to other schoolmates that I had lost contact with. The establishment and reestablishment of my relationships was not a difficult process, especially because most of the people thought of me as a *kypselioti* (a local person from Kypseli) and they were interested in the subject of my study. As a result, many discussions, informal interviews, and a period of six months of participant observation were conducted without any difficulties.

Antonis is in his late twenties, and he studied economics at one of the private American universities of Athens. He is the only child of a family that has lived in Kypseli since the 1960s. His father is the owner of a vegetable store in the central vegetable market (*lahanagora*) of Athens, and his mother is a housewife who spends most of her time preparing meals for her husband and her son and watching her favorite programs on television. Antonis is still living with his parents, as his economic situation does not allow him to rent his own apartment. This is the case for the majority of my low-income interlocutors from Kypseli, who earn or receive as a salary 700 to 800 euros per month. Antonis has been working for at least six years at an economic newspaper since he graduated from university. Despite his full-time productive work, he is not able to make more than 800 euros. With his salary he pays for his cigarettes, his mobile phone bills, the Internet, his lunches and sometimes dinners out when he is working, the taxis he commutes with (there is no access to his work by public transport), and his outings to bars, *ellinadika,* and sometimes *bouzoukia.* In addition, he takes good care of his appearance and his clothes and also spends part of his salary on expensive branded clothes for his work and his outings. When discussing *bouzoukia* he usually says, "I wish I could have more money to spend there and go more often to the nightclubs I like." In any case, he goes out once or twice a week and spends between 30 and 60 euros for an outing in an *ellinadiko* or in *bouzoukia.* To remember the good nights in *bouzoukia* and to make his music style clear in his own space, he has several photographs with friends from nights out in *bouzoukia.* "This is an evening out in Lepa (lefteris Pantazis) and this is from Mazonakis," he states about the photographs he has in a corner. Each photograph represents not only a memory but also one of Antonis's favorite singers, as he is an admirer of most popular Greek music singers in *bouzoukia.*

In his room he has small posters of Cutty Sark Scotch whisky, a Johnnie Walker metallic statue, and a couple of bottles of Scotch for his guests. He usually serves *ouiskaki* (literally meaning a small Scotch, to sound more familiar with the beverage) and smokes his Lucky Strike cigarettes if he gets visitors in the evening. He will play a CD of contemporary popular Greek music in the background or sometimes watches one of the Greek music channels on television. When I ask, "How come you only drink whisky?" he says, "I am a dog (*skylas*)," claiming a connection between the beverage and the popular scene of *skyladiko* and *bouzoukia*.

Kostantina and Maria (the high-income women whom I mentioned earlier) belonged to a second network of informants from Northern Athens (*Voria proastia*) and claimed a similar relationship between whisky and *bouzoukia*. I was able to meet them during their summer vacation on the island of Skyros, where I had explained my research to them, and gradually I was given the opportunity to have several informal discussions and meetings with them in Athens. They are both Scotch whisky drinkers, and they both claim an assertive femininity that identifies with a style of entertainment in *bouzoukia* and *ellinadika*. They own their own cars and apartments, and they can afford to go out more often than can Antonis. When I asked Kostantina about her drinking preferences, she stated, "I drink Scotch because I like the contemporary Greek popular music scene. This is the drink for our night outings to these clubs."

During my regular visits to Maria's home, I was faced with the same Scotch ritual that Antonis offers to his guests. She has a large selection of malt and blended Scotch in her small bar next to the living room, and she serves the beverage on the rocks. She puts on a CD of contemporary Greek music in the background, and we discuss her outings to *bouzoukia*. "I am a night person," she states. "I like going to hear my favorite singers in *bouzoukia* and I like going to *skiladika* even more, because they are more authentic and not so commercial. After a few bottles of Scotch with my company you can imagine that I'm dancing on the table and we throw flowers on the singers."

Likewise, the men that I met from Antonis's group, such as Giorgos and Sotiris, emphasize their style with dancing. Sotiris, for example, who is a good dancer of *zeibekiko*, a kind of dance regularly performed in *bouzoukia*, takes the opportunity to stand up and perform when he feels like it. His style also identifies with contemporary Greek popular music, and he is a regular Scotch whisky consumer.

Sotiris studied in the same university as did Antonis, and after he finished his studies he served in the Greek army for one year. As a matter of luck, Antonis happened to be doing military service at the same time, so they reestablished their relationship from university. Since then they have been very good friends, and they regularly go out together. Sotiris works for Vodafone, a mobile telecommunications company. Unfortunately, with his low salary he is still living with his parents in a small apartment in Kypseli and is saving most of his money to buy a motorcycle so he can commute easily to his job. Part of his salary goes also to his night outings to *ellinadika* or *bouzoukia* almost every Friday and Saturday. There Sotiris will always order or reserve a bottle of Scotch.

One of the regular outings on Saturday for Sotiris, Antonis, and their friends is to an *ellinadiko* that mixes Greek and oriental music. As mentioned earlier, *ellinadiko* is a form of club that literally means Greek-like, and Greek popular music is usually played there, though the music is not performed live as it is in *bouzoukia*. The club is located in Psiri. Psiri is a newly developed area of Athens, situated next to Monastiraki and Thision, and is now an in and trendy place to be throughout the year. The smell of spices from the shops in the small streets next to Athinas Street makes this area quite recognizable and distinctive. Until the end of the 1990s, Psiri was almost a forgotten area of Athens, full of small shops selling tools, leather, antiques, carpets, and cheap consumer goods in general. The shops were old and run-down; some buildings in the area were falling apart; and most of the population living there were immigrants. Within a few years it was completely transformed into the most commercial and fashionable area and the place to be in Athens. Psiri filled up with bars, clubs, and restaurants of all kinds.

The club we usually go to is situated quite close to the area's central square. It is a huge club with face control (as Athenians call this kind of selective customer strategy) at the door (*porta*). This is a widely used technique among many clubs in Athens. Usually, one or two inflatables (*fuskoti*)—or in other words, thugs—make sure that only people who are dressed well, who are not in the category of a man unaccompanied by a woman (*bakouria*), and who fulfill the aesthetic stylistic criteria of the club may enter. As a result, patrons try to follow the accepted style of clothes when they go out to such clubs. A shirt, a good pair of trousers or blue jeans, a pair of leather shoes (not sports shoes), and a good brand of jacket or suit are considered ideal. This selective customer strategy that guarantees the style of the customers is a common technique found in many clubs in Athens. Depending on the musical scene, people develop their style of clothes according to the club they go to and their night entertainment.

The style of the club is a materialization of Edward Said's book *Orientalism*. There are cushions everywhere, the architecture combines Eastern lines with an Athenian aesthetic, there are water pipes that customers can order to smoke, and—most extraordinarily—there are women dancers dressed up in oriental clothes, dancing *tsifteteli*. *Tsifteteli* is derived from the Turkish *Çiftetelli*. The term also refers to oriental music in general. Furthermore, the music of this place is a combination of Moroccan, Egyptian, Turkish, and popular Greek sounds, making clear the connections among the cultures. Other similar cafes and clubs exist in Psiri, and these are very popular.

When we arrive inside the club, a bottle of whisky is already waiting on the table Sotiris reserved for us. After a while, the waiter brings the ice and Coca-Cola to mix with the whisky. My interlocutors place their cigarette packs on the table and stand up. The first drinks are served, and the men comment on the female dancers. The girls in our group start dancing next to the table when the spirits are high. My interlocutors dance with them while holding their glass of whisky and their cigarettes. The disposition of the body and the style of masculinity are clearly centered on these two objects of consumption. The cigarette as well as the glass is held in a performative manner. Both are held high, and the group circles the table with the whisky and the cigarettes.

Generally speaking, the women in our group dance without drinking to get drunk. The fear is *methi,* the biological intoxication of alcohol that is believed to entail a loss of control over oneself. For the women, this is highly inappropriate, as a loss of control might result in not being in control of their sexuality. Whisky is considered a very strong masculine beverage that should be diluted with Coca-Cola to become lighter. Some men from the group drink it without mixing it with Coke, and they consider this practice more masculine. While neat whisky or whisky on the rocks is considered a man's drink, whisky with Coke is considered a woman's drink. Some of my interlocutors stated that they liked "taking whisky gay-style" (*to pinoume ligo pustiko*),[10] meaning that they like mixing their whisky with Coke. In the context of a *bouzoukia* or *ellinadika* with popular Greek music, whisky with Coke might also be consumed by men.

For men, *methi* is also undesirable when they go out because they might be viewed as woman-like, as women supposedly get drunk easily. The expressions of *methi* for men also have feminine connotations and express an inability to be masculine and in control. *Alifi* (ointment), *Lioma* (melted), and *tifla* (blinded)—only a few of the words used to describe this undesirable state for men—express a softness/passivity and therefore a kind of femininity. The idea of passivity and its relationship to femininity is also expressed in the Greek word for a male homosexual referred to above, *poustis. Poustis* is conceived as a female-like character that is not *energos,* or active, but *pathitikos,* or passive.[11]

Despite similarities in the conceptualizations of the customers of such clubs in relation to drinking, the social and economic differences are visible on our way out of the club. The keys of a BMW are handed to the owner who is coming out to take his car, a man in a Porsche convertible is waiting for his girlfriend, and a few other groups are heading to a major avenue to find a taxi or a bus. Despite the common stylistic references and significations such as body language, clothes, the consumption of Scotch, the smoking of American cigarettes, the dancing to contemporary popular Greek music, and the preference for that style of entertainment, significant socioeconomic differences divide Athens both spatially and socially.

Going Out in *Bouzoukia* in Athens

In addition to *ellinadika,* another regular destination for the group from Kypseli as well as for my other interlocutors was the *bouzoukia* or sometimes the *skiladika.* In this context, the consumption of whisky by club patrons is institution-

Map 4.1. Center of Athens: A indicates the center of Athens. Iera Odos begins on the left side of A and ends in Aegaleo; Kypseli is situated on the left side of the area of Galatsi in the direction of A (All rights reserved by Google 2009, Google maps).

alized and deeply interrelated with particular forms of spending. Such venues can be found in Iera Odos, Aegaleo, and Kypseli, areas of Athens with major nightclubs.

Night entertainment (*nihterini diaskedasi*) in Athens varies from expensive *bouzoukia* in the center, in which singers such as the well-known and popular stars Remos and Vandi perform, to cheaper places in which less well-known artists appear.[12] These *bouzoukia* usually open at midnight and close at seven or eight o'clock in the morning. The major drink consumed in most *bouzoukia* is Scotch whisky. Only rarely do people order other spirits, and *ouzo, raki,* brandy, and Greek-produced spirits in general do not appear on the menu. In short, whisky is almost synonymous with night entertainment in *bouzoukia* in Athens to the extent that prices are expressed in terms of the beverage.

To illustrate: one night I consulted *Athinorama* magazine in an effort to decide along with my interlocutors which *bouzoukia* we would visit. *Athinorama* is the oldest and most informative magazine about entertainment in Athens. The magazine is divided into several sections: cinema, theater, music, bars and clubs, *bouzoukia* (*pistes,* stages or dance floors), and food (*gevsi,* or taste). A television guide is also included at the end of the magazine. The difference between the category of bars or clubs and *bouzoukia* is the fact that *bouzoukia* present live Greek music and target an audience with a mainstream popular lifestyle. The *bouzoukia* section is divided into the famous *bouzoukia* (*megala programata*) and the less known *bouzoukia*, which are described as musical scenes (*musikes skines*). The other categories are the hot clubs, dance floors (*pistes*), *rebetika*/popular music (*rebetika ke laika palka*), oldies, small nightclubs (*bouat*), traditional, taverns with music, and clubs to book. Among these sections, the first five categories are the biggest and most popular. The category of *rebetiko* usually represents venues where food is served, while the majority of *bouzoukia* do not offer anything except alcoholic beverages, wine, and champagne. Interestingly, all club categories express their prices in terms of whisky. For example, in the first category of *bouzoukia* (*megala programata*) we read (see figure 4.3):

Fantasia
Entrance inclusive drink at the bar 15 Euros, bottle of whisky, 160 & 190 Euros (inclusive). Friday-Sunday, Posidonos Avenue 5, Elliniko 210 8940203, 2108940302

The same style of entry is used by all the other clubs, though prices differ. The price expressed in terms of a bottle of whisky, which represents the price of entry, refers to what a company of four people would have to pay, while the price of a bottle of wine refers to what just two people would pay. However, nowadays most clubs have small whisky bottles for two people. The bottle of wine, it could be argued, represents the price for couples and women, while whisky relates to bigger groups of friends and men. Furthermore, the bottle of whisky is the representation of the cost of the outing to *bouzoukia* and most nightclubs, a key symbol of night prices and alcohol consumption. This is reinforced by the social activity of booking a table. The booking should clearly state whether a regular or a special whisky is required. In various *bouzoukia*, regular whisky is served after the arrival of the customers, whereas special whisky is placed on the booked table, distinguishing the customers from the rest of the *bouzoukia*.

This division between two and three or four people in relation to drinking that is produced by the *bouzoukia* corresponds to a cultural conceptualization widely used in Greece. Going out (*vgeno* or *vgenoume)* in a couple is not considered a company (*parea*). A *parea* is a social group of three or more friends who come together to socialize. The bottle of whisky corresponds to the *parea*, whereas the bottle of wine corresponds to the couple (*zevgari*). Discussing this observation with my interlocutors, I came to understand that the context of the *bouzoukia* is intimately interrelated with the bottle of whisky. The bottle is a form of booking as well as the major commodity bought on a night out. Most of my interlocutors would not think of going out without buying a bottle of whisky in such a club, despite its high price. When, for example, I suggested to Antonis one evening that we go to a *bouzoukia* and just have a few drinks, I received the extraordinary answer, "Are we gypsies or what?" (*ma tsigani imaste?*). Other interlocutors gave similar responses. Their reaction encapsulates the fact that going out corresponds

FANTASIA Ο Νίκος Βέρτης, ο νεότερος gentleman του λαϊκού τραγουδιού με το «αστεράτο» προσωπικό ρεπερτόριο, επιστρέφει στο χωροταξικά υποδειγματικό στέκι του, ενώ η Τάμτα ανεβάζει την ένταση με την ποπ εκρηκτικότητά της. Είσ. με ποτό στο μπαρ € 15, φιάλη ουίσκι € 160 & 190 (κομπλέ). Παρ.-Κυρ. >> Λεωφ. Ποσειδώνος 5, Ελληνικό, 2108940203, 2108940302.

FEVER Διαφορετικής γενιάς, αλλά με μεγάλη εμβέλεια και οι δύο στο είδος τους, ο Σταμάτης Γονίδης και ο Νίκος Οικονομόπουλος κορυφώνουν τη λαϊκή ένταση με μεγάλες επιτυχίες. Φιάλη ουίσκι € 160 & 180 (κομπλέ), κρασί € 80 (κομπλέ). Παρ.-Σάβ. >> Λεωφ. Συγγρού & Λαγουμπτζή 25, Νέος Κόσμος, 2109217333.

[30%] FRANGELICO Ο Κώστας Καραφώτης παραμένει στις επάλξεις της παραλιακής και το χειμερινό σχήμα αποκτά ανεβασμένη νεανική διάθεση με τη Χριστίνα Κολέτσα και τον Νικηφόρο. Είσ. με ποτό € 15, φιάλη ουίσκι € 130 & 150 (κομπλέ). Τετ.-Σάβ. >> Λεωφ. Ποσειδώνος 35, Καλαμάκι, 2109843630, 2109843250.

ΙΕΡΑ ΟΔΟΣ Ερωτικός, χορευτικός και κοινωνικά προβληματισμένος, ο Νότης Σφακιανάκης βάζει την προσωπική σφραγίδα του σε ένα πρόγραμμα με έντονη γυναικεία παρουσία από τις Φανή Δρακοπούλου και Πηνελόπη Αναστασοπούλου με τους Mamacita On Fire. Είσ. με ποτό στο μπαρ € 15, φιάλη ουίσκι € 150 & 170 (κομπλέ), άνω διάζωμα € 100 (κομπλέ). Παρ.-Σάβ. >> Ιερά Οδός 18-20, Γκάζι, 2103428272-5.

κρασί /2 άτομα € 80 (κομπλέ). Πέμ.-Σάβ. >> Λεωφ. Ποσειδώνος 18, Ελληνικό, 2108941033, 35.

REX Ο Νίνο και ο Κωνσταντίνος Αργυρός ορίζουν το νεανικό χαρακτήρα του προγράμματος, η Άντζελα Δημητρίου βάζει τη σφραγίδα της πείρας, ενώ το μπαρ με τα cocktails φτιάχνει clubbing διάθεση. Ποτό στο μπαρ € 10, φιάλη ουίσκι από € 100, κρασί από € 50. Παρ.-Σάβ. >> Πανεπιστημίου 48, κέντρο, 2103823269.

[30%] ROMEO Το σχήμα με το φετινό ρεκόρ μακροβιότερης σεζόν (και κεφιού) ανανεώνεται προσκαλώντας σε after hours διασκέδαση με τον Χρήστο Χολίδη, τη Θέλξη, τον Κωνσταντίνο Γαλανό και τον Αλέξανδρο Νότα. Ποτό στο μπαρ € 10, φιάλη ουίσκι € 140 (κομπλέ), κρασί ανά δύο άτομα € 70. Παρ.-Κυρ. >> Ελληνικού 1, Ελληνικό, 2108945345.

SENSE STAGE Σε έναν ολοκαίνουργιο χώρο, το κεφάτο πρόγραμμα καθοδηγούν οι ευέλικτες φωνές της Δήμητρας Μεταλλινού, του Άγγελου Ανδριανού και του Γιάννη Μωραΐτη. Ποτό € 7, φιάλη ουίσκι € 90 & 100 (κομπλέ). Παρ., Σάβ. >> Λεωφ. Αγίου Δημητρίου 1 & Λεωφ. Βουλιαγμένης 224 (έναντι στάσης μετρό Δάφνη), 2130253222, 6945848935.

TEATRO MUSIC HALL Ο λαϊκός των λαϊκών Βασίλης Καρράς και δύο φαινόμενα της εποχής, η Πάολα και ο Παντελής Παντελίδης, καλύπτουν όλες τις εκφράσεις του σύγχρονου λαϊκού τραγουδιού. Είσ. με ποτό στο μπαρ € 15, φιάλη ουίσκι € 160 & 180 (κομπλέ), κρασί € 90/τα δύο άτομα. Παρ.-Σάβ. >> Λεωφ. Ποσειδώνος 26-28, Τζιτζιφιές, 2109400726-7.

Figure 4.3. *Pistes.* Section of *Athinorama* magazine with prices expressed in terms of whisky (Source: *Athinorama* magazine, 20–26 December 2012).

to spending money on at least one bottle of whisky; otherwise, you would look poor like a gypsy (a metaphor for poverty).

At other times, my interlocutors told me, "I have *cava* in that *bouzoukia* so we should go there." *Cava* here means that a bottle (*boukali*) or half-bottle (*misoboukalo*) is stored there under the customer's name. The next time he goes there, he can order his *cava*, which is already paid for. This happens when the bottle is bought but not finished or when the *parea* might leave for some reason. The bill will be paid and the remaining bottle or half-bottle will be stored for another time. This practice is usually applied for known customers who entertain themselves regularly in a specific *bouzoukia*. Some *bouzoukia* also sell half-bottles, which cost half the price of a bottle. If two men visit the *bouzoukia* and do not wish to drink heavily, they might order half a bottle.

In many of my interlocutors' narratives, the bottle of whisky (*boukali*) emerges as a major reference for entertainment, pleasure, and celebration. Interlocutors do not talk about drinks or alcohol as such, but mainly about bottles. Expressions such as "We ordered our bottle" or "We drank our bottle" and questions such as "How many bottles did you have?" express the major role of the object in contextualizing the activity of drinking in a *bouzoukia*. The bottle should also be understood as a concept that expresses masculinity and the ability of a man to drink a lot yet still be able to control himself. Drinking a bottle or bottles is a characteristic of a capable masculinity that invests in alcohol and in the pleasure of drinking. More importantly, the bottle acquires its quasi-sacred character by the way it is placed in the physical context of the *bouzoukia*. The tables at the front, even if they are empty, should always have the symbol of pleasure and night entertainment on them, the bottle of whisky.

One of the clubs that my interlocutors visited regularly was the Athenian.[13] Antonis, Sotiris, and Giorgos are regular patrons of *bouzoukia*, and this one is their favorite as long their favorite singer is performing there. The club is situated on a central avenue in the Aegaleo area. This area is full of car and motorcycle repair businesses, spare parts for cars, retail stores, tool shops, and similar businesses. However, the Athenian's customers do not necessarily come from this part of Athens, as the popularity of a singer might bring people there even from far away in the countryside.

At the entrance of the club is the *maitre,* who welcomes the customers and takes them to their table, which has usually been booked in advance. The role of *maitre* is very varied. He knows the customers, and therefore he decides which table is to be given to each company. There is a hierarchy of tables in the club. The tables closest to the stage are higher in status, and the first row is usually the most prestigious. On the first tables there are usually bottles of special whisky that have already been reserved. Each club has a variety of blended and special whiskies. The special whisky brands are usually Johnnie Walker Black Label, Chardu, Dimple, and Chivas Regal, and the blended are Johnnie Walker, Famous Grouse, Dewar's, Cutty Sark, Bell's, and Jack Daniel's. The tables behind the stage and in the center are next in the hierarchy, and the lowest class of tables are the ones to the sides of the stage, especially those at the back. The logic of this hierarchy depends on two basic concepts: access to the stage (for dancing or throwing flowers) and the ability to have a good view of the performers. The *maitre's* selection of the table is related to a number of different factors. One important factor is his relationship with the customers, which can be friendly or close to impersonal. Apart from the network of patrons who might come from the close social environment of either the performers, other people who work in this context, or the *maitre* himself, the majority of people must build up their relationships in these clubs. Relationships are built over time and with the amount of money spent during a night. Regular customers who spend a lot are highest on the *maitre's* list and will be given a table next to the stage.

Antonis, Sotiris, and I enter the *bouzoukia* with the *maitre,* who walks us to our table. The hall is rather dark and empty. A stage is in the center, and dozens of tables for four surround the stage. On the stage, a small orchestra is playing popular Greek rhythms while two singers sing. The reserved front tables have bottles of special whisky on them, even though nobody is sitting there. In a few hours the hall is full, as it is a Saturday night. People are smoking and looking at each other while drinking. Most are silent, as the music is too loud for talking. They glance toward the stage (*pista*) and wait for the singers to appear.

The center of the *bouzoukia* is the stage. The stage is so important that *bouzoukia* themselves are also called stages (*pistes*). The stage is where the singers perform, and, perhaps more importantly, it is the space where the customers dance *zeibekiko* or *tsifteteli* when spirits are high (*kefi, ftiaksimo*).[14] *Ftiaksimo* (coming into being) is an emotion that requires drinking (moderate or excessive, depending on the occasion), and whisky in particular is considered a beverage that brings the interlocutors to such a state. The emotion of *ftiaksimo* builds up gradually in such contexts, interrelated with the music program of the *bouzoukia.* Spirits are high when the singers know how to keep them high; particular singers are known to create more *kefi* in comparison with others. (The word *kefi* is also used in relation to liking or disliking a person, an object, or a situation and in relation to personal attraction.)

Kefi is expressed by patrons singing along to songs that they know, sometimes dancing to a song that they like, and—more importantly—spending money to throw flowers, open champagne, or, in rare cases and limited clubs in the countryside, break a glass or a plate. However, complete alcoholic intoxication is not considered part of *ftiaksimo,* and drunkenness (*methi*) is undesirable even if losing oneself (*hasimo*) with whisky is desirable. When someone is completely drunk (*methismenos*), he loses face before his friends as he loses control over himself. The control of masculinity in the context of the *bouzoukia* also means control of drunkenness, despite the fact that in some cases two bottles of whisky might be consumed by a single group of four people.

When the singers start to perform their *programa,* the younger, less famous, and less experienced artists are the first to appear. They try to warm up the atmosphere and build up the *kefi* of their customers. Audiences are less enthusiastic with these preliminary artists and do not dance as much while the younger singers are singing. When the atmosphere has been prepared, the lights are lowered, the stage is emptied, and the big-name singers (*to megalo onoma*) appear on the stage with one of their famous songs or with the question "Is everything all right tonight?" The orchestra accompanies their appearance by playing a characteristic rhythm.

While we are watching the orchestra's performance, the waiter comes to take our orders, asking, "What would you like to drink?" Antonis orders a Johnnie Walker for our table, like the majority of tables in the *bouzoukia*. After a while the bottle comes, along with four glasses for the *parea,* a big bowl of ice cubes, and a small bowl of dried nuts. As time goes by, most groups drink their whisky straight and sometimes they mix it with Coca-Cola. At my table, most men do not mix it, as whisky with Coke is thought of as a female drink. Whisky should be straight—like the men themselves—and is usually drunk with ice.

As the *kefi* builds up and the patrons begin to recognize the songs, someone stands up to dance *zeibekiko*. His girlfriend and his friend are on their knees clapping. The man makes continuous performative turns while dancing in the center of the stage. His friends clap even more enthusiastically when the performance comes to an end. A man who dances a good *zeibekiko* is a *magas,* a man who expresses his masculinity. *Zeibekiko* is considered a highly masculine dance to be performed mainly by men; in various contexts it used to be considered an insult if a woman among a certain company of people danced it.[15] In one of my interviews, a woman who was part of the network of my interlocutors of Aigaleo stated,

> At the end of the seventies I was a rock and punk fan and I was very daring. I would dress like the other fans of the scene and I was against most institutions. On one outing with the older men of my neighborhood we went to a place in the Koridalos area where a lot of underground figures and outlaws used to hang out. That was the place where prisoners would go outside of Koridalos [the area of Athens where the prison is located]; they would go there to get together again with other outlaws or ex-prisoners and entertain themselves. The evening we were there I heard a song that I liked a lot. It was a *zebeikiko.* The stage was empty so I stood up and went to dance the song. The older men of the company did not react fast enough to stop me, as I had rushed very fast to the stage. Then, while I was dancing, a man came onto the stage and threatened me. He said he would harm me because I was embarrassing a masculine dance. The older men in my group stood up and said I was one of the young rockers who don't know these rules. My protectors said it would not happen again.

Gradually, *zeibekiko* became a dance to be performed by women as well as men, and feminine dances also came to be performed by men (occasionally on the outings of my group women would dance a *zeibekiko* and men a *tsifteteli*). This gender emancipation became possible after the 1970s, when the number of women in Greek universities increased and shifting social and political conditions influenced the redefinition of gender and womanhood in general.

My *parea* (drinking company) is observing the performance of the singers and of those dancing while they slowly drink their whisky. There is very little speech; my interlocutors are focused on the music and the performances on the stage. Comments are made about the style of dancing, the dancers' movements, and body gestures.

The bill increases as customers spend on champagne and flowers. The practice of opening champagne is very widespread, especially in the second-tier clubs. Usually the customer orders a few bottles of champagne or even more. Then a waiter opens the champagne on the stage while the singer is singing and serves the singer. The singer never drinks the champagne, but simply takes the glass and waves to the customers who treated him, while holding the glass up to them in a gesture to wish them good health. The champagne is usually a fake champagne called Bolero, which is produced in Greece especially for this kind of practice in nightclubs.

More recently, this practice has also been seen on popular television programs on days of celebration, in which usually a studio is transformed into a tavern or a *bouzoukia* and famous artists, actors, or other famous people in the star system perform. While the singers are performing, several flower women (*lululudes*) circulate around the audience with baskets filled with flowers. When the *lululudes* receive the order, they are either paid immediately or keep track of the customer's bill. A basket of flowers ranges from 20 to 50 euros, and a man who wants to throw flowers over the singer will buy at least two or more baskets.

Depending on the song and the singer, people buy the baskets and throw the flowers or even the whole basket on the singer. The surprising gesture of throwing the actual bamboo basket on the singer is usually practiced by men, who do it in a performative manner, while women usually throw only the flowers. It is also usual for the flower women to walk onto the stage and throw the flowers on the singer while pointing at the customer who paid for the them. The singer will nod or throw one of the flowers back to the table that treated him or her to the flowers. The most popular singers in each club receive flowers, and the quantity of flowers thrown each time is a way of gauging a singer's popularity.[16] Sometimes flowers are also thrown gradually while a woman of a group is dancing *tsifteteli,* or each basket might be emptied on her head in a performative act.

The amount of money spent in such a context is variable. Customers might spend from 140 euros, which could be the price of a blended bottle of whisky, to 300 or even more for a special.[17] The group usually shares the costs, but in cases of personal celebration one person alone will pay the bill. In some cases, Antonis and Sotiris even saved money for a week to spend on one night. When Antonis, for example, received his degree, he saved for months to be able to pay for one night out at *Asteria.*

Maria and Kostantina, on the other hand, never saved to go out to *bouzoukia*. Their high income enables them to entertain themselves regularly in various *bouzoukia*, and they are proud of spending on flowers and Scotch. Other high-income patrons of such clubs are also able to express their budget in such excessive practices.

The status of a company at a table that spends a lot during a night is affirmed by the club in various ways: in the service (which is faster and much more polite), by the orchestra or the singer (in drinking and toasting to the health of big spenders), and in the photographs that are taken to be kept as a reminder of the big night. In almost all popular *bouzoukia* where big-name singers perform, there is a photographer cooperating with the club who takes photographs of patrons while they entertain themselves, moving from table to table. The photographs are usually placed at the entrance of the club, and patrons buy them on their way out. Thus the memory of spending gloriously is preserved and may even be displayed conspicuously in the homes of those who socialize in *bouzoukia*.

Despite the personal ostentation of those who spend lavishly, there are also people in *bouzoukia* who cannot afford to spend as much as my interlocutors. However, when going out with my interlocutors, Antonis as well as Sotiris follow this style of entertainment and spend on Scotch and flowers even when they cannot afford to spend as much. Prestige is not the only motivation behind excessive consumption, as the small spenders simply cannot compete with the big spenders. In my group, for example, most of the time none of them was able to afford to pay for the bottles alone.

Therefore, keeping up with a style of entertainment is a process that requires a lot of investment. Material constraints might limit the ability of some of the interlocutors to perform their style regularly, but when they decide to invest in it they are able to bring it off successfully.

Thus Scotch has been localized within the context of *bouzoukia* and has become part of a specific style of modernness in entertainment. Reserving a table with whisky, throwing flowers, and opening champagne are practices that express an excessive consumption style in the context of *bouzoukia* and constitute cultural aspects of a style of entertainment deeply entangled with contemporary Greek popular music. This can also obscure the socioeconomic inequalities of urban social life, as the patrons of *bouzoukia* differ between low- and high-income salaried workers and professionals.

Emotionality and Anti-Domesticity in Drinking

One of the most excessive performative practices described by a group that I socialized with and interviewed in Aigaleo is demolition (*katedafisi*). Dimitris, a divorced retired public servant who has spent time in *bouzoukia* almost all his life, described it thus:

> I remember I used to go out with a guy who owned some apartments blocks in Glyfada. We would go to Dilina, where Litsa Diamanti was singing, and we used to get a table right next to the scene because he knew her. We would order a bottle of whisky but he couldn't drink a lot because he had heart problems. In any case the waiters would bring the bottle and the fruit and after a while he would throw the table with all the stuff and the bottle onto the stage. Afterwards the waiters would bring the table back again with a new bottle and fruit, but he would throw the table on the stage again. He was in love with her (*kapsouris*).[18]

According to my interlocutor Antonis, excessive practices in *bouzoukia* outside the context of partying (*glenti*) can also be explained when someone is deeply in love (*kapsouris*). When somebody is in love, whisky is the drink that gives them courage, relaxes them (*se stroni*), and helps them get over past or present disappointments.[19] According to Antonis, "If you are *kapsouris,* you will drink whisky." *Kapsura* is an emotional state that literally means *burning*. It describes the emotion of loving someone without receiving any emotional stimuli in return. The subject then is trapped in this one-sided affection, which might last for years. The metaphor of fire and burning is used regularly in the Greek language in relation to failed and unconsummated love relationships, such as *me ekapse*. Such phrases usually are used in reference to a man's feelings for a woman, but can also be applied to a woman's feelings for a man. *Kapsura* (or *burning for a woman or a man*) is a major motive for the consumption of Scotch that legitimates excessive actions in the context of *bouzoukia*. Similarly, the dancer Alexandris refers to various examples of customers who would spend fortunes in a night because they were crazy, or in *kapsura,* over a female singer or a woman from his dance group (Alexandris 2000: 67). The notion of *kapsoura* has been so important in this genre of contemporary popular music in the context of *bouzoukia* that many Athenians call *skiladika kapsourika* or *kapsourotragouda* (songs with *kapsoura*).

Dimitris clearly explained that this demolition was not the result of drinking whisky or alcohol in general. Rather, demolition expresses an unfulfilled erotic relationship, a disappointment, a divorce, or in general a situation that upsets a person's soul. In this case, then, the destruction of the bottle of Scotch whisky becomes the means to express such feelings of *kapsoura*. Similarly, many songs in this genre are about unfulfilled and destroyed relationships, illegal love outside the context of marriage, divorce, and betrayal of women or men.

The style of entertainment in *bouzoukia* has inspired various filmmakers in modern Greek cinema. The contemporary director Voulgaris, for example, narrates a scenario in which the anti-domestic discourse and the excessive consumption (the making of the self through style) are condensed in a case of a divorce

(*Ola Ine Dromos,* 1998). A family man in his fifties who lives in rural Greece spends his evenings in a *bouzoukia*. One day his wife, disappointed from his lifestyle, his excessive consumption in the *bouzoukia,* and his anti-domestic sexuality in this sphere of entertainment, decides to leave him, taking their child, and asks for a divorce. That night the man decides to go to the *bouzoukia* again to let off steam. First he orders a special Scotch, and then he breaks all the plates in the club. When no more plates are available he is willing to pay to smash the toilets. After smashing the toilets there is nothing left to break, so he decides to buy the *bouzoukia* club the same evening and demolish it with a bulldozer. As the bulldozer demolishes the *bouzoukia* he soaks his coat in whisky and sets fire to it while dancing. At the end he throws away his burned coat with a performative gesture and continues his *zeibekiko.* Setting fire to whisky and thus symbolizing the negation of domesticity was indeed widespread in *bouzoukia* before 1973. Petropoulos has described this habit taking place in the underground *bouzoukia* of Athens: a man would spill some whisky on the floor and then set fire to it while he danced (Petropoulos 1987: 133).

A typical story of a ruined relationship that became materialized in Scotch whisky was told to me by Dimitris and later by his daughter. Dimitris from Aigaleo, a man in his early sixties whom I met through a colleague of mine in Athens while conducting research and whom I interviewed on two occasions, has spent all his life enjoying whisky and entertainment in *bouzoukia*. His daughter described him as a man of the night (*tis nihtas*) and as someone who has squandered his life in whisky. Dimitris was a public servant who married in the 1970s and a few years later had a daughter. His relationship with his wife was not very successful, as he spent most of his evenings in *bouzoukia* with his friends, a situation that led to many conflicts. His wife decided to move to a new house with her daughter and end the marriage in divorce. Since then he has let off steam through whisky and *bouzoukia* and has tried to recover by spending his last savings.

The concept of destruction has a major significance in the night entertainment in *bouzoukia*. Songs such as "*Gremista Ola Pia Skliri Kardia*" ("Destroy Everything, Harsh Heart!") are typical examples of the idea of destruction in popular music and night entertainment. Destruction might also take the form of burning banknotes, throwing whisky on the floor and setting fire to it, breaking a bottle, breaking chairs, and pulling off the tablecloth.[20] However, such practices are not encountered very often and have been largely replaced (as noted) by the institutionalization of symbolic destruction in the form of throwing flowers.

In second-rate *bouzoukia*, excessive consumption might be actively promoted by the staff and the women working there. For example, the term *damage* (*zimia*) means the bill that an individual runs up in a night in reference to a particular person or singer or artist. Alexandris, who was a singer in many different *skiladika* all over Greece, stated about one of his employees who was a dancer that "He supported me with the damage he did for me." He meant that this person (customer) was so *kapsouris* with her that he did excessive damage in his effort to express his feelings (2000: 62). It is also of interest that the expression "I held a funeral" (*kano kidia*) means that the female artist is smart enough to cause damage of at least 300,000 drachmas, an amount estimated to be at least 1,000 euros (2006: 62).

Another realm outside of *skiladika* and *bouzoukia* where whisky is interrelated with an anti-domestic mentality is the sex bar (*bar me consommation*). The word *bar me consommation* is derived from the American word for bar and the French *consommation,* meaning sexual intercourse and consumption.[21] Women who work in such bars are expected to keep company with each man who enters the bar. Men accordingly buy drinks for the women and thus also buy their time. The majority of men in these sex bars drink whisky (Abatzi 2004: 152). More interestingly, wine, *ouzo*, or other Greek beverages are never consumed this context.

Similarly, whisky is the main beverage in other bars that offer sexual services, *stiptitzadika* (strip shows), or *koladika* (sex clubs), a masculine underground form of leisure. One evening after returning from a *bouzoukia*, Antonis suggested to the remaining group of men that we visit such a place, situated behind the Hilton hotel in central Athens. His main argument was that the owner of the bar was obliged to him because Antonis had fixed his computer, so we would not have to pay for any drinks. The major difference between normal bars and the bars of the above category is that the center of the bar is a stage for strip shows, and sometimes some sort of sexual services are offered on the spot. Most of the women employed there are from outside Greece (mostly from Eastern Europe) and do not spend a long time talking with the men, as they do not speak very good Greek. Such spaces are usually very dark, tables are spaced far apart, and there is usually a bottle of whisky on the table. If the customer buys the bottle to drink it with one of the women who works there, the woman might offer him manual sexual services. The women present themselves very sexually. Those who dance take off all their clothes, and at the end of their performances, they sit down again with the men who are paying for their company. Customers who want to be more private will move to tables situated at the back of the bar where it is totally dark. Some men have sex in public in the dark corners of the underground club; others masturbate accompanied by the women. In such places, whisky is a form of payment for the women's sexual services. Men who do not buy a bottle are allowed to treat women to a few drinks, but for more sexual behavior they must spend more money on alcohol.

Consumption and Style in Night Entertainment

Rather than expressing the imaginaries of the mediascape of marketing and advertising that projected it as a symbol of modernity, Europeaness, female emancipation, and companionship, this trajectory of Scotch whisky became precisely its reverse. Within this context, Scotch became interrelated with a Greek oriental-ism, a Greek popular music, and the underground and marginal style of night-clubs, all expressed in an anti-domestic mentality. Gradually, Scotch became part of the popular entertainment in *bouzoukia* and became representative of this form of entertainment, even to the extent (as already noted) that the prices of such nightclubs are represented in bottles of Scotch whisky.

The emergence of contemporary popular Greek music and entertainment is deeply interrelated with the genre of *rebetiko* and the immigrants who identified with it. It was within this context that the *bouzouki,* a stringed musical instru-ment, was imported into Greece at the beginning of the twentieth century. The arrival of *rebetiko* transformed the music entertainment of the capital of Greece, especially because this genre and this urban style of entertainment were popular-ized and indigenized in the postwar spaces of *bouzoukia,* where *bouzouki* music was widely performed. Part of the commoditization process was the Europeaniza-tion of the music, the spaces of entertainment, and the beverages consumed. As a result, Scotch whisky, in the process of becoming a symbol of modernity (the American way of life or Europeanness) for the Athenians, was slowly adapted and adopted in an Eastern style by subverting the dominant notions of modernity in the heterotopias of *bouzoukia* and *skyladika* (Foucault and Miskoweic 1986). As Foucault has argued, heterotopias function in an anti-utopian and anti-hege-monic way, and they constitute the space of otherness. They are sites that relate to all other sites in a way that neutralize and invert the set of relationships that des-ignate and reflect. As such the sites of *bouzoukia* and *skyladika* contradict all other sites by subverting a rational, emancipated, and disciplined leisure of modernity with an excessive and out-of-control mentality materialized in Scotch. Within this context, Scotch becomes a negation of the social and economic responsibili-ties of Athenian middle class.

The establishment of contemporary popular Greek music and entertainment during the 1980s and the 1990s with *firmes,* well-known *bouzoukia* and *skiladika* localized Scotch to the extent that their prices became represented in terms of the beverage. Within this context, Scotch became intertwined with this scene and style of entertainment.

It follows that my interlocutors who identify with this type of popular music make themselves through whisky and claim a relationship between the beverage and their style. However, not all consumers of Scotch identify with this style; some new cosmopolitans, for example, try to differentiate themselves through single malts.[22]

In addition, the cultural style that is associated with entertainment in *bou-zoukia* in recent decades is based on an excessive unproductive mentality that includes opening a bottle of special or a bottle of Scotch, throwing baskets of flowers at singers, opening champagne, and running up enormous bills for a bottle of whisky. Similarly, the *firmes* who represent the new Greek popular music scene and perform in *bouzoukia* spend their wealth conspicuously and publicly (Varouhaki 2005: 83). Although my interlocutors identify with this style of entertainment and these forms of conspicuous consumption, they are divided by major socioeconomic differences that are both united and obscured under this modern urban style.

Finally, large socioeconomic differences and power relationships are also evident in the heterotopias of sex bars or sex clubs, in which *consommation* and prostitution take place. There, prices for sexual services are represented in terms of alcoholic beverages and Scotch whisky, a further realm of the localization of the beverage.

Notes

1. For more information on *rebetiko,* see Kotaridis 1996, Damianakos 2003, Oikonomou 2012.
2. While orientalism in Europe has been a way of exoticizing the other for many centuries, in Greece an ambivalent relationship with the East created the superior meaning of the West or Europe and the familiar otherness of the East. Herzfeld has argued that Greece has been viewed as a polluted vessel, the cradle of civilization and conversely the country that was part of the barbaric, exotic East, the Ottoman Empire (1989). This European view of Greek culture profoundly influenced the way in which Greeks view themselves and also the way in which they employ the concepts of the West and Europe. The essentializations of Europeans became part of a selective memory in Greece, and Western products and ways of thinking and behaving gradually colonized the population. The Greek word *xenophile,* denoting the liking for *xeno* (things that are foreign), expresses the passion for otherness that is manifested in consumption, representing the materialization of the symbolic domination of modern Greek identity and the ambiguities that social identities entail in everyday life.
3. *Tekke* in Turkish is a building used as a retreat and a spiritual center by the Sufi or Tariqa brotherhoods. The term was adopted into *rebetiko* slang and signified the semi-illegal socializing places of musicians and other *rebetes,* where alcohol, hashish, and other drugs were sometimes consumed. Possibly the term was adopted in this manner because the Orthodox Muslims of Turkey did not identify with the mysticism and the values of Tariqa; thus the *tekke* was stigmatized as a place of sin of those Sufi who were imagined to consume alcohol and hashish, going against Muslim tradition.
4. The interview with Tsitsanis was included in the television series *Paraskinio,* broadcast in 1976. The musician stated *"Kovame ta bemolia"* ("We would avoid Eastern climax") in relation to rhythms that would undergo censorship.
5. Examples of this kind of club were Embassy (situated in Panepistimiou and Amerikis Streets), Ritz (located in Stadiou 65), and Arizona. Of Ritz, Kerofilas writes: "It was a nightclub with German staff occasionally, a magnificent juggler and the 'queens of sex,' Sabine and Iris" (1997: 205).
6. It is very possible that whisky was also the main drink of consumption in cabarets and sex bars in various areas of Athens and more particular in the area of Truba before and after

World War II. The sex bars are spaces in which the company of women is exchanged for the offering of alcoholic beverages by the customers. According to Abatzi, the bottle of whisky was found in various sex bars before the dictatorship (2004: 58).

7. According to Cowan (quoting Petropoulos), *magas* was a masculine identity constructed by Greek immigrants from Asia Minor who lived at the margins of Greek society and who would criticize all aspects of conventional social values. For example, he would never get married and never hold his girlfriend's hand in the street. He never wore a tie and never had an umbrella; he smoked hashish, hated the police, and regarded going to jail as an honor (Cowan 1990: 183).

8. The term *ellinadiko* appears mainly during the 1990s and refers to a form of club where *ellinika* (Greek popular music) is played by a DJ. Therefore, in *ellinadiko* no live music is performed.

9. As Abatzi (2010) has observed, I have also encountered similar examples of people who say, "I always drink my whisky with two ice cubes." The number depends on the person, but the choice of ice becomes a very personal matter of identification. Many people drink the same whisky brand, but it is not always the case that they have the same number of ice cubes. Ice therefore becomes one more parameter of social distinction.

10. The *poustis* is considered to be a passive male gay figure in various contexts of social life in Greece, and the word is also used as a highly inappropriate discursive insult. If somebody is considered not to be moral or is regarded as scum, this term may be applied to him. The concept might also have more neutral connotations that describe illegal practices that are not considered significant, especially in relation to the state.

11. However, someone who is active might not be considered a *poustis* because he is the penetrator and therefore masculine. Sotiris, for example, who is assertively masculine, described a sexual encounter he had with a *poustis* in the army. He stated that he (Sotiris) penetrated him and thus does not consider himself homosexual/*poustis*. The rest of the men in the group considered such behavior eccentric, but in no way was he thought to be a homosexual or *poustis* because he had a sexual encounter with a man. On the contrary, Antonis claimed that such behavior could be highly masculine, and he stated Sotiris "is fucking everything that moves" (*gamai oti kinite*).

12. Lesser known successful singers include for example Efi Thodi, Sabrina, and Terlegas.

13. The pseudonym *Athenian* is used for a music hall with live contemporary Greek music situated in the area of Aegaleo.

14. According to Papataxiarchis (1991: 170), *kefi* derives from the Arabic word *keyif* or *keyf,* meaning pleasure and delight, or humor, a healthy state as well as a state of slight intoxication. The villagers of Mouria use the word to refer to an ideal mood of joy and relaxation, achieved when problems and social conventions are banished.

15. A *zeibekiko* song might be a *paragelia,* that is, a request from a customer. In the past, a *paragelia* was usually danced only by the customer who requested the song, but the custom has gradually changed. The request was once so highly valued that during the dictatorship a customer called Nikos Koemtzis knifed three policemen and killed one in a music hall when one of them tried to interrupt his dance.

16. On Christmas and New Year's Eve in 2006, several television programs presented studios as *bouzoukia* with flowers being thrown to the singers; I observed similar phenomena in 2007.

17. Prices are given for the research period of 2005 and 2006.

18. The bill in that instance was 500,000 drachmas, which would translate as a sum between 1,500 and 2,000 euros nowadays.
19. For more information on the subject see Abatzi (2004).
20. A song associated with this practice says, "*tha ta kapso ta rimadia ta lefta mou*" ("I will burn my damned money").
21. The word *consommation* perfectly describes the consumerist ideology of the commodification of sex.
22. This aspect of single malt consumption seems to confirm Stewart's early points about class distinction (1989), as whisky is not necessarily rejected by the elite once a broader section of the population begin to drink it, but some new pattern of consumption is found to continue to claim a class distinction.

CHAPTER **5**

The Location of Whisky
in the North Aegean

Men's traditional breeches have turned into blue jeans. Our vineyards
have become illegal constructions and the wine has become whisky.

—*Skyriana Nea* 1993: 4, issue 204.

Introduction

In the recent past, various new beverages have become part of the social life of the
inhabitants of the island of Skyros in the North Aegean. Among these commodities, imported alcoholic beverages and more specifically Scotch whisky stand as a
sign of the specific forms that modernity takes on the island. The increasing presence of imported beverages is evident in several aspects of the social life. From
bars to *kafenio* (the Greek coffeehouse) and nightclubs, *parees* (companies) of inhabitants form to go out and drink whisky, whereas others use the beverage while
they play *poka* (a local version of poker). However, such consumptions habits are
not viewed by all Skyrians as constructive and socially accepted in a way as they
are by a large majority of Athenians.

On the island of Skyros, various consumers of alcohol and whisky live in a
dialectic relationship with imported beverages; people make themselves through
alcohol and at the same time drinks/beverages are identified with particular persons. The locations of whisky vary, as do the styles of the islanders who drink the
alcohol. Vagelis, for example, who owns the Makedonia *kafenio,* which serves
mainly whisky to its customers (amounting to up to 90 percent of the total consumption in his shop), claims "Whisky is the national drink of Greece and the
favorite beverage of my Skyrian customers." Moreover, whisky accounts for 40
percent of the imported alcoholic beverages on the island, at least according to
Stamatis, the owner of the island's only liquor store, and the employees of the

multinational alcohol companies Diageo and Pernod Ricard, who come regularly to the island to arrange imports. Conversely, the majority of Skyrians might claim that they prefer to drink wine and *tsipouro* in the traditional *kafenio* (the coffeehouse), in the *konatsi* (the shepherds' country dwelling), and in various other locations. Such gatherings are usually characterized by commensality, and they are constructive and constitutive of social relationships.

Therefore, this third trajectory of the study of Scotch whisky—on the island of Skyros—investigates the ways in which the processes of the consumption of the beverage are distributed across the social life (in contrast to wine and *tsipouro*). To understand this trajectory and the meanings of consumption in each context, it is necessary to outline the ways in which the islanders make themselves at home, drawing on local history, geography, and my anthropological fieldwork before focusing on the places that Scotch takes up on the island.

Moreover, I have chosen to describe in detail the inhabitants of the island, their history, social relationships, and consumption habits in relation to Scotch. These relationships have been crystallized in time into some major social conceptions, such as the notions of shepherdness (a style characterized by the moral values of shepherds) and laborhood (a style based on the alternative moral universe of laborers). Such notions have influenced the gender styles of the inhabitants and their relationship to matrilocal residence, household domestication, or anti-domesticity. The meanings of gender style that one chooses to perform and the consumption practices in each occasion and social setting are also invested with modernness (*moderno, sihrono*) or tradition (*paradosi*), concepts that are of major importance in the distribution of alcohol and whisky in the social life of the inhabitants.

The Journey from Athens to the Island of Skyros

In the North of the Aegean, close to the islands of Alonissos, Skiathos, and Skopelos, lies the island of Skyros.[1] The area of Skyros measures almost 209 square kilometers, and the population of the island is estimated at 2,602 residents.[2] Several mountains are on the island as well as a big forest of pine trees. Valleys are used for agriculture, and sheep and goats are herded on rocky landscapes. The island is actually divided into two different types of landscape. The northern part of the island is more fertile and less mountainous, whereas the southern part is full of mountains with relatively dry and rocky land.

The endless blue sea, which can be calm and transparent in summer and foamy and choppy in wintertime, separates the island from the mainland. The islanders feel that their island is unique, and they are very eager to talk about their customs, traditions, and the old ways and to revive them. They say that their lives have been changing, that the past is no longer part of the present and the future, and that everything is transforming. Their local idiom is slowly vanishing, and the young do not know the old ways anymore; the young leave for Athens, and traditions are lost. "We have become modern now," say many islanders in a bitter and disappointed tone, yet they still believe that they are traditional in comparison with outsiders. Within this context, tradition has been a major concern for various agents ranging from those connected with the European Union and state projects to local cultural associations for the preservation of tradition, folklorists, and anthropologists. Tradition is usually seen as something static and stable, which has to be preserved and well kept, like a dusty room in a folklore museum that has the smell of the past or a chest containing the old things (*ta palea*) that is opened once a year during Carnival.

The journey from Athens to Skyros begins at the Evia bus station in Tris Gefires, where the buses stand in a row according to their final destinations. Trips to Chalkida, Kimi, and Aliveri are only a few of the usual daily journeys of the passengers who are waiting in the new waiting room filled with plastic chairs. The few shops around are the last resorts of supplies for the passengers. A bottle of water and a packet of cookies or some chips are regular purchases for the short trip. The bus sets off. The driver is listening to contemporary popular Greek music on Evia local radio as he drives through the narrow streets of various villages on his way to the port of Kymi. After three hours the bus arrives at the small port, where the new ship belonging to the local company Skyros Lines is moored. Next to the ship there are many small fishing boats waiting for their next adventure. The passengers from the bus run to the ticket kiosk. Within a few seconds a long queue has formed. Some passengers find acquaintances, good friends from school or from the army, and neighbors or kin, and groups take shape. People move onto the ship after buying their tickets and sit on the deck; others prefer to have a few drinks in the café/bar of the luxurious common room. Some truck drivers order whisky while a company of fishermen drinks beer. The café/bar is packed with bottles of whisky of various sizes and brands, placed in the glass showcase like sports trophies.

Within two hours the ship has arrived at Linaria, the harbor of Skyros. Linaria is a small settlement with a few houses, some fish taverns, a few shops, and a petrol station. Some relatives and friends of the travelers are waving from the harbor while shop owners and newspaper distributors wait for their commodities. Dozens of cars start up their engines in the ferryboat garage, which fills up with fumes. A long line of trucks, buses, and cars is now heading toward the village. A few kilometers away a huge rock becomes visible on top of the hill by the sea. As the bus reaches the village, white houses can be sighted, which spread from the top of the hill to the bottom. After passing Agelis's gas station we enter the village, and after a while the bus parks opposite the neoclassical building that houses the primary school. The high school is a hundred meters away. Between the two schools is Paneris's supermarket, a reminder of the recent shift from neighborhood food stores (*bakalika*) to supermarkets selling all kinds of imported commodities and luxury goods. A few meters away, on the edge of the market, is Vagelis's *kafenio,* Makedonia, where the island's middle-aged laborers watch their football games, bet on poker games (*poka*), and take their whisky. Opposite Makedonia is another *kafenio* called Sinantisis, where building professionals meet up early in the morning to drink coffee or beer before leaving for work. Next to Makedonia is a car rental firm and a small office called KEP (Citizens' Assistance Center), a relatively new institution promoted in all municipalities of Greece by the Ministry of the Interior to help citizens overcome bureaucracy.

Most travelers walk toward the *agora,* the main market street of the village and the center of the social life of the island, and then disappear into the tiny streets to the left and right, called *sokakia,* which spread all over the hill like a labyrinth. The first thing visitors notice when they enter the *agora* is the *platia,* the central square where some of the modern bar-club hybrids and *kafenio* are situated opposite the town hall and the municipal library. Taxis are parked in the small parking space next to the square, and the taxi drivers are drinking *frappe* (ice coffee) as they wait for prospective customers. On the *platia* are also two newsstands, where newspapers and magazines are available. Next to the press point on the square is a clothes shop, owned by a new Chinese family, and the National Bank of Greece, the only bank on the island.

Further up is Maritsa's *kafenio,* where shepherds and farmers spend their time in card games and discussion. Recently, Maritsa's son Manolis tried to inject a more traditional esthetic into the space with renovations and added a sign saying "Paradosiako Kafenio" (traditional *kafenio*) at the front. Next to Maritsa's is a bar/club/café, which was a *kafenio* until a few years ago. This modern café/club stands side by side with Maritsa's traditional *kafenio.* The two establishments are separated by a real as well as a symbolic boundary: a small wall keeps separate the worlds of the two cafés and the imaginative categories of modernity and tradition.

Across the street is the shop owned by Stamatis Ftoulis, selling traditional pottery art, a form of ceramic that has come to be known as Skyrian in recent decades even though most objects are replicas of seventeenth- and eighteenth-century Dutch, Italian, English, and Chinese porcelain created for the European market. Although plates and ceramics are bought by tourists as souvenirs, local women regard these objects as inalienable wealth in their dowry, which is transferred from mother to daughter and displayed conspicuously in most households in the village. Houses are usually open, especially in summer, and local women are very proud to show off their material culture to the tourists. A less friendly spot where ceramics are also displayed is the cemetery. Very often women dressed in black walk through the backstreets of the market to the cemetery to light the oil lamps placed in front of the graves of their loved ones and clean what they think of as their last homes that symbolically resemble their real houses. The cemetery is situated a few minutes away from the market street and marks the boundary of the village as its entrance is on the village's main asphalt street.

Beyond Ftoulis's shop we find the first crossroads of the market street. The alley that crosses the market street leads on the left to the police station, the village parking lot, and the cemetery. To the left the alley is narrower and descends to the area of Kohylia, which was the poorest part of the island until a few decades ago. On the corner of the market street is Stamatis's *cava* store, a cosmopolitan alcohol store that sells bottled Greek wines, various types of whisky, and a variety of imported beverages. Stamatis runs the only alcohol store in the market and is the main distributor of alcoholic beverages on the island. On the other corner of the crossroad is another relatively new *kafenio,* where middle-aged shop owners from the market, artisans, and public servants spend their time in chat, card games, television, and backgammon.

I continue my walk toward the ancient acropolis, or castle of Skyros, called Kastro, which lies at the top of the hill and houses the Monastery of Saint George, property of the monastic community of Mount Athos. The steep stone path extends to Rupert Brooke Square and then comes to the oldest neighborhood of the island, known as *megali strata,* where the Skyros elite lived until the beginning of the twentieth century.[3] The neighborhood is surrounded by Byzantine churches attached to each other and stone arches. The biggest church is Virgin Mary of the *arhontes,* or *Arhontopanagia,* meaning Virgin Mary of the noblemen. Neighbors sit and chat on the stone benches on the sides of the church.[4]

At the end of the road is the front entrance of the acropolis and the gate to the monastery. Next to this gate, where an Athenian lion made of white marble lies as a reminder of the influences of classical Athens, is the house of my matrilineal uncle Mihalis, who gave me hospitality and provided precious information and contacts during my research. The view from this area is magnificent, and the visitor can see most of the settlements on the island, including the structure of the village. On the western side, on the balcony of the monastery of the ancient acropolis, I can see the *agora* and the Kohylia area. Kohylia surrounds the western part of the village up to the market street, the *agora,* and it is the lowest area of the settlement. This is where many laborers and farmers reside. The area between the *agora* and the *Arhontopanagia* is the second major part of the village, which used to be—and still is—where most of the shepherds dwell. The area above the church of the Virgin Mary, which surrounds the rock of the ancient acropolis and the monastery, is known as Kastro. The elite inhabited this area in the past. After the dictatorship, the area gradually became a ghost town, occupied mainly in summer by Skyrian-Athenians and the foreigners who have bought houses in the area.

The small square next to the entrance of the monastery, called Kamantou, is a wonderful spot with a view on the east part of the Aegean. Standing high on the hill, the viewer can see an endless horizon filled with the blue of the archipelago and a few fishing boats far below in the sea. On the north side is a lowland (*kabos*) where vineyards grew until most of the local production was destroyed by phylloxera in the 1970s. Nowadays the whole area stretching from the edge of the lowland down toward the sea is built with the new-style houses of Skyros. A garden and a garage at the front, sometimes a lawn, and usually two floors are regular characteristics of the houses in this area. The rapid tourist and economic development has transformed the area between the sea and the *kabos* into a holiday resort for many foreigners, Skyrian Athenians, military personnel, and, lately, also inhabitants who prefer to be close to the sea. The change in the landscape after the 1960s and 1970s included the construction of various hotels and houses, the Xenia Hotel, and, more recently, beach bars and rooms to let, all over the seashore.

The seashore is divided into three main settlements that no longer possess borders. The oldest settlement is Magazia, which is on the southern part of the seashore. Magazia was also the first area to develop tourism, with the Xenia Hotel being built there in the 1960s. The first bar on Skyros, owned by Stamatis Ftoulis, opened there, and some others followed later. Nowadays the area is booming with hotels, bungalows, and rooms to let but has kept a local character. After Magazia is the area of Molos, which used to be the largest community of fishermen on the island. Molos is recognizable by the small fishing port situated in front of an old white windmill that has been transformed into a tavern. In the winter, several boats are hauled onto the shore next to the small harbor to be protected from the winds and maintained by the fishermen. The rest of the time, fishing boats of various colors are in the water and can be seen leaving and entering the harbor early in the dawn and in the afternoon. When there is no wind, their old petrol engines can be heard kilometers away with their slow hypnotic pulse that resembles the social life of the island. The last and newest settlement of the seashore is Girismata. More than a decade ago, the largest hotel on Skyros, the Skyros Palace, was built there, and various other houses followed that spread toward the *kabos* (lowland) area. However, the proliferation of houses, rooms to let, and small hotels has resulted in a chaotic buildup that has not been supervised by the municipality or any other authority.

On the rest of the island are some smaller settlements of farmers and shepherds and an increasing number of houses owned by wealthy Athenians or inhabitants who prefer to stay on their own estates. The area of Kalamitsa, for example, in the southwest next to the port of Linaria, has been transformed into a tourist, Skyrian-Athenian, and Skyrian-American settlement with a bizarre pseudo-elitist aesthetic and is full of small villa estates. The development of the area has also resulted in the establishment of a small mini-market and a new Athenian-style restaurant.

On the north side of the island is a military and civil airport, part of a large army base. The transformation of social life on Skyros was also influenced by the construction of this military air base, which began in 1970 and was completed in 1976 (*Skyrian News* 1979: 1–7). The farmers who owned the land and the laborers who had bought land in the Trahi area received an indemnity from the state. Skyrians received considerable amounts of money that were subsequently invested in tourism and in buying apartments in Athens, which could be given as dowry. A network of roads was constructed, and the population of the island increased as several of the military construction workers married Skyrian women and stayed on the island. Nowadays the airport serves the charter flights from the Netherlands and Olympic Airways' flights from Athens and has recently been renovated. Next to the airport are a few agricultural areas and a large pine forest, which covers the largest part of the northwest side of the island. The eastern side is the driest part of the island, where shepherding takes place and the highest mountains stand. The area of Vouno, for example, is the highest area of the island, with a relatively large goat and sheep population and many shepherd families. [5]

The Cultural Construction of Place and Identity on the Island of Skyros

On Skyros, there are various small settlements, but the majority of the islanders live in the only town-village, called the *horio*. In the *horio* houses are packed one over another in a cubistic style from the top to the bottom of the settlement. The heart of the *horio* is the *agora*, or market street. Life in the *agora* begins between eight and nine o'clock in the morning and continues till nine to ten o'clock in the evening, with an afternoon break of four to five hours, usually from one to six. During summer, however, shops stay open longer, as there are tourists on the island. Public events take place in the *agora* all year, including Carnival, political debates, and festivals. Within this context, men frequent the bar, the *kafenio* (sort of coffeehouse), and the tavern. Women tend to socialize more often inside and around their houses, where they also dominate the family affairs. In some ways, then, "women are houses" (Stewart 1991: 49). This perspective is especially the case if they are matrilocally settled in their dowered house. There they are responsible for keeping men and things in order, saving money (*oikonomia*), and organizing family life in general.

The *horio* is the center of the social life of the island and, as such, is also called Skyros. The *horio* is divided into Kastro, the *agora* (the shopping street including bars, *kafenio*, and mini-markets), and Kohylia, though there are no clear boundaries between these areas. The *agora* is the major point of reference in the *horio* when somebody is giving directions and is the most public and busiest place both day and night. Leisure is almost synonymous with the *agora*, and people ask "*Pame stin agora?*" ("Shall we go to the *agora*?") when they want to invite you out or have a drink with you. The village is divided into *pano* (up) and *kato* (down), with the *pano* area usually referring to the Kastro area and *kato* to the *agora*, Kohylia, and the seashore. In daily conversations in terms of space, islanders also distinguish between *ekso* and *mesa*. *Ekso* means the outside and includes everything that is situated outside the village except the seashore in front of the castle with the areas of Molos and Magazia. The term is also associated with nature and wilderness as well as with supernatural beings and the devil, the *okso apo do*.[6]

Interestingly, the meaning of *ekso* has shifting meanings among the shepherds, who refer to Athens and to the outside of *horio* (including their spaces of labor in the countryside) as *ekso*. Outside the *horio* (*ekso*) can be found, for example, the *konatsi* or shepherds' country dwelling.[7] This is male property and is viewed as a male space. It is where the shepherds or farmers sleep when they have long working periods; it is where tools and wine are kept and where male drinking gatherings take place. The *konatsi* provides a solution for socializing for shepherds who cannot afford to drink and entertain themselves *mesa* in the matrilocal residence, the property of women. Socializing in the house is usually a privilege of the matrilineal kin. The center of the household and the nuclear family in the village is *mesa* in the house, which is property of the women and is thought of as female space.

By contrast, Athens might be also referred be as *mesa*, or inside, by various people who claim a closer relationship with the Greek capital. This reference to Athens as *mesa* is not accidental, as will be demonstrated. Athens as an imagined place is related to the values of cosmopolitanism expressed in a specific style adopted by present or past migrant-laborers and Skyrian-Athenians. As such it has been appropriated as *mesa* and therefore close, part of the style of those who come and go between Skyros and the capital and those who want to be identified with Athens. It is worth stating, then, that meanings of place—such as the dichotomy of *mesa/ekso* in the case of Skyros—are translocal and subject to the cultural style with which each network identifies and makes itself at home. Claims over cultural styles relate to the construction of places and their cultural meanings and associations (Ferguson 1999: 82–122).

With regard to property relationships and inheritance, male shepherds usually do not inherit anything *mesa* in the village. As a result, they usually own their flock and the land *ekso*. Women, on the other hand, inherit the house and the fertile land, and they remain in control of the economics in the household. So in terms of space, property relationships that can be articulated in the house, bilateral reckoning, matrilocality, and the village structure are expressed in the cemetery (Bampilis 2002), and new income differentiations are related to the area where a person lives and entertains herself or himself. Within social space human action is organized in its relation to boundaries such as the *mantra*.[8] Inside and outside (*mesa-ekso*), *fridatsi*, or up and down (*pano-kato*) are symbolic boundaries that define the neighborhood, the household, the grave, the professional space, and the property.[9] The social space organizes human action in various contexts such as the village, the market, the church, the household, or the *kafenio,* all of which express different types of social relationships.

Despite the effectiveness of symbolic boundaries, their fluidity is unquestionable. For instance, the yard of a house—which I initially thought to be a private space—becomes a public space in the summer; houses that are closed in the cold evenings of winter open up in spring and summer; the *fridatsi,* which is not visible in the winter, is repainted and becomes visible in the spring; and the *kato* of the market during winter transforms into the seashore and the fishing port during summer. The social categories of space change their meanings according to the occasion, time frame, and relationship.

In terms of sociality, male gatherings take place in the market, the *kafenio,* the bar, the *konatsi,* or the homes of single men. Men are expected to be social through drinking and sometimes singing. Women also sing, and especially in the context of *panigiria* (religious festivals) there is competitive singing of local songs, a practice that has continued for generations. Dance and dancing are not usual and tend to take place at weddings or in clubs and bars. As the inhabitants say, "On Skyros we sing and drink."[10] Songs, small poems that people compose to use in everyday life, local sayings, and generally the idiom with its local color are the major social contexts for reproducing and expressing the cultural particularity of the island. For instance, after I had spent almost a year on the island, many Skyrians spoke to me in a very local idiom and expected me to answer back in the same vein.[11]

The inhabitants identify themselves as Skyrians mainly because they were born and live on the island of Skyros. Very long lineages called *soia* (kindred) are not a prerequisite for a Skyrian identity, even though they are of major importance. On the contrary, there are Skyrians who do not have a long lineage because they are descended from migrants who have traveled in the Aegean for several hundred years. However, there are various levels of Skyrianness.[12]

One of the first things the islanders asked me when I was introduced was "*Pianu ise?*" ("What is your family name?"). Another similar question could be "*Ti soi ise?*" meaning "What is your lineage?" The *soi* is reckoned both matrilineally and patrilineally and is of great importance in socialization and establishment of social relationships. Already from school age, children are indoctrinated by their parents about the *soi* and their social relationships. Socializing with cousins and close relatives is desirable despite the fact that children do not follow these social conventions. *Soi* is also of great importance among the occupational partnerships such as the associations (*smihtes*) of shepherds who come together for milking and producing cheese and wool. Generally speaking, the matrilocal or sometimes neolocal habitation results in extended relationships of the male partner with the male affines of the maternal lineage. In this sense, the male affine relatives are likely to cooperate and establish bonds. Another term that inhabitants use for *soi* is *sira,* meaning *line* in Greek. However the term *sira* also represents the appropriate web of social relationships for each individual, including marriage, and social groupings related to other forms of socialization, such as the school and the army. When I was present at discussions concerning the proper marriage for my uncle, for example, my grandmother would say, "She is in your line" (*Ine tis siras su*) or "She is not in your line."[13] Therefore, *sira* in that specific context expresses the appropriate marriage for women and men coming from similar socioeconomic backgrounds.

Ekso as a term may also be related to *eksoteriko* (abroad), everything situated outside of the geographical area of Greece. *Eksoteriko* usually refers to Western Europe and the United States, where most tourists come from. As such, *eksoteriko* is highly valued, as life there is considered to be progressive and advanced. In addition, commodities might come from *eksoteriko,* and these usually bring a high status. Scotch, for example, is from *eksoteriko* as are other imported beverages. However, the most common representation of *eksoteriko* relates to the English and Dutch tourists who come regularly to the island during the summer. [14]

While Greek *xeni* are accepted and at certain occasions included in the community many immigrants from Albania find it more difficult to be included unless they become baptized as Greek Orthodox, they speak Greek, and they become similar to the islanders. The second-generation immigrants, for example, who have been to Greek school, have been baptized, and speak fluently Greek are viewed as islanders despite the fact their parents might not share these characteristics. Those who are not able to perform those stylistic criteria and reproduce their own cultural habits are usually excluded from the social life of the island. Therefore the identity and the relationship between host and guest is a continued negotiated process that obscures the unequal differences of the two parts and it might be able to change.

In all cases, *xeni,* or outsiders, coming from *ekso* are considered to be enjoying the benefits of Skyros without return. As the shepherds say, the outsiders "*Afinoun tin kotsilia tous ke fevgoune,*" meaning they leave their shit and go. Athenians especially are considered to have this mentality of snobbery and disregard for the social life of the countryside, not to mention that they are sometimes viewed as the cause of all the problems in the community. Despite this uneasiness about the Athenians, various networks identify with Athens as a value and a style, as will be demonstrated in the coming chapters.

Social Stratification and Social Differentiation

For hundreds of years, the ecclesiastical authorities and the noblemen would rent their land to the rest of the Skyrians, mainly to shepherds and farmers, and would receive products and money in return. As a result, the political and religious elite was able to keep the social status and indeed become wealthier without coming into conflict with the other social strata that followed the rules of conduct with religious devotion.[15]

The social differentiation on Skyros was evident until recently, with a hierarchical social stratification expressed in the terms of *arhontes* (noblemen), *tis agoras* (men of *agora*), *tsopanides* or *kotsinogonati* (shepherds), *agrotes* (farmers), *psarades or xsipoliti* (fishermen), and *Kohiliani* (laborers). Each occupational group had a distinct identity, which was expressed in clothing, residence, and symbolic capital. The reckoning of cognatic descent in combination with relatively flexible endogamic rule resulted in the reproduction of this hierarchical social stratification, which remained part of the social life of Skyros for hundreds of years (de Sike 1978, Zarkia 1996). While social class has been changing with time, a new formation is being shaped at the moment based not so much on ownership but more on symbolic capital, a process similar to the case of Meganisi (Just 1994).

The political power of a ruling group was evident from the political bodies that were already constituted from the sixteenth century. The noblemen, called *arhontes,* first appeared in a written source in 1515 (Zarkia 1991: 33).[16] The noblemen were the only ones who could read and write; they were the first to wear Western-style clothes, and their consumption habits were very distinctive.[17]

Figure 5.1. Horio. The shepherds neighborhood and agora in the 1960s (Source: Archive of Giannis Venardis).

Women decorated their houses in an elaborate display of expensive porcelains and silver pieces from all over Europe and the Mediterranean, a custom that was later copied by other Skyrians. The distinction of the noblemen was also expressed in the *prikosimfona* (dowry agreements).[18] The *aloni* was given from the mother to the daughter as part of her dowry and still today constitutes symbolic and material capital in the form of antique European porcelain, plates, pottery, and embroidery.[19]

The hierarchical social relationships of production were expressed in space.[20] The *arhontes* lived in the area of the Kastro and Sarous, the shepherds in the area of the *agora* and *Agia Anna,* the men of *agora* in the *agora* and in Kohilia, the farmers in Kohilia and in the countryside ("outside," or *ekso*), and the laborers in the Kohilia area. The few fishermen always lived close to the seashore in *Molos.* Of all these groups, the *arhontes* had the strictest endogamic restrictions to retain control of the means of production, a mentality that gradually changed.[21] Still today remnants of the past hierarchical differentiation are reproduced in local sayings.[22] Furthermore, until recently there were conflicts between the occupational groups, and Mayor Labrou is recorded stating in his election speech in 1951 that "We have to remember that the usual fights between the shepherds and the laborers/peasants in relation to agricultural damage often resulted in killings."[23]

Those who lived in the Kohylia area, the lowest part around the castle hill, were called Kohiliani, and they would take care of all kinds of hard work, particularly hard manual labor. They were hired by the noblemen and the shepherds to cultivate their land and to assist in milking and other shepherding and goat herding activities. They did not own any property or land, and therefore they had no access to the means of production. They worked as farmers, artisans, carriers with mules, woodcutters and builders, and in any kind of heavy labor. Their payment was not always satisfactory. For example, when they worked for shepherds, they would receive yearly only ten goats and a pair of *trohadia,* the shepherds' handmade sandals (Zarkia 1991).

These laborers were considered to have low status in Skyrian society, and they were called *grunia,* which literally means pigs. Marriages with women from this area were not welcomed by the other strata on Skyros, as these women would have no dowry and would bring nothing but their reproductive capacity to the marriage (they came with only "*to mni sto heri,*" only their vagina in their hand). The men were not respected, as their wives would have to participate in the process of production, and this was considered shameful, as ideally women should focus on childcare, the household, embroidery, and religious ceremonies. Today such terms are still used by the shepherd families of Skyros to refer to the *parakatianous* (those without social status) who lived in Kohylia.

Gradually, the property of the *arhontes* was transferred to the shepherd and laboring families.[24] The international economic crisis as a result of the two World Wars and the scarce agricultural and goat/sheep products raised the value of the

Figure 5.2. Kohilia. View of the area of Kohilia in the 1960s (Source: Archive of G. Venardis).

labor of shepherds and laborers. The state agricultural reforms from 1917 to 1922 resulted in more ownership of the land by laborers, farmers, and shepherds (Zarkia 1991: 36).[25] The shepherds and laborers were slowly able to buy the windmills, the olive fields, the vineyards, and the shops of the market, and they started decorating their houses with the *palea,* the symbolic capital of the noblemen.

After World War II, those laborers who were not able to find work on Skyros left the island to work on the mainland, became seamen, and received an education to make a career in the army or in public administration. Girls and women were employed in domestic service in Athens by extended families (*psihopedia*), wealthy Athenians, or Skyrian noblemen in Athens. Many of these migrants would return to get married and build their households on the island, and some would keep houses there for their vacations.

These processes of migration and enrichment continued after World War II and affected the social life of the island.[26] More importantly, these processes resulted in the repatriation of economically successful laborers who preferred to leave the mainland and return to Skyros (de Sike 1978: 69–78). Those who returned wanted to express their upward economic mobility and also tried to claim upward social and cultural mobility. Especially the laborers began during the 1960s to invest in the land, the old symbolic capital, small businesses, and tourism, but they did not manage to climb the social ladder, which was under the political control of the merchants and shepherds. Gradually land lost its social symbolism of traditional hierarchy, and the division of space in the village was no longer related to social stratification. Those farmers and merchants who bought houses in the Kastro area did not become members of the local elite. On the contrary, extreme wealth was seen as a threat to traditional values, despite the fact Skyrians admired material possessions. The successful laborers who bought land close to the Trahi area and close to the seashore became even wealthier because in the first case they were able to sell their land to the Greek army for the construction of the large military air base and in the second case sold strips of land to Athenians, Skyrian-Athenians, Skyrians, and foreigners.[27] Laborers who traveled regularly to the mainland invested in small businesses such as taxis, night entertainment, and shops in the *agora*. Among this group of laborers, various individuals were gamblers who would come together to play *poka* in several *kafenio*. Gambling was gradually introduced on the island, and after a few years the first shop with football betting and national lottery tickets opened. Trade developed as a result of the increased population through the permanent personnel in the military base and the first ferryboat (Skyraki) was bought by the newly established and locally based shipping company in 1980.[28]

The newly rich Skyrians would spend their money on new consumption goods or property in Athens, and in some cases they would leave the island for the city (de Sike 1978: 77). The city (Athens) became a symbol of well-being and a comfortable life, and an urban Athenian style was widely appropriated by newly rich laborers who were not able to become members of the political establishment of shepherds. Within this context, the modern became an expressive tactic of consumption of urban Athenian aesthetical forms among many Skyrians since the 1970s. This mentality stood in opposition to the tradition of the shepherds and farmers, which according to Persidis, was based on a nonconsumerist lifestyle (1984: 7).[29]

Making a Living on the Island

As noted in the previous sections, social life on Skyros was dominated by the *arhontes* for at least four hundred years and was gradually transformed during the nineteenth and twentieth centuries. The socioeconomic changes affected the position of the elite and new occupational groups appeared on the social landscape. The *arhontes* disappeared and shepherds as well as farmers were able to gain access to the traditional means of production. Laborers tended to migrate and work in various other areas of Greece after World War II. However, they returned and gradually developed into an economically successful group that took up opportunities for innovation in tourism, construction work, entertainment, and trade (Zarkia 1996: 144–173) and claimed an urban style. More specifically, "they were the first to receive the tourists, the first who had to cope with them, the first who realized that things were changing. ... As their situation was favorable they were the first to invest in 'rooms to let,' bars and restaurants, sometimes simply by converting their shop to a supermarket or their workplace into a souvenir shop. Having long been somehow 'culturally marginal' they became the innovators in their society. ... Their capital was small, as was their investment. But in fact their decisions were advanced and innovating" (Zarkia 1996: 150).

Despite their innovations and their economic success, laborers do not usually have access to the political structures of Skyros and the large lineages of shepherds. Furthermore, their long cultural marginality produced an urban style that adapted practices and consumption habits favorable among the Athenian style of entertainment. This process of claiming and practicing an urban style has been a relatively new pattern among those who cannot and do not want to identify with the matrilocal domesticated shepherds. For example, N.T., a regular consumer of Scotch who has adopted an urban style, is descended from a poor Skyrian family of laborers and has become a successful and wealthy laborer and businessman. He described his life as follows:

> I was born in 1949. I come from a poor family of four boys and two girls. I was the fourth. I went to school here but I had to work with my father, who was a fisherman. As a result I had to quit school because I had to spend a lot of time selling fish. We were so poor that we had to steal oil from the church to eat. Gradually I started working as a construction worker and got paid very well. I survived like this for some years until I went into the army. After the army I decided to work as a sailor and I liked it a lot. I traveled all over the world and I saw a lot of new places. After a few trips I came to live on Skyros.

N.T. is one among several new rich Skyrians who has been able to make a living as a seaman and later as a carpenter. He left Skyros during the 1970s to live and learn his craft in Athens. However, after a few years he decided to become a seaman so he could save some money and start a family. During the time he was working as a seaman he met his wife on the island of Skyros (she was from abroad), and they decided to get married and live in Athens. After a few years in Athens N.T. changed his mind and decided to go back with his family and live on Skyros. Unfortunately N.T.'s marriage did not last, as he was not able to deal with several problems that arose in the relationship with his wife. He continued his work as a carpenter and decided to invest his profits in some rooms to let and later in a bar and a nightclub. These leisure spaces in which he invested his money are identified with his Athenian style of entertainment and his preference for Scotch whisky and imported beverages.

Despite the upward economic mobility of many laborers, these networks were not able to access the social hierarchy and take part in the political life of the

island. On the contrary, there has been a cultural marginalization of many laborers that is expressed in local sayings such as *parakatianos* (second-rate class).
For example, in one interview N.T. made the surprising statement: "I am not a
Skyrian. Everybody on Skyros belongs to a kin group or is related to the extended
shepherd families. I don't have a large lineage [*soi*]. How can I be a Skyrian?"

Another major distinction is between *eksohinous* (those who work *ekso*) and
horianous (those who work *mesa* in *horio*). Those who work *ekso* are usually the
shepherds and the farmers, whereas those who work *mesa* are usually the men of
agora and the laborers. This distinction implies that those who are *eksohini* are
expected not to be in control of the money earned. Women will be in control of
the economics of the matrilocal household and of the money earned by the men.
On the other hand, the laborers and the men of *agora* are in contact with commoditization and exchange money regularly. As a result they are expected to be
in control of their money.

The men of *agora* own or rent retail shops, mini-markets, *kafenio,* restaurants,
bars, and similar businesses, which are all situated in the *agora.* Other occupations in the market include traders in various commodities, shop owners, and
professionals. Those who work in the *agora* are usually the best educated of the
island and include enterprising migrants who, like the migrant laborers, have
returned to the island. The men of *agora* have usually studied outside Skyros at
technical schools or universities, and as such they are the most cosmopolitan.
They are also likely to speak a foreign language, usually English.

The state jobs are related either to the army or to public services such as the
municipality (*dimos*), the National Bank of Greece, the National Telecommu-
nication Company, the Public Electricity Company, and so on. These are considered the most secure occupations, and to become a public servant (*dimosios
ipalilos*) is the ultimate value of many islanders. The pension scheme, the permanent contract for each position, and the average salary are considered the most
rewarding aspects of these occupations.

In many cases, shepherds are also employed as public servants. Laborers and
fishermen rarely have access to this type of public occupation, which requires
connections to the large lineages involved in politics. The shepherds are the most
likely to acquire a position as public servants on the island. The long *soi* lineages
determine the results of the local elections and influence deeply the political life
of the island. As a consequence, members of a large *soi* lineage are more likely
to receive positions as advisors of the municipality and find state jobs and state
indemnity.

Those shepherds who are employed in state jobs, for example, divide their
time between their flocks/herds and their major occupation. However, those
shepherds who are also public servants are less interested in their fathers' occupation and have neglected to learn the local systems of animal classification, the
production processes for cheese, and the rules of conduct. In one of my visits to a

shepherd's *konatsi,* for example, I encountered a conflict between the son and the father. The son of N.K., one of the shepherds of Vuno, works in a state job offered by the municipality. Talking about the future of their occupation, the father said, "The young do not know the job anymore; there are many things that they don't know how to do." The son replied, "When my father dies, I will have to divide my life between shepherding and my full-time municipal job. Even though this is going to be difficult, I will have to do it because others will laugh in my face if I sell my father's flock. What else can I do? ... Whatever I do, how am I going to find a woman if I am a shepherd? Women nowadays don't like that."

Those who get state jobs no longer regard shepherding as a priority in their working lives. On the contrary, they are very critical of this occupation, which is considered by the Athenians to be backward and not modern. In that sense, many young shepherds try to imagine more possibilities and attractive occupations to raise their income. They feel that they should also be modern to succeed in their lives by leaving aside this profession, which is for the uneducated and for the *vlahus* or *kotsinogonatous,* as they say.[30] The term *kotsinogonati* means "those with red knees" and is used as a pejorative expression for those shepherds who have shepherding as a way of life and as a mentality. (The most reasonable explanation I was given for this name is the fact that most shepherds move their flocks in areas where there is red ground, specifically in the Vuno area, and as a result their feet and knees are colored red).

An additional source of income for the shepherds is EU funding, which supports both their own production and feed for their animals. Lately the KEP (*kentro eksipiretisis tou politi*), or Citizens' Assistance Center, has played a vital role in the incorporation of state subsidies into the local economy. New business plans and tourist projects have been partially or totally funded, and as a result a number of new hotels and businesses have been established on the island. However, the result of funding for shepherding has been to increase the herds without any modernization of the production of cheese or other products, because shepherds are paid according to the number of animals they own. Thus the flocks do not have as much space or food as they had in the past because resources are limited and their population has increased significantly.

The number of farmers gradually becoming landowners has been reduced, especially since the main agricultural areas of Trahi and Kabos were sold to the Greek army. The few farmers now live outside the *horio,* mainly in the Trahi and Kalamitsa areas. They grow potatoes, seasonal vegetables, and fruits, and they also have a few animals, such as chickens, sheep, and cows. Most of the farmers' children leave for Athens to work as laborers, receive an education in technical professions, or work in the army. The family of Tzanis, for example, who grew potatoes in the Trahi area for many decades, moved to Athens after their father passed away. The older son, Giannis, decided to start a career in the army and Giorgos, the youngest, has become a laborer in construction work.

The last occupational group is the fishermen, also mockingly called barefoot (*xsipoliti*) by other Skyrians because they tend not to wear shoes when they are working. Another possible explanation is that the word *barefoot* connotes their relative poverty and an inability to dress themselves properly. Their incomes are relatively low in comparison with the other occupational groups on the island, as during winter the strong winds are an obstacle to fishing, and there is no stability in the production process. Generally speaking, the number of fishermen has decreased, and the younger men do not want to be fishermen.

Gender Styles

As Ferguson has noted, the term *cultural style* refers to practices that signify differences or to processes of social differentiation (Ferguson 1999: 95). Styles are not total modes of behavior but tools of imagining and belonging with a wide range of referential categories, mechanisms of placing, and placement into social categories, such as gender. While femininity and masculinity stand as opposing categories, this opposition does not guarantee their homogeneity. On the contrary, there is a plurality of gender negotiation as various authors have argued (Archetti 1999, Papataxiarchis 1998).

On Skyros, gender styles are deeply influenced by the conceptualizations and the practices of persons in relation to the household and their domestication, issues that are widely discussed on the island. While a large majority of Skyrians identify with these values, a *parea* of laborers who practice an urban style of entertainment identified with the Athenian contemporary popular musical scene challenge these dominant notions. Within this context, such anti-domesticity is a major value.

For example, past or present migrant laborers who have been moving between Skyros and *mesa* (Athens) identify broadly with the popular culture of Athens, the *laiko* musical scene, the consumption of whisky, and a style of dominant or assertive masculinity. Within these networks, assertive masculinity is a form of symbolic capital in opposition to the disciplined and ordered domesticity of manhood as expressed in the values of the matrilocal household of shepherds, public servants, or the majority of the men of *agora*. Domesticated householders represent the mainstream values of the community in opposition to the mainstream Athenian style of entertainment, and they cannot afford economic excesses, gambling, drinking, or extended sexual relationships outside the context of marriage. Laborers, on the other hand, not only negotiate their masculine identities through an assertive sexuality but also divorce in some cases.

A major consequence of the anti-domestic style is courtship with foreign women who can accept nonmarital relationships, with the men avoiding extended matrilineal kin sociability and bilateral obligations. For instance, among the laborers I encountered two cases of men who were not married but had children (one with a foreign woman and one with a Greek woman) and also many cases of divorce. Although in the past divorce was not usually considered an option, I recorded more than fifteen divorced couples on Skyros. However, couples who have had children and divorced once the children were grown up are seen as more productive and are more socially accepted.[31] In particular, a divorced woman who has given birth and raised the children is much more valued and respected than a divorced woman without children. As various ethnographers have elaborated, womanhood is fulfilled and structured in relation to birth (Campbell 1964, Papataxiarchis 1991: 6). This differentiation should also be understood within the context of motherhood and sexuality. As Loizos and Papataxiarchis have argued, the sexuality of married women who do not give birth is viewed as threatening to the social order and the household, while mothers seem to have fulfilled their proper role (1991b: 223). The value of motherhood is central within all Greek communities and especially in areas where the Orthodox Church has customarily projected the Virgin Mary as a symbol (Campbell 1964).

Despite the anti-domestic discourse of laborers, the general morality is for a person to be valued as *nikokiris* (meaning a man or a woman who is focused and looks after the household and the family), as *timios* (an honest person), and *kinonikos* (a social and community-oriented person).[32] As *Thia* Maria, the wife of a shepherd who lives in the neighborhood of my matrilineal uncle, told me, "a good man or a woman should be polite, devoted to his or her family and the children and put the household as a priority over his life. This is a moral and communal obligation. The man should be *nikokiris* and the woman *nikokira;* they should be hardworking, economic-oriented and social."[33]

A typical expression of embarrassment and nonsocial behavior in the Skyrian dialect is *"gia mana nikotserio"* ("What a household!"). The social disapprobation for those who reject *nikokirio* shows the social significance of the institution and the symbolic status of the concept. Marriage is a central rite of passage for an individual on the island, and once a man and a woman come together in holy union they are expected to stay together for the rest of their lives in a nuclear family. Accordingly, divorced men and women are considered to be unsuccessful and an embarrassment for their families. In particular, those who practice matrilocal residence cannot afford to lose their households, their family, or property transmitted through *iso* agreements.[34] Despite the social criticism and the difficulties involved, however, the number of divorces has gradually increased in recent years among laborers who do not relate to a matrilineal matrilocal residence.

Among the shepherds, a man who is considered *nikokiris* is supposed to have his own wine and should offer it in drinking sessions. Getting drunk is considered embarrassing, however, and is not encouraged among friends. The only cases where drunkenness is accepted are saints'-day celebrations (*panigiria*), weddings, Carnival, and all-male drinking gatherings outside of the village. Laborers, on the other hand, are more likely to get drunk, gamble, entertain themselves until late in the night, express their economic success in conspicuous consumption, and establish relationships with foreign women. In other words, they are more associated with excess and an unproductive eroticism. When such networks go out, they have the habit of booking a table with a bottle of whisky in a club, a practice that imitates the Athenian popular style. That is the case, for example, at Tzivaeri, a seasonal *bouzoukia* with live Greek music.

Although the elders and the domesticated shepherds and their families do not consider these practices constructive, this assertive masculinity can attract social criticism. One evening, for example, I was sitting with my neighbors *Thia* Maria, her husband, her daughter, and her son-in-law. The son-in-law, who is a domesticated shepherd in his forties, offered me some whisky, and after a while he started saying that when he was young and unmarried he was able to go out and drink with his friends. After marriage, however, he could no longer come home late at night, couldn't drink as much, and couldn't enjoy himself as he used to do in the past. His wife became very upset and slightly embarrassed and said, "Why don't you go out? You can go any time!" *Thia* Maria, the wife's mother, disapproved of her daughter's anger and tried to calm things down by saying also that he should go out (*volta*). After this scene, *Thia* Maria spoke to her son-in-law in a motherly manner, saying, "What do you want to do in *agora*? Can't you see that it is for the young and for people who don't have households?" The market street is therefore used as a metaphor for an unproductive mentality of drinking and gambling, which opposes the household values. In cases like this, Skyrians will talk about you (*se kouventiazoun*), as my grandmother always says to my uncle and her son, a seaman in his forties (*naftikos*) who has a relationship with a woman but is not married. The fact that his girlfriend is Ukrainian and works in a bar complicates the family tensions. "What are the people of the island saying about you now? Is that a *nikotserio*?"

Generally speaking, the majority of metaphors in contemporary Skyros (as in many other areas of the world) are related to food and drink.[35] For example, when I was involved in endless political discussions about the mayors of Skyros I often encountered the expression "He ate everything" (*ta efage ola*), accompanied by a symbolic gesture to convey eating. The meaning of this expression is that the mayors took advantage of the treasury and the money of their municipality and spent public funds. Drinking might also have negative connotations when used in a literal form; "He is drinking," I was often told, and a disapproving gesture would also allude to the inappropriate character of this habit. Drinking is considered a major socializing activity but when someone is drinking (*pini*), or goes around (*girnai*), meaning someone regularly consumes large amounts of alcohol, this is a threat to his household and to the community. As such, drinking might express a highly anti-domestic persona that threatens the values of *nikokirio*.

Drinking alone is a highly stigmatizing activity. It is rarely encouraged, as it can be seen as a problem; people who do it are socially excluded and rarely taken seriously, as they can become *bekris* (drunkards) and *alkolikos* (alcoholic). This fear should be understood within the general context of drinking alone and drinking with a company (*parea*), a division that has been described by various ethnographers of Greece (Gefou-Madianou 1992, Papataxiarchis 1991, Cowan 1990). Drinking with a company (*parea*) is a high value, and it is the major practice of socializing among men. This practice of drinking with a *parea* has been understood as a constructive activity that reproduces social relationships and constitutes a major arena of gender negotiation (Gefou-Madianou 1992).

Although the alcoholic beverages that Skyrians consume depend mainly on gender and occupational group, there are some common terms in relation to drinking that are widely used among the participants of this study. The concept of *parea,* mentioned earlier, refers to the group of persons who come together to socialize in various contexts. However, in the matrilocal and in some cases neolocal society of Skyros, women tend to socialize more often *mesa* (in the house and neighborhood) with their kin and establish matrifocal alliances. This has as a result the socialization of most men *ekso* in other spaces outside of the home, in which relationships are constructed more on the basis of occupational background rather than kinship. It has been observed that in similar communities where male leisure is excluded from the household, men establish emotional attachments of friendship in opposition to kinship (Papataxiarchis 1991).

Although women might socialize more *mesa* and men *ekso,* this does not imply that men are public and women private.[36] As will be demonstrated, shepherds and farmers prefer to be private when they drink heavily in the *konatsi*. Similarly, the consumption of whisky among the laborers might take place in private spaces such as the back room of the *kafenio* Makedonia (or at least be concealed) to the extent that drinking is accompanied with gambling. Women, on the other hand, avoid drinking heavily in public but might drink in moderation during church festivals. Women also consume alcohol at communal events such as weddings, name days, and celebrations of saints, and the majority might also drink at home with food or on visits of friends, relatives, or neighborhood members. Generally speaking, women are not heavy drinkers, and they are stigmatized as immoral if they are seen drunk in any context. Gefou-Madianou has noted that in various areas of Greece, female drinking is interpreted as a lack of self-control and self-respect, which is an indication of an uncontrolled sexuality and hence threatens the household by exposing it to social critique (1992: 16).

Moreover, gender styles are reproduced through material culture and more specifically through the exchange of alcoholic beverages and food. In many cases the alcohol exchanged and consumed by women is usually a sweet liqueur, which is homemade and is considered a female drink (*ginekio poto*). The sweet liqueurs are usually consumed on visits by friends or at family gatherings, and they are given as treats only to women by the housewife. These liqueurs are made from several fruits and are very high in alcohol content. Fruits such as cherries, morellos, mandarins, mulberries, quinces, and pomegranates are the basis of the beverage.[37] Other drinks that might be exchanged among women in a household include Scotch, brandy (cognac), and sweet wine. Although drinking in such contexts is encouraged among women, the consumption of alcohol does not usually take place in the presence of men. The beverages are usually drunk during *sperisma,* the late-afternoon/early-evening gathering of neighborhood members and matrilineal female relatives. Although men are not necessarily excluded from such contexts, it is more common that they will socialize in the market or in more private places with their friends. On all these occasions the bottles of cognac, sweet wine, and sweet liqueur are kept in the liquor cabinet of the house, a female domain. Furthermore, alcohol is not to be consumed in the house except in moderation. For that reason the household alcohol store is under the supervision of the women, who will decide under what circumstances the beverages are going to be consumed. Liquors, imported beverages, and whisky are thus be consumed only on visits by neighbors (*episkepsis*), celebrations (*giortes*), at evening gatherings (*sperisma*), during construction work as treats (*kerasma*) to construction workers while having breaks, and at weddings and funerals.

Especially among the domesticated shepherd families and men of *agora* families, the alcohol is kept by the housewife in a concealed place of the household in the *sala* (living room), usually a small dusty cabinet in a hidden corner next to the sofa, under the television, or in a place that is not easily accessed by the men of the house. Therefore, in a matrilocal domesticated household, that is, in a *nikokirio,* women have the power over the sphere of alcohol, which is used in a domestic manner. Within this context, men cannot access and drink the alcohol, which is property of the woman.

One of the beverages of major importance among women is *cognac,* the Greek brandy, which is the base of the homemade female liqueurs.[38] Brandy has become embedded in Greek social life and is a main drink of socialization in various communities. More importantly, it is the spirit used in many rituals and home gatherings among family members. Papataxiarchis has observed the same processes on the island of Lesbos, noting that coffee and cognac are usually used among family members (1992: 233). On Skyros, as in other areas of Greece, cognac is also a symbol of death. It is used during the night when family and friends lament the dead and is also drunk after the funeral in one of the market's *kafenio.* In addition, cognac is consumed by both men and women in domestic contexts. The spirit is also a gift for family celebrations and family visits. Formal occasions require a good bottle of cognac, which is kept in the liquor cabinet for future family gatherings and formal visits. In this context, cognac has emerged as a symbol of family continuity, collective drinking, and family union and is deeply entangled with domesticity, especially among the shepherds and the men of *agora* families.

Another division on Skyros that reproduces gender styles is between beverages *me meze* and *horis meze,* that is, drinks accompanied by small quantities of food called *meze* and drinks to be taken on their own without food. *Meze* on Skyros is usually consumed by men and consists of a piece of Skyrian cheese (*kefalotyri*), some olives, and bread. *Meze* is usually consumed outside the home, *ekso* in the countryside or in the *agora,* and it symbolically opposes the sphere of food, which is a feminine and a household based domain. So-called real food is considered to be the food made in the household by the housewife, in contrast to the *meze* offered in the *kafenio* or even the meals prepared by men in the *konatsi,* such as fried eggs, cheese, and olives. Meals in the home are prepared only by the women (the housewife, sisters, and daughters), and the housewife usually serves the food. There are rarely any guests, although family meals are not totally a private context. The table is a major activity where family disputes, tensions, hierarchy, status, and conjugal relationships are expressed.[39] Dinners among friends are not common, although a drinking session might be accompanied by food or *meze.* In everyday life, exchanging gifts of food is not a common practice, but food is usually offered as a gift at religious ceremonies on saints' days, at weddings, and for death rituals. Alcoholic beverages, however, are regular gifts among the community, as will be discussed below. The alcohol consumed with *meze* is usually wine, but *tsipouro* and *ouzo* should also be consumed with *meze.* By contrast, women do not exchange or eat *meze.* The alcoholic beverages exchanged by the women are usually cognac or fruit liquor, which are usually offered with a sweet (*gliko tou koutaliou*) or a *chocolate* candy (*sokolataki*) or a Turkish delight (*loukoumi*). However, they might also be offered without any sweets. Similarly, in recent times, beverages (*pota*) that are consumed by men in the bars and *kafenio* of *agora* are not drunk with *meze.* In one of the first bars established in the market (Renaissance), for example, the owner (a sailor working on trade ships) said, "My bar was probably one of the first, and for that reason customers did not know how to drink imported beverages. Customers would come in and say 'You don't have any *meze;* how are we supposed to drink without eating?'"

A major differentiation between food exchange and alcohol exchange lies in *kerasma.*[40] *Kerasma* is a customary offering of alcohol to people, which might follow the Maussian structure of offer-acceptance-return depending on the context and the relationship. According to Papataxiarchis, "[T]he very gesture of friendliness is articulated as a treat to a drink" (1991: 64). This gesture might also take the meaning of greeting, but in general it is for treating friends. It follows that *kerasma* is reciprocal, but it can take the form of a gift without return.

Traditionality and Modernity Inside Out

> One is not born traditional; one chooses to become traditional by constant innovation.
>
> —Latour 2002: 76

According to Zarkia, Skyros went through three phases of transformation in relation to conceptualizations of modernity and tradition (1996: 159). The first phase was that of urban attraction, which was characterized by an urban aesthetic influenced by conceptions of city life and its new elements (1960s). Skyrians wanted to see and construct themselves in opposition to peasants, the village aesthetic, herding and agriculture and the local identity, expressed in clothing and architecture. For example, after World War II, most shepherds started to wear blue jeans and many houses were furnished with imported Athenian furniture, plastic chairs, and aluminum frames. New houses adapted an urban style with new spaces and small gardens, and the Kastro and Agora areas were gradually transformed. Many Skyrians wanted to be modern—and as such urban—in their everyday lifestyles. This shift resulted in a negation of signs connected with peasants and herders that had been part of the Skyrian settlement for hundreds of years. There are stories of peddlers exchanging precious antique objects from the *aloni* and the interior of houses for Athenian clothes or small gadgets. In short, tradition was regarded as a backward and negative concept and involved an inferiority complex of the peasantry.

The second period was characterized by an imitation of what was conceived as a Western European and urban aesthetic, which was further expressed in various aspects of social life (1970s and 1980s). Zarkia describes a gradual shift in the mentality of the inhabitants and the migrants from Athens who initially avoided the ambassador's *kafenio* because it was a place for shepherds and farmers.[41] However, tourists thought the *kafenio* was an authentic traditional place, and therefore its clientele increased. The Skyrians gradually imitated the foreigners and became aware of others' interest in tradition. This period coincided with the development of tourism on the island and also with the foundation of the Skyros museum of folk art. That was the period when things became objects with a price, when the cultural aspects of Skyrian life started to be of great interest for outsiders and became part of the national heritage of Greece. Islanders realized that there was a possibility that they were not peasants but rather a living museum of tradition, an island with culture. Tourists coming from afar paid to see them in their environment, filmed them, and studied them; this meant that Skyrians were interesting—or at least this is what outsiders such as tourists and folklorists thought.

A transitional voice from these times has been traced in the local newspaper *Skyrian News* (*Skyrian News* 1984: 7–9). The paper became a stage for many debates between traditionalists and modernists. For example, an article was published about the negative aspects of tradition: tradition was presented as a mentality that had brought a difficult and hierarchical life to the poor on Skyros in specific historical periods. Mr. Persidis, a local folklorist and historian, published an argument against this materialistic interpretation in his article "What is Tradition and What is its Value?" ("*Pia I Paradosi Ke Pia I Aksia Tis?*"). He argued that tradition is a national good, claiming that it represents a better past in comparison with the modern present and is a culture created by the people for the people, in opposition to the modern culture created by companies and television.

Persidis's arguments resembled those of the majority of the folklorists who played an active role in convincing Skyrians that "tradition is the materialized expression of the mental and material life of people, an expression of their cultural idiosyncrasy, their national identity" (*Skyrian News* 1984: 7).

In the third and most recent period came the actual capitalization of tradition (the end of the 1980s, the 1990s, and the first decade of the twenty-first century). Objects made by artisans became traditional artifacts, rituals such as Carnival were organized in such a way as to attract more outsiders, Skyrians became proud of their herding and farming heritage, architecture was sometimes adapted to foreign taste, and tradition emerged victorious over the stigma of peasantry. In the past decade, local associations for the preservation of tradition have been established, local traditional artifacts have proliferated, and the traditional Aegean aesthetic of the Cyclades—the most touristy of the Greek islands—has been used by entrepreneurs in their new hotels and guest houses. As a consequence a local style as a mode of signification has successfully been reproduced in contrast to the Athenian style that many laborers perform.

Clearly the shifting meanings of modernity and tradition have been influenced by the relationship between outsiders and insiders. Skyrians gradually realized that they wanted to present what outsiders thought was their tradition. Moreover, Skyrians wanted to rediscover and preserve it, as various local historians and folklorists have argued (Persidis 1984: 7–9). To be modern was not as good anymore, or at least not good in relation to outsiders.

Nowadays these categorizations are extended to various aspects of social life, such as food and drink. Stamatis Ftoulis, for example, a traditional pottery artist, had a cosmopolitan style in the past, as he was the first bar owner (1967). Now he has adopted a local style and views tradition as his own innovation. Nowadays, Stamatis sells his Skyrian wine he produces himself, together with his Skyrian pottery.

In a contrasting case, Stamatis the *cava* owner, who has adopted an urban style, has an extensive collection of Greek wines in his alcohol store and claims a distinctive knowledge of tasting, gained through his long experience. He stated, "Skyrians do not know how to make wine," and he thinks that the local product in general is not comparable in quality to his own imported bottled wine. Despite the fact that his brother is a local artisan who also makes his own wine, Stamatis wants to differentiate himself from rural production and the local taste. In the eyes of Stamatis, tradition is not found in the production of the Skyrian wine but in the local bottled wines around Greece. Another form of differentiation for Stamatis is the narration of his travels abroad (in *eksoteriko*) that were sponsored by the large multinational corporations Diageo and Pernod Ricard. A certain volume of sales is rewarded by the large alcohol multinational corporations with gift trips to the Americas, Southeast Asia, or Europe, depending on the season. When we met with Stamatis, he always liked to talk about the luxurious hotels of

Asia, the foreign and cosmopolitan new tastes he discovered on each continent, and the luxury of his travels. In addition, he has an elaborate collection of single malts in his store, and he always drinks imported beverages when he is in a bar. The majority of his profit is from imported beverages and specifically whisky, which is sold in the island's bars, clubs, supermarkets, and *kafenio*. The alcoholic beverages he sells are from *eksoteriko* and as such fit his cosmopolitan aura, which is focused on the various conceptualizations of *ekso*.

Those who do not identify themselves with the cosmopolitanism of Stamatis, with *eksoteriko,* or products from *ekso* capitalize their style with the local, traditional wine. Stamati's brother Giorgos, for example, makes his own Skyrian wine despite the fact that he buys the must from mainland Evia. While an increasing number of Skyrians are buying must from Evia, there is a claim that this is their wine and their product. This selective memory of the production process, the most important aspect of the creation of wine, is not necessary felt as alienating; rather, it is dressed with tradition, locality, and personal identity.

This transformation from an innovative and new form of making wine to an authentic and traditional product should be understood within the context of the capitalization of tradition and the adoption of a local style. Giorgos, the brother of Stamatis the *cava* owner, claims to be a traditional artisan who was taught the art of carving on the island and has run his own wood-carving business since then. The business has been financially rewarding, especially because in the past few decades more and more Skyrian-Athenians and outsiders have become interested in making their houses traditional with a local aesthetic. Giorgos does not associate himself with his brother's cosmopolitanism and believes that tradition is the highest value. "Being a traditional artisan is a way of life," he told me at one of our regular *tsipouro* meetings in Manolis's *kafenio*.

Similarly, Takis, who is the owner of Rodon, one of the most popular bars in the winter, makes his own wine from his vineyards. After November his wine is sold in the bar next to the bottles of whisky and rum, and for the majority of the customers it is the most preferred beverage. Takis, who is also descended from a family of farmers, believes that wine is the most authentically Skyrian drink and does not produce and sell it to make a large profit; on the contrary, he claims that there is not so much profit with his own wine as with the imported beverages. While his style has a cosmopolitan aura because he owns a bar and he plays and listens to a wide range of ethnic and electronic music, he has adopted also a local style. He is very proud of his farming background and the fact that his father was the owner of a *kafenio*. He imagines Rodon as a modern *kafenio,* an extension of the tradition of the past, which is expressed in black-and-white photographs of old traditional Skyros on the walls. Wine is part of this local identity, and this is what he would always offer to his customers if the commodity chain of whisky was not so successful. He identifies himself against the cosmopolitanism of Stamatis, despite the fact Stamatis is his importer, and on the last day before my departure from the island to return to the Netherlands he told me, "If you really want to know about whisky, you should understand that Stamatis started it all. He's the one who imports and delivers it and he is the one who tells us what to buy. That's why we drink whisky now instead of wine." Takis's reaction can be interpreted in the context of his dislike for the changes in drinking habits. However, he does not want to imagine himself as one of the innovators on Skyros despite the fact the he has owned one of the most island's successful bars since the 1990s. Furthermore, he is married to a woman from abroad (*ekso*) and, like Stamatis, he is a regular traveler to *eksoteriko*. Takis also frequently refers to his travels, and he often receives postcards from his foreign clientele, which he places on the wall next to the bar. While Takis is able to move easily between cosmopolitanism and localism, the laborers or shepherds of Skyros do not have this competence.

Regular customers of Rodon who are shepherds prefer to order Takis's wine, which is placed next to the bottles of imported beverages and whisky. They will rarely get drunk (unless there is a celebration or festival), and they will regularly discuss the Carnival, a festival that expresses shepherd culture (Amanatidis 2005, de Sike 1993). Regularly also local political discussions take place during the evenings, in contrast with the football discussions that laborers have in the *kafenio* of Makedonia and Synantisis. In short, the style of discussion among the shepherds focuses on Skyros as a place, whereas the discussions of the laborers relate to national and popular culture subjects. This mode of signification is also evident in the names of *kafenio* that these two networks socialize. The *kafenio* of the shepherds is called after the owners, Barba Giannis or Maritsa. Another *kafenio* where shepherds and men of *agora* socialize is called To Paradosiakon (The Traditional). Laborers, in contrast, socialize in Makedonia, a name that was chosen to express the Greekness of the geographical area of Makedonia in the national political debate about the cultural identity of the Republic of Makedonia.[42] Although laborers are not necessarily nationalistic, they claim a connection with the national, as they cannot claim a connection with the local politics. The ancient sun of Makedonia found in the grave of the father of Alexander the Great is placed strategically next to the name of the *kafenio* Makedonia in the entrance door.

Moreover, most laborers—unlike the shepherds—can afford to express their urban style with new cars, gambling, expensive clothes, their own houses, and expressive drinking habits (manifested in whisky). N.T. exhibits a characteristically assertive masculinity and a breach with domesticity and identifies with the cosmopolitan popular style of Athens expressed in music, his leisure habits, and whisky. When we spend time together he is usually not wearing a shirt, and he talks very proudly of his masculine body. His expressive sexuality is also evident as he talks about the women he had in the past and the women from Eastern Europe who work in his hotel. He is also very proud of the endless sexual adventures of his young son, who has more opportunities now in his bar, saying excitedly, "Maria Mavrikou the filmmaker said she wants to make a film about *kamaki* and she is going to film my son! Isn't that amazing?"[43] Therefore N.T.'s urban anti-domestic style is also expressed in the practices of his son and more specifically in his *kamaki* strategies and male seduction techniques.

By contrast, shepherds and men of *agora* families think about what others say about their style, and they do not want to be discussed (*den thelume na mas sizitane*). The community and the household are values that they think need to be taught to younger children, and the children of shepherds especially are willing to get married and set up a household early in their lives. Expressive sexuality is not encouraged among younger shepherds in their relationships, as assertiveness in the domestic sphere might bring problems in the matrilocal rule of residence. Laborers, in contrast, who identify with anti-domesticity (and anti-matrilocality), learn to express their assertiveness and masculinity freely.

Drinking *Mesa* and *Ekso*: The Consumption of Alcohol in the *Konatsi, Kafenio,* and Bar

The Konatsi

Generally speaking, the social life on Skyros, as in most areas of Greece, is structured around commensality and large-scale drinking and eating occasions. The dinner parties or the drinking sessions that take place among men are basic socializing rituals and are fundamental for the establishment and reproduction of social relations. In most cases it is unthinkable to maintain a social relationship without drinking and eating. The absence of men from companies on such occasions can be harshly criticized.

The dominant urban and local styles on Skyros are reproduced and manifested in the organization of space in *agora*. The association of space with social life has been a dominant theme in anthropology and in Greek ethnography. The major example is the division between women/private and men/public, which has been criticized by various scholars such as Papataxiarchis (1991). As will be demonstrated in this part of the study, men are also very private in relation to drunkenness and femininity is also negotiated publicly in the spaces of the bar and *cafeteria*. In this section, I limit my examination to some particular spaces that have been overlooked by Greek ethnography and, more particularly, the men's country dwelling (*konatsi*), the *kafenio,* and the bar.

A major division when Skyrians are drinking alcohol is between drinking *ekso* and drinking *mesa*. Laborers are very likely to drink *mesa* at home until the early hours of the morning while their children and wives are asleep. I have been present at various such cases of heavy drinking of Scotch that could last until the morning when the laborers have to leave for work. In addition, drinking *ekso* among the networks of laborers is related to heavy drinking when going out in *agora* and might include booking a table of whisky in a small club or bar.

Shepherds, on the other hand, have a different style of drinking. The expression "Come for a wine" (*ela gia kana krasi*) expresses an open invitation to visit someone and share food and wine with him or the group accompanying him. As noted at the beginning of the chapter, the categories of *mesa* and *ekso* represent a spatial division that extends to various aspects of social life. While drinking *mesa* might imply drinking in the house, the domesticated male householders who have to follow the rules of matrilocality cannot afford to drink at home. Drinking in the presence of parents and the women of the family is considered restricting, as men cannot enjoy and cannot express their inner problems and thoughts. Exceptional cases are family celebrations, religious ceremonies, and various rituals.

Drinking *mesa sto horio* might also mean drinking in the *agora*, and this is the more usual scenario for most men. However, as noted in the introduction, drunkenness is not an accepted social practice in public, especially for shepherds. For this reason, when shepherds want to drink heavily, they drink *ekso* of the *horio*. The space used for such purposes is the *konatsi*, the shepherd's country dwelling. Most such dwellings are very simple constructions built out of stones with a wooden ceiling. There is usually only one large room where beds, a table and some chairs, and a fireplace are situated. Usually the *konatsi* is a space where only men come together, and as such it is a context in which masculine identity is reproduced and negotiated. Women are not welcome there, especially on days when work has to be done. The *konatsi* is the property of the man and is transmitted patrilineally to the sons of the family, as opposed to the house in the village, which is transmitted matrilineally to the daughters. As such, it is part of the property of the shepherds and the farmers together with their lands and flocks.

The *konatsi* is also the place where wine is stored. On Skyros there are no cellars. The wine is usually placed in a wooden barrel facing the north in what is supposed to be the coolest area of the house. The wine requires cool or even cold spots, and in that sense the north-facing part is considered ideal. The wine is used after working or when taking breaks from work with food. More importantly, it is used extensively in parties (*mazoksi*), usually during autumn and winter months. Most male gatherings take place during winter, and the saying goes that "Wine is drunk in the months that include the letter *r*," excluding the four spring and summer months.

In the matrilocal and bilateral society of Skyros, the *konatsi* is a resort for the domesticated shepherds and single men who cannot socialize, drink, and make a noise in the female-dominated houses of the village. In contrast to the house, the *konatsi* provides an ideal opportunity for men to come together with friends from similar age groups, to drink, sing, and discuss (*kouvenda*). According to Papataxiarchis, "[K]*ouvenda* is an ongoing commentary on events or people, premised on an already shared point of view. The expression *kouvenda na yinete* suggests a purposeless discussion that leads nowhere: the words exchanged in *kouvenda* carry no binding force" (1998: 172). Similarly, on Skyros, *kouvenda* is the major activity of table companions. Usually men sit around the fireplace with wine and discuss in this way. After a few glasses, the interlocutors start cooking.

The drinking parties in the country dwelling take place among the most intimate friends, and drinking in such contexts is a highly bonding communal activity. The real friends are the drinking partners on such occasions who know how to keep private the investment of emotions and experiences. Drunkenness may be a part of the gatherings at the *konatsi,* and in that sense it is a private matter. The fear of drunkenness in public spaces is a metaphor for fear of a state of female passivity, an ideology that also exists in various other areas of Greece as well as in Athens (Paptaxiarchis 1991).

The food in the *konatsi* depends on what the participants bring with them. Drinking without eating is a highly inappropriate activity. It is usual for cheese, bread, and olives to be stored in the *konatsi.* The guests bring five or ten-liter containers of wine, usually from their own production. The amount depends on each interlocutor. There are cases where drinking parties have gone on for three days, sometimes including naps and a rest in the evening. In these drinking parties the most desired dish is rooster with pasta (*petnes me makaronia*). The rooster is a metaphor for masculinity in many contexts. For example, Skyrian embroidery depicting a rooster is a common gift from mothers to sons or newly married grooms. If the owner of the *konatsi* does not have a rooster, there is a possibility to steal one from a neighboring coop. This practice is considered appropriate for such occasions (and was even more so in the past), and many interlocutors referred to it with enthusiasm.

Herzfeld has observed the institutionalization of the stealing of goats and sheep among the shepherds of Crete, who create enemies or partners on the basis of stealing (1985). This activity on Skyros is not only found among shepherds but also among farmers. In the past, the stealing of animals between farmers and shepherds was more widespread but the stealing of animals is still practiced nowadays, especially as the goats and sheep on Skyros are not kept in pens but can roam freely on the mountainside and on the northeast side, on the mountain of Kohylas. The man who steals the animal is considered a cunning and capable man who takes risks that reward both his reputation and his stomach. Such actions can be interpreted within a general context of anti-commodification that friendship and male bonding entails among shepherds. In the *konatsi,* the wine should not be a commodity but the product of one's own labor and food ideally should be stolen or be part of the flock.

The Kafenio

Drinking in the *agora* might take place in a *kafenio* or a bar. According to Cowan, the *kafenio* is a major space for male socializing, and "[I]t is here that manhood is expressed, reputations are negotiated, and social relationships are enlivened through endless card playing, political debate, competitive talk, and reciprocal hospitality" (1990: 71).[44] In addition the *kafenio* is in a way what the house is for the women, it is the "house of men" (Paptaxiarchis 1988: 205–250). Whereas in the past the island's market was filled with *kafenio,* gradually they disappeared, and now there are only two left in the main market and another two at the entrance to the village. According to S. F., who was the first bar owner and later owner of a nightclub:

> I was the first one to open a bar on the island, in 1967. It was a time when youngsters would come to the island and only find traditional *kafenio.* The *kafenio* would serve food and wine. Wine was produced by each *kafenio* so the customers were used to each distinct taste. I remember more than thirty *kafenio* in the market and now there are only bars. I left the island in my twenties and went to Athens to become a singer but my career wasn't so successful. In Athens I indulged in the life of bars and clubs and there I decided I should open a club on Skyros. My first bar was Magia, which was close to the sea. We were a company of forty youngsters and my friends supported my project despite the fact that the club was not so professional. After a while the people in that neighborhood began complaining about the noise and they pushed me out. As a result I opened a new place close to my house, the Ipokambos. A few years later I bought a very big club which is still the major club for entertainment, called Skyropoula. The main drinks were vermouth and whisky. While I used to buy vermouth very cheaply, whisky was much more expensive. But I bought it from a guy who used to work in the coast guard and he had access to cheap imported authentic whisky. However, most Skyrians didn't like the imported beverages in the beginning and they called them *kolofarka,* meaning that these drinks were for *poustis* [passive male homosexual] and for *aderfes* [also a passive male homosexual with an expressive feminine style]. They didn't know the taste; that's why they said this. … Gradually, though, this changed and as time went by Skyrians insisted on drinking whisky and imported beverages. In 1974, I decided to rent the club to Sideras because I wanted to focus on traditional pottery. Since then I have my shops with Skyrian art and Sideras rents the club from me.

Nowadays in the Agora there are seven bars, four *kafenio,* and two cafeterias in which the various networks come together to socialize over alcohol or other beverages. Each place has different regular customers, but the customers at the bars circulate from bar to bar, whereas the customers of *kafenio* tend to remain devoted to one place. In addition, whereas the patrons of bars and cafes are more mixed in terms of gender, age, education, and professional background, the *kafenio* are male spaces in which the social codes of inclusion and exclusion are appropriated and practiced.

The most popular *kafenio* is the one belonging to Manolis, called The Traditional, and situated in the center of the market opposite Stamatis's *cava*. No doubt the *kafenio* has adopted a local traditional style that is expressed in the simple chairs and tables (found in the older *kafenio* of Skyros), the nostalgic photos of old Skyros, and the beverages that people drink there. Usually the *kafenio* is run by Manolis's wife, who is responsible for cooking and taking orders. Although women are excluded from most *kafenio*, it is acceptable for them to work in the *kafenio* if they are part of the owner's family. Most inhabitants who socialize there are shepherds, public servants, shop owners, farmers, and artisans who engage in card playing (usually without betting or betting in exchange for small treats), backgammon, and discussion. The television is usually on in the background, with the daily news at eight being the center of attention. The main beverages served in this *kafenio* are coffee, soft drinks, beer, *ouzo*, *tsipouro*, and wine, and whisky is not the most popular drink there. Manolis stated, "I always buy a bottle of whisky for the *kafenio*, usually Johnnie Walker. There are customers who ask for it and I have to serve it," meaning that nonregular laborers who have an urban style might request Scotch if they go there. The bachelors of the island also socialize in this *kafenio* with the married men of a similar or older age. Soft drinks are usually drunk by Manolis's children when they play there after school, by his wife and by older men who do not want to take coffee or alcohol. Greek coffee (*ellinikos*) is usually drunk in the mornings and during the afternoon by most customers, whereas wine is drunk when there is a good *meze* in the kitchen and especially when Manolis's wife has cooked. Beer, *tsipouro*, and *ouzo* are drunk regularly with or without *meze*; however, *meze* usually accompanies the drinks if a group of men starts drinking.

The next *kafenio* is situated a few meters away from Manolis's, and it is the place where customarily the older generations of Skyrians socialize. It is the older of the market's *kafenio*, dating back to 1956. The style of this *kafenio* has not changed since the time it was established, and only recently the son of the owner added new traditional tables in it. The owner, Barba Giannis, passed away a few years ago, and his widow, Maritsa, is the only one left on the island to keep up the business.[45] During the summer months and Carnival, their sons come to the island to run the business. The *kafenio* is empty most of the time while Maritsa is usually asleep in a chair or watching television. Unfortunately, she cannot walk very well, so ordering is a long and painful experience for her. Even so, Maritsa is always in the *kafenio*, which is almost her home or, as she claims, her life. The beverages drunk in Maritsa's *kafenio* are traditional and usually include *ouzo*, wine, *tsipouro*, brandy, and beer. Coffee and tea are also served in the morning and in the afternoon, whereas most alcoholic beverages are drunk in the evenings with card playing.

The other two *kafenio*, called Makedonia and Sinantisis, are situated in the margins of *agora*. They have modern, urban styles and are opposite each other.

Both *kafenio* have Athenian-style chairs and tables, whisky advertisements on their walls, and proper bars to serve the beverages. This is where groups of laborers come to spend some of their time. Kostas, the owner of Sinantisis, is a man in his sixties who has been doing this work for at least twenty years. He has lived most of his life Skyros, working as an unskilled laborer in all kinds of jobs. After he got married he decided to invest all his money in this small *kafenio*, which is under his house. Kostas is regularly in the *pro-po* (football and betting agency), and he likes taking risks. In his *kafenio* there are regular card bets when patrons play *poka*. He is a regular whisky drinker, and the beverages served in his *kafenio* are usually beer and Scotch. Sinantisis (meaning *the meeting*) is a place where people from the building trade (construction laborers and traders) spend their time. The place can be busy from early in the morning when builders come together before they go to work. Coffee and sometimes beer are taken in the morning hours, whereas whisky and other beverages are drunk in the evening. Sinantisis is less popular and busy than is Makedonia.

Makedonia is even more urban and Athenian than Synantisis. It has a big television screen for sports and more comfortable tables to play cards and backgammon and drink coffee and other beverages. This is the *kafenio* where laborers and some shop owners of Skyros come together to socialize and play cards, betting on their games. The semi-legal character of card games with large sums of money and property involved (in the concealed room at the back) is the main reason for the owner's skepticism in relation to newcomers. In my case, I was introduced to the *kafenio* by the owner's son Giorgos, and thus I was able to spend time there and regularly discuss several issues.

According to Vagelis, the father of Giorgos and the boss of Makedonia, "my shop has been open for fourteen years. Whisky is the main drink consumed here and more particularly Cutty Sark and Johnnie [Walker]. It is usually drunk by men over forty years old. In general, Skyrians and my customers drink mostly whisky; this is our national drink."

Makedonia, the property of Vagelis, serves mainly whisky to its customers during the evenings and is thought of as a concealed place by many Skyrians. Takis, the owner of the Rodon bar, for example, and my matrilineal uncle Mihalis, characterized Makedonia as a modern card club because betting with cards takes place there. The style of the *kafenio* is based on the cosmopolitan aesthetic of Vagelis, who has added a bar next to the entrance and high stools, imitating the bars on the island. Behind the bar various different types of whisky are on display, along with a few bottles of Vodka. In an attempt to explain the aesthetic of drinking, Vagelis said, "Here we like foreign drinks [*xena pota, apo ekso*]. Skyrians look down on Greek drinks; you can't go to the bar and order an *ouzo* ... they'll snub you. You'll say, give me a Scotch." Thus the cosmopolitan style of Vagelis's *kafenio* is expressed in the consumption of whisky, which comes from *ekso* and is connected to a superior aesthetic in relation to locally made beverages. Greek alcoholic products are not prestigious enough and are considered by the networks of Makedonia to be the habit of old and poor men.[46]

Vagelis is not originally from Skyros. He migrated to the island during the 1980s from mainland Evia, and since then he has established an extended network of customers who are mainly interested in whisky drinking and betting. Sports are also a regular point of reference, and when there are football matches the *kafenio* fills up with men watching the games on the big screen next to the entrance. Betting is also part of football games, and bets are usually placed before the match.

Vagelis, like his customers, has adopted an urban style that is identified with contemporary popular Greek music and an Athenian style of entertainment. However, he does not enjoy the seasonal *bouzoukia* of Skyros, which is rarely open. He prefers when he has free time to go *mesa* to the urban centers of Athens or Chalkida to find a good *bouzoukia*. Similarly, the laborers who are regulars there, such as N.T., go out to the local bars but prefer Chalkida or Athens for big nights, as there they can find the singers they prefer there.

The Bar

The distribution of alcoholic beverages before the 1970s was based on the local network of *kafenio* and taverns, which would receive the wine from the producer. The amount of wine distributed was much greater than today, and wine was also exported to the mainland. *Ouzo* and *tsipouro* were not made on the island but were imported and sold in grocery shops. A few islanders would make homemade *tsipouro,* the amounts of which were very small. It was not distributed but kept in homes to be offered to guests. Whisky was not found in *kafenio* or other spaces of the *agora,* and it was a luxury good imported by a few Skyrian-Athenians and the laborers who traveled *mesa-ekso.* One of the transitional voices is N.T., who lived through the change in consumption practices and is himself a regular whisky drinker and a customer of the Makedonia *kafenio.* He recalls:

> The first time I saw whisky was in 1959. A friend of my father's called Vlaikos owned a *kaiki*[47] and he used it to transport stone and retail goods from Volos. On some trips he would bring back a bottle of whisky and he would drink it with my father. Before I went into the army around 1967, *Ipokambos* was founded. There whisky was only drunk by a few people as it was a bit expensive for us. Later on, another bar opened, called *Moreno,* and that stayed open until 1977. However, both bars were outside the island's market.

Most imported drinks became widely available during the 1970s when the first bars and discos opened on the island. On the Rocks was a place where inhabitants would dance disco and drink whisky, rum, and other imported drinks. Most tourists at that time would spend time there, and it was also an important socializing place for younger Skyrians. The place was open in the summer, like all the nightclubs. After 1984, however, its owner, Stamatis, decided with his colleagues to close the place and invest in a *cava* with imported drinks, as there was no importer on the island and their club had to order all its drinks from Athens. The *cava* opened in 1986, and since then Stamatis has been the only distributor on the island.

During the 1980s, the first supermarkets also began to appear. Skyrians who used to be grocers decided to sell more processed consumer goods and expand their business. The first grocer who made his shop into a supermarket told me, "I opened the supermarket in 1981. I used to stock wine, *tsipouro,* and *ouzo,* as the islanders didn't use whisky and imported drinks at that time. At the end of the '80s I had to sell whisky as well because there was a demand for it." In the 1990s, more bars opened in the market, whereas several *kafenio* were closed down. *Rodon* and *Artistico* are two of the bars that opened during that period. Today almost ten bars are in the main market of the island and only four *kafenio* are left.

Therefore, a major institution that emerged on the island of Skyros during the 1970s and capitalized on Scotch whisky for its style is the bar. The bar represents an Athenian view of leisure, which first became popular in urban contexts in Greece during the 1970s and gradually became part of the countryside too. Bars are socializing spaces for both men and women (in contrast to the *konatsi* and the *kafenio*), and the main alcoholic beverages are foreign (*xena pota,* or beverages from *ekso*) spirits such as rum and whisky. The first bars on Skyros appeared in the market during the 1970s, and their number gradually increased to nine. The center for socializing is the actual bar in which customers order their drinks. Next to the bar there are always high stools and tables for two or four customers. Nowadays the bars on Skyros are open all seasons except Kalypso, the bar where the foreigners, Athenians, and cosmopolitans (or would-be cosmopolitans) spend their time during summer, Easter, and Carnival. Some inhabitants usually avoid this bar, which they regard as being for snobbish people who are not related to Skyros and do not participate in the social life of the island—despite the fact that it was one of the first bars opened in the market.

Although some anthropologists in Greece have thought of bars as modern and *kafenio* as traditional, this division does not apply in the case of Skyros (Cowan 1992, Papataxiarchis 1998, Papagaroufali 1992). Takis's bar, Rodon, for example, has appropriated a more local style. He thinks of his own bar as a form of *kafenio,* a continuation of the career of his father, who was also a *kafenio* owner. In addition, in the place where the bar is situated there used to be a *kafenio* before World War II. The style of the bar expresses this type of aesthetic with its painted green wooden tables and chairs, wood stove in the center, and Takis's local wine, which he produces himself. Furthermore, activities that are usually part of the *kafenio* also take place in the bar, such as card playing (though not as often as in Makedonia), backgammon, and political discussions.

Vagelis, on the other hand, who is the owner of Makedonia, has adopted a bar style for his *kafenio* and has even added a bar to serve imported beverages and Scotch to his customers. The beverages in his *kafenio* are the beverages that are usually served in a bar, and the modern style of the chairs and the tables imitates an Athenian cafeteria.

Whereas the age group in Rodon varies, in Makedonia and in most *kafenio* the men are usually between thirty-five and sixty years old. The bar clearly expresses youthfulness, despite the fact that all age groups between eighteen and fifty are regularly there. However, the bar is a rite of passage from childhood to adulthood, especially for men, and the place that teenagers learn to perform a style of modernness. Teenagers in their groups gradually attend the drinking sessions of older islanders in these spaces, and gradually they learn to drink; they embody the dispositions of drinking but above all they learn their limits and obstacles because they must be in control of themselves as their elders are. Drunkenness is not encouraged in these contexts. Girls might accompany these groups, but they are moderate; like most women, they avoid drinking heavily.

A slightly different setting from the bar is the *baraki,* a smaller and cozier setting where customers mainly stand and do not sit, as there is not enough space for tables.[48] A typical example is Artistico, situated just a few meters away from Rodon. Artistico is usually packed, as it can hardly accommodate twenty to thirty standing persons. Nevertheless, it is the place where inhabitants dance to island Greek music and the owner, Sakis, prefers to play Greek popular music on most occasions. Sakis has adopted a cosmopolitan style, with clothes inspired by American Westerns and the rock scene, such as high boots, and he is always drinking whisky and smoking Marlboros. Similarly, the bar has an American style, with photographs of New York and a saloon door as an entrance to the toilet.

Leisure gatherings in all bars take place in the evening only, and mostly on weekends. Bars might be open until four or five o'clock in the morning (especially Sakis), depending on the customers and the season (summer, Carnival, Easter, etc.). In any case, most bars will be full after eleven or twelve on Saturday evening unless the bar is also a cafeteria.[49] The bar-cafeteria is a new kind of leisure space, initiated by Makis Trahanas, who was the owner of a similar business in Exarhia in Athens. After he closed down his business in Athens, he invested on Skyros. Makis's cafeteria is also a hybrid of traditional and modern space, incorporating Athenian design with an old bicycle hanging from the ceiling and built-in wooden elements reminiscent of the houses in the village. During the day, the cafeteria is the socializing place for schoolchildren, soldiers, and inhabitants and serves coffee, hot chocolate, tea, and other beverages. At night the place gradually transforms into a bar, which also serves European and American drinks and plays foreign music.

Although bars and cafeterias are for mostly men, the *zaharoplastion* (sweet shop) on the island is a common family (domestic-oriented) space for various inhabitants, both men and women, especially during summer. The sweet shop is a space where local and other sweets are made, including *baklava, kantaifi,* and *pastes,* and these are usually served with juice or soft drinks. Alcohol is not regularly served there despite the fact that the shop sells a wide variety of whiskies and liqueurs. According to the owner, "The beverages and more specifically whisky are usually bought as gifts to accompany sweets for *epsikepsis* [visits] or *giortes* [celebrations] in the community." On name-day celebrations, birthdays, or family gatherings, it is customary to offer some sweets with an alcoholic beverage, and inhabitants will buy their gifts from these shops. Whereas in the past cognac was the main gift on such occasions, nowadays whisky is the rule. Both sweet shops (the second one is situated in the shopping street) sell whisky such as Cutty Sark, Dimple, and Johnnie Walker, which are the usual gifts for a man. In case of a female celebration, Campari and vodka are usually preferred.

The Symbolism of Scotch Whisky in Gambling

Various anthropologists have observed the value attached to card games on the islands of the Aegean and the competitive or reciprocal aspects of different games (Herzfeld 1985, Papataxiarchis 1991). Papataxiarchis, for example, notes that on the island of Lesbos,

> The card game of *poka* (poker) and the throwing of dice are popular avenues for competition among men. *Xeri,* however, is markedly different in many respects. First it is the only card game that remains part of the realm of commensality, since no money stakes are at use. What is at stake in *xeri* is the right to *kerasma,* awarded to those who lose. *Xeri* then, focuses on the honorific side of *kerasma.* The defeated side honors the winners by offering them a brandy or a soft drink. The treating becomes a penalty for losing that does not require future reciprocation. (1991: 166)

Xeri (a popular card game in various places in Greece) is played in Manolis's (the Traditional) and Maritsa's *kafenio,* where there is no money stake but the losing parties pay the bills of the winners. In winter Maritsa's *kafenio* has few regular customers, who are mostly domesticated shepherds. They are between fifty and eighty years old, with sunburned and wrinkled faces from their work, and they spend most of their time outside of the village (*ekso*). In the evenings, usually between six and nine o'clock, men gather next to the wood stove to play *prefa* or *xeri.* The shepherds usually drink *tsipouro* or *ouzo* while they play, which are the main alcoholic spirits for consumption in the *kafenio.* As in Manolis's *kafenio,* good friends come together in pairs to play *xeri.* During the game and depending on which round, the losers will ask Maritsa for shots of *ouzo* or *tsipouro.* However, because Maritsa is not able to move quickly, as she has problems with her feet, one of the losers will bring the drinks. At the end, those who lost each round will pay the cost.

The losers of the game will be obliged to buy the *tsipouro* or *ouzo* for the winners as an honorary gesture, an offering that does not require immediate return or future reciprocation. However, the rivalry of the game will be continued in the following days or weeks, and the position of the loser will shift with the position of the winner, making the offering of the drink a regular form of exchange among friends who play cards. The reciprocation of the rivalry of the game results in the unspoken obligation to play cards again and again and therefore to return the stake (Mauss: 2002 16–18). The obligation to give and the obligation to receive can be understood as forms of exchange over long periods of time that strengthen the bonds of the players of the teams and reproduce the sentiments of friendship.

The refusal to play cards again and thus return or receive the stakes might result in the weakening of social relationships, as card playing is one of the major activities of the *kafenio*. Furthermore, the participants in the game cannot be exempt from such a relationship, as they might be viewed as exempting themselves from mutual ties and reciprocation. Once the drinking gift is given in a card game, there are several expressions that might be uttered by the losers, such as "We'll see next time" ("*Tha dume*"). These create a time continuum in relation to the game. Such expectations from the side of the losers express their willingness to reciprocate. However, the players are not interested in the actual monetary value of the stake but in their reputation as winners.

Generally speaking, when persons come together regularly, the inhabitants of Skyros say that these persons receive and give (*ehoun pare dose*), meaning that a person has regular interaction with someone. The expression might also refer to any form of social relationship, including friendships, sexual affairs, economic affairs, and even legal cases. As such, to receive and to give is viewed as a characteristic of social relationships within Skyrian society.

Makedonia *kafenio,* by contrast, where the consumption rate of whisky is an average of twenty-four bottles per week (90 percent of the total consumption being Cutty Sark), the central card game is *poka* (poker), which is not necessarily related to friendship. On the contrary, the players of the *poka* table should not be good friends or relatives. Ideally, the players know each other but do not have regularly *pare/dose*. Compared with the players of *xeri,* a few Skyrians are gamblers (*tzogadori*) and participate in the gambling circle of Makedonia.

Poka is a highly competitive game with money stakes that sometimes expand to property and pieces of land. The game is highly individualistic and never involves cooperation with other players or playing in groups (as in *xeri*). Participation in the game is limited to a few times a month, or sometimes these are spaced with long periods of time, as the losers of the money stakes cannot afford to play very often. As a result, the constitution of the group of *poka* players changes regularly. The players usually show up in the evenings after seven o'clock, and the games continue until late, sometimes till the morning hours.

The busiest gambling periods take place in the wintertime and, more specifically, during December, January, and February, when laborers do not have to work as much (mainly because of bad weather conditions). The period before New Year's Eve is especially competitive, as gambling during this period is an institutionalized practice all over Greece.

During the busiest periods of gambling, there might be big games (*megala pehnidia*). What characterizes big games is the number of participants at the table, their socioeconomic status, and the amount of money involved. Sometimes big games might involve total stakes higher than 1,000 euros per person (which is the average monthly salary of an unskilled laborer), but there are cases in which pieces of land are the stake. In one of my regular visits to the island's notary, I was informed that there are at least five cases of property transactions every year as a result of gambling. In addition, the son of the owner of Makedonia referred to a story of a man who is the owner of a *zaharoplastion*. He told me that K. is a regular and experienced *tzogadoros* and managed to make a large profit in a big game. He was able to win a large piece of land close to the *horio*, and nowadays he is using it for his own business.

During the big games the doors of the *kafenio* are closed, and sometimes the door might be locked from the inside. Vagelis, the owner of Makedonia, conceals the game from unwanted customers late at night. In addition, there is a second kind of concealment, which is more regular. At Makedonia there are two *poka* tables, one in front of the entrance and the other in a semiprivate room at the back of the *kafenio*. The concealed room is behind the bar of the *kafenio;* it has small curtains on the two windows facing the bar, a large table with a green cloth, and leather sofas. The front table of Makedonia is used by the regular players for small stakes and is busy most of the time. In both settings, players bet with plastic counters given by Vagelis. At the end of a game, Vagelis will exchange the counters for cash unless the stakes are high enough. In that case, the loser will pay the money individually to the winner.

At both tables, whisky plays a central role. Usually all players drink the beverage, and Scotch is considered an integral part of the style of a player. Whereas at *xeri* the right of *kerasma* (treating to a drink) is awarded to those who lose, in *poka* this right is awarded to the winners. The amount of whisky should always be limited to five or maximally six drinks during the evening because more alcohol is considered to bring drunkenness, which is not desirable within the context of the *poka* game. Whisky is usually served diluted with water and ice to make it lighter. The amount of ice is different for each customer, a detail that is known to Vagelis, who serves the beverages. Vagelis is always asking the customers about their drink loudly in an affirmative manner such as "Cutty Sark with ice and water?" and then the customers will agree. This process of naming the exact way that someone drinks the beverage (despite the fact the owner of the *kafenio* knows this) is also a way of asserting an individual identity and making it public. In *poka*, winning is a gradual process that might take a long time, especially when there are many players in the game. As the winner proceeds, he is obliged to invite his fellow players to a drink. The dialog is usually "Will you drink something?" The other party answers with a short yes, and then the winner loudly announces the drinks for his table: "One for Giorgos, and one for Giannis." It is clear, then, that within this context, whisky is an obligation in the moral code of the winner.

According to Vagelis, the owner of the *kafenio,* this treat is a way of balancing the unequal relationship between loser and winner, and in that sense it effects a smooth game. Within this perspective whisky is seen as fuel for the game as it keeps the players calm (*psihremia*), a necessary condition of *poka.* This drinking gift will be without return, as the accumulation of the money of the players by the winner requires a minimum kind of compensation. This form of gift is therefore expressing the success of the winner and is a form of exchange that transcends the utilitarian calculus. Such gifts can be the gifts of pity, such as those given to street beggars and those who are desperate, or gifts in the form of charitable donations and voluntary work. As Bataille has argued such heterogenous things, such as Scotch, open the space of contradiction in the production of deliberately squandered gestures (Bataille 1991). Heterological practice is movement of un-productive expenditures to abject things to the extent that it refuses the power of domination and mastery to which has been added.

Generosity, then, is a characteristic of a good gambler who is able to give by taking the risk to lose. The good gambler will be able to spend (*eksodo*) outside of his household, he will treat (*kerasma*) other players to a Scotch, and he will be in control of his economics (in contrast to the domesticated shepherds). In any case, gambling is an *eksodo.* It would then be relevant to state that the concept of spending, namely *eksodo* (the verb is *ksodevo*), "derives from *eksodos,* exit, and im-plies an outward movement. In some sense, then, money 'comes out' in gambling" (Papataxiarchis 1988: 268). This suggests that gambling is symbolically placed *ekso* in contrast to *ikonomia,* the savings of the household that stay *mesa* in the house. To save and to give the money *mesa* is a characteristic of the domesticated householders who look after their *nikokirio,* whereas to spend and to give money *ekso* is an anti-domestic practice that characterizes conspicuous consumption and consumption in general. In most cases, to consume (*na katanalono*) is viewed as the same practice as *ksodema.* Consequently, consumption is also placed *ekso* of the sphere of the household and might be viewed as a highly anti-domestic activity.

As already noted, women are in control of the economics of the household among the matrilocal domesticated householders. As a result, they are the ones who usually manage the male income, which is used for the needs of the house-hold and for *ikonomia* (savings). Gambling is not viewed as an integral part of the household needs, and no income or property will be used in such a context unless the amount spent for taking a risk is small (such as in a lottery called a *lahio* or a *pro-po* football bet). Small amounts might be regularly spent in the lottery store of the *agora,* but they are not viewed as *tzogos* (gambling).

By contrast, the network of gamblers of Makedonia, who are mainly skilled or unskilled laborers and *horiani,* avoid and are avoided by the matrilocal residence rule; they might marry women from *ekso* and from *eksoteriko,* some are divorced, and those who are married are in control of the economics of the household because the income they receive comes from *merokamato* (daily work) labor, construction work (with payment depending on what was constructed), and market occupations. The first two spheres require the total administration of the economics by the men, as they need money to buy tools, building materials, and other goods to be used for their work. Moreover, these two spheres are opposed to the matrimonial system because they are not related to the land transmitted to the women or to any other valuables as in the case of shepherds. With regard to the occupations of *agora* there is a similar logic with the occupations of laborers, with one major difference. Whereas most shops in *agora* are property of shepherds, some are rented to descendants of *Kohiliani,* some to descendants of farmers, and some to Skyrian-Athenians who arrived on the island during and after the construction of the military airport. Among those who rent the shops, a few Skyrian-Athenians who do not follow the matrilocal rule and are in control of their own shops (usually their wives do not work in their shops) are also gamblers, as they are able to gain an excess profit from their work and they can afford the criticism as a result of their Athenian background. In all cases, the matrimonial property of a woman is inalienable, and as a result no gambler who might have a matrilocal residence is able to afford the social criticism if he *ksodepsi* (spends) his wife's property.

Therefore, in the context of card playing in the *kafenio,* two distinct forms of consumption correspond to two different forms of spending on beverages. The first stake, which is evident in the Traditional coffeehouse, is related to a socializing experience among friends. There the domesticated householders and the unmarried shepherds and men of *agora* come together to play *xeri* in pairs, and those who lose will spend on buying the *tsipouro* for the winners. They will avoid Scotch or cognac, which are consumed on extraordinary family occasions and are kept in the liquor cabinet of the women. The *tsipouro* will mean that the food becomes *meze* (Papataxiarchis 1991), and as such it will reproduce the masculine ideology of the *kafenio.* However, the gender style of the men who play *xeri* is not based on an assertive masculinity and is not related to the urban style that many laborers claim. In addition, the matrilocal rule and the kinship obligations that follow this relationship limit the amount of money that the patrons of the traditional *kafenio* can spend. A major cause is the fact that "Men do not have money" (*oi antres den ehun lefta*), as *Thia* Maria told me, meaning that married shepherds give the money they earn to the household and therefore to the woman. Similarly, the unmarried shepherds and the men of *agora* will give a part of their money to their family or sisters (common bank accounts are a very common strategy) to save for their own shake. As a result the participants will pay small amounts of money for the *kerasma,* and their stakes cannot be excessive, as they should be looking after their household, saving, and not spending their wives' money.

Clearly, gambling opposes the spheres of shepherds' domesticity, the *nikokirio mesa sto horio,* and the mainstream family values of the inhabitants of the island. In addition, gambling might seem like an irrational practice if viewed under the light of economic theory or, more importantly, if it is understood as the opposite pole of constructive card playing and drinking, evident in *xeri* and *kerasma.* However, such heterotopias like Makedonia *kafenio* are outside of all places even if they have an actual location and constitute a contrast to utopias (Foucault and Miskoweic 1986). Such places function like mirrors as sites of counteraction in the position that the other occupies in them. In most cases, heterotopias include those individuals whose behavior is deviant in relation to the required mean or norm, and they form the space of the other. Therefore, especially within the context of gambling and anti-domesticity, Scotch is also a form of deviation because the control of economics and the domesticated householders are the rule.

The laborers and the men of *agora* who are patrons in the Makedonia *kafenio* are *horiani,* and they are in control of their own money in their neolocal residence or in their divorced or unmarried life. They might have an excess of wealth as a result of their upward economic mobility since the 1970s, and they are willing to spend it more conspicuously in whisky in their nightlife to invest in an urban Athenian style to oppose the matrilocal and kinship obligations. Moreover, they are willing to risk their excess wealth in betting in *poka,* an anti-domestic practice that opposes the spheres of the matrilocal household. Gambling should therefore be understood as an integral part of the style of those who want to make themselves through taking risks, by opposing the matrilocal management of the money and the disciplined domesticity of the values of the shepherds and of those who are *eksohini.* By investing in an urban Athenian style of modernness evident in their excessive consumption habits, they oppose a major value of *nikokirio,* the *ikonomia* (savings). As a result, Scotch whisky, which is a *kseno poto* and comes from *ekso,* is intertwined with an Athenian modernness. Moreover, the association of the beverage with gambling and the fact that it is given as a treat by the winner materialize Scotch into a symbol of profit. Within this context, the *kerasma* of Scotch becomes a gift without return that expresses a profit (an amount of money), which is not returned and not reciprocated.

As Malaby has argued, gambling is directly tied to claims about personal status and identity in Greece (2003). Gambling is especially a context for negotiating manhood, and a gambler might demonstrate his *egoismos* (self-regard) by showing indifference to money and material wealth. Simultaneously, a man has to provide for his *nikokirio,* and the gambler who bankrupts his family has no *filotimo* (honor). Gamblers skillfully walk this thin line by trying to seem free of money's burden and not also jeopardize their family when they are married.

Therefore *poka* as well as the drinking gift of whisky in the context of the card game is opposed to the obligations of *nikokirio* because it involves spending large amounts of money outside the context of the family. In addition, in the sphere of the household, there are no gifts without return, as exchanging food and beverages is a major form of socialization and a way of reproducing social relationships. Conversely, within the *soi*-based society of Skyros, the shepherds do not accept those card game challenges that go against their matrilocal and domesticated character; they cannot afford to be discussed (*na tus sizitane*) and lose large amounts of money (that usually they cannot afford as *eksohini*). Therefore, the gift of Scotch should be interpreted as a symbolic practice that deconstructs the material constraints of the players and affirms their upward economic mobility, which is not necessarily related to the political and social privileges of the domesticated shepherds. In that sense, the consumption of Scotch challenges the hegemonic cultural values of the socially powerful domesticated shepherds, and the beverage is placed at the center of an alternative heterotopic moral universe that promotes consumption or spending and relates to the realm of Athens.

Consumption and Cultural Marginality

The socioeconomic changes that took place on Skyros until the beginning of the twentieth century resulted in the decline of the elite group of *arhontes* who were the main owners of the means of production and the landowners together with the ecclesiastical elite of the monastery of St. George. Gradually the extended lineages of shepherds, the *soia,* were able to acquire the land, the shops of *agora,* the old symbolic capital of the *arhontes,* and they became the most influential occupational group in the political and social life of the island. By contrast, those who were known as *Kohiliani* and *parakatiani* became laborers, and some among them migrated to Athens and abroad. Among those laborers who had migrated *mesa* (to Athens), those who were successful with their work returned to the island and continued their skilled labor. The gradual increase of the value of labor and the economic success of the laborers who had migrated to Athens resulted in their upward economic mobility. However, this upward economic mobility did not bring any political and social influence. On the contrary, the laborers remained politically and culturally marginal.

Moreover, the conceptions of cultural coherence held by the inhabitants is radically different between laborers and shepherds. This dichotomy has invested the meanings of shepherds with traditionand locality and the meanings of laborers with modernness and *ekso.*

Furthermore, the notions of shepherd and labor culture noted above are related to the gender styles that persons choose to perform. On Skyros, gender styles are deeply influenced by the conceptualizations and the practice of persons in relation to the *nikokirio* (household) and their domestication. The general morality is for a person to be valued as *nikokiris* (meaning a man or a woman who is focused and looks after the household and the family), as *timios* (an honest person), and *kinonikos* (a social and community-oriented person). These widely shared cultural values are claimed and performed among the matrilocal shepherd householders, who use the matrimonial capital of their wives and are obliged to focus on matrilineal kinship relationships. Within this perspective, consumption (*ksodema*) outside of the context of the household is viewed as contradictory to the values of *nikokirio* and the savings of the family.

However, among the single, married, or divorced laborers, there are some who do not identify with the *soi*-based society of Skyros and the matrilocal domestication, and they avoid the obligations that such a marital relationship might entail. They express an assertive masculinity, they might engage into courtship with foreign women (from *ekso*), they drink imported beverages (from *ekso* or *ksena pota*), and they do *eksoda* (they spend and consume). They can afford conspicuous consumption, and they can express their breach from domesticity by gambling or staying up late at night in the bar and in the *kafenio*. The majority of those laborers consume Scotch whisky in an anti-commensal manner.

Day, Papataxiarchis, and Stewart have argued that such oppositional identities might be observed among various marginal groups who wish to define themselves in contrast to the dominant cultural values of more powerful neighbors (1999: 1–24). This is done in a systematic and conscious manner, which can be understood as an adoption of a style (Ferguson 1999). In such cases, marginal networks consider themselves as outside society beyond the reach of the prevailing neighbors, and they place themselves at the center of an alternative moral universe in contrast to the dominant one. As a result, they are able to replace the experience of dependence with the notion of cultural difference (Day, Papataxiarchis, and Stewart 1999: 1–24). Within this context, marginal people are able to challenge or even transform the hegemonic practices and interpretations by denying the social hierarchy in favor of feelings of autonomous and equal social relationships. In addition, such marginal people have a focus on the present moment because any future transcendence such as religious belief and practice is associated with the dominant order and might be conceived as a strategy for control and authority (Day, Papataxiarchis, and Stewart 1999: 1–24).

Among the Skyrian laborers, for example, a minority are gamblers (*tzogadori*) who focus even more on their own marginality and the luck of the moment. The gamblers come together in Vagelis's *kafenio*, where they play *poka* and place at stake large amounts of money and property. There they bring off their urban and anti-domestic style, as they totally oppose the sphere of the household, the *oikonomia* (saving and being rational in their economics), and the matrilocal obligations of domesticity. By taking large risks and finally by treating or being treated to a Scotch whisky, they express an anti-domestic discourse as well as an upward economic mobility. As a result the gamblers of the *kafenio* localize Scotch as a heterotopic beverage of excessive consumption (*ksodema*).

The domesticated shepherds, in contrast, and the majority of the men of *agora* prefer to socialize in the traditional *kafenio* and in Maritsa's establishment. When they drink heavily as a group, they prefer to drink wine in the *konatsi* in a private sphere. When they spend time in the *kafenio,* they prefer to discuss local politics, playing backgammon and *xeri*. The game of *xeri* lies in diametrical opposition to the game of *poka*. The players involved in *xeri* are friends, they play in pairs, and the losers of each game pay small stakes of *tsipouro* or *ouzo* to the winners. In the game of *poka,* the players are not friends, there are no partnerships, and each player is highly individualistic. There are large stakes each time (at least in comparison with *xeri*), and the winner treats the losers to Scotch whisky.

Thus, Scotch whisky is a heterogeneous and heterotopic beverage for the *horianous* and for those who are in control of their own economics. It encapsulates the notions of modernness and laborhood (especially in relation to Athens), and it opposes the values of domesticity and rational economic constructiveness. Furthermore, it expresses an outward movement (*ine kseno poto, apo to ekso-teriko*), which is appropriated and localized by the laborers who make their style with *ksodema* (spending) and identify with the popular culture of Athens.

Notes

1. The island of Skyros is part of the group of islands called Sporades, which includes Skiathos, Skopelos, and Alonissos. Skyros is twenty-two miles from the harbor of Kymi on the island of Evia, which is the daily destination of Skyros's only ferry boat.

2. Whereas most anthropologists of Greece, such as Campbell (1964), Danforth (1982), Friedl (1962), Herzfeld (1985), Papataxiarchis (1988), and Stewart (1991), have conducted fieldwork in very small communities, this ethnography deals with a slightly larger community.

3. The English poet Rupert Brooke, who was commissioned into the British Royal Naval Force, passed away from pneumonia on 23 April 1915 on his way to Gallipoli. He was buried on the island of Skyros, where his grave remains today. A few years after his death, the Greek state founded the Square of Eternal Poetry on Skyros, where the statue of a young man was placed in his memory.

4. On Skyros the stone bench attached to the house is called *pezoula*. It is usually painted white and is considered a continuation of the house where the outside sociability of the early evening, known as *sperisma*, takes place. *Sperisma* derives from *espera* or *speros*, meaning the early evening time, and it is the context for neighbor or maternal kin sociability.

5. The island's economy nowadays is based on tourism, sheep and goat herding, small businesses, and the army. There are at least 222 shepherding and goat-herding families and almost 38,000 sheep and goats on the island. The rest of the inhabitants make their living

as shop owners, laborers, farmers, fishermen, and public servants. The shepherd families own most of the shops in the *agora,* and the politics of the island are still influenced by their large lineages. Names such as Mavrikos, Fergadis, Xanthoulis, and Mavrogiorgis represent the largest extended shepherd lineages that own most of the property, land, and the animals on the island.

6. For a detailed analysis of the meanings of *ekso* on Naxos island and its relationship to the mythical creatures of *eksotika* see Charles Stewart (1991) *Demons and the Devil,* Princeton University Press.

7. A *konatsi* is a small, simple construction usually made of stone and wood with a few small beds and a fireplace. In some cases there is also a vegetable garden next to the dwelling. Families associated with goat herding and shepherding usually own at least one *konatsi.*

8. In opposition to the *fridatsi,* which is considered a female boundary, the *mantra* is a male boundary that covers the shepherding and herding spaces of milking and cheese making. It is usually a wall made from stones and branches of various trees and plants. The *mantra* boundaries incorporate religious symbols, such as crosses painted on the wall, which protect the flock.

9. The *fridatsi* (meaning *small eyebrow*) is a thin blue-gray line that surrounds almost every house in the village and is a symbolic boundary of the household. The line is always painted by women and is usually taken as a symbolic image of a woman's eyebrows. It is painted once or twice a year, usually in spring and summer, and the same figure is also found on the graves in the cemetery. In the eyes of local women the *fridatsi* indicates the existence of a woman, and usually of a family. A well-kept *fridatsi* is also a symbol of a clean, tidy, household-focused woman, thus expressing the central values of the gendered social life on the island.

10. *Stin Skyro pinoume tse tragoudoume tis tavlas.*

11. According to Herzfeld, language has a central role in the reproduction of social relationships and locality within the context of "cultural poetics" (1985). The local dialects and idioms are therefore major processes of shaping and expressing cultural contexts. With urbanization, central education, and the gradual shift toward the "formal Athenian accent and dialect," the local idioms have been diminishing. However, the persistence of younger people has resulted in a renegotiation of local identity through the practice of idiom in everyday life. Folklore studies and publications have also influenced further the reproduction of the language by younger generations.

12. A so-called real Skyrian is a person who has a Skyrian mother and father—but anybody can claim a Skyrian identity by bilateral reckoning, either from the mother's or the father's side. Being born on the island is not a necessary requirement, especially in recent decades when parents have decided to go to Athens or Evia to give birth in a proper hospital. For example, people are still considered Skyrian even if they were born in another city or town and returned to the island as a newborn baby. The most important aspect is the level of kinship association, and people are readily considered to be Skyrians if one parent comes from Skyros. Miltiadis Hatzigiannakis, for instance, who is currently the mayor of Skyros, is considered a Skyrian despite the fact he lived in Athens for most of his life. The major reason is that his maternal kin comes from the island. Likewise, in my case I was considered a Skyrian because my mother, Anna Christodoulou, was born and grew up on the island.

13. Similarly, Papataxiarchis has noted in the case of the island of Lesbos that "the term *sira* is used in different contexts, to refer to the order of marriage priority among sisters, the turn of treating to a drink, or even as an indicator of class status. In all cases, therefore, a kind of rank order is implied, and the individuals are differentially placed in accordance with it" (1991: 172). This rank order applies also to the island of Skyros. Furthermore, on Skyros *sira* refers to the social position of the person in relation to the past hierarchical social system or the contemporary class differentiations. As such *sira* relates to social hierarchy and social differentiation.

14. A major division that exists in almost all communities of Greece is that between inhabitants (*ntopious*) and outsiders or *xenous*. This division can be understood as a continuation of the boundary between *mesa* and *ekso*, as inhabitants are from *mesa* and foreigners from *ekso* and a prerequisite for the hierarchical construction of the idea of *philoxenia* meaning hospitality (Papataxiarchis 2006). Although the term *xenos* is a highly diverse term and its hierarchy depends on the problematic relationship of host and guest, guests are distinguished by their origin. Immigrants, for example, from Albania are not viewed as the desired guests, whereas tourists from Western Europe are always welcome. On Skyros, outsiders are usually divided among Greeks, immigrants, and tourists, whereas foreigners who stay longer on the island might be our *xeni,* meaning our *familiar foreigners.* Greek *xeni* are usually divided between Athenians and the rest but are categorically different from *xeni* from *eksoteriko,* as they share the cultural ingredients of similarity, namely Orthodox religion, Greek language, and Greek nationality. Other Greek *xeni* are the brides and grooms of inhabitants who come from other areas of Greece. Male *xeni* are usually *fantari* or *aeropori* (soldiers or pilots who work in the military airport). Another category of Greek *xenos* is the person who comes from another area of Greece and is employed on Skyros as a public servant (*dimosios ipalilos*).

15. Traces of the history of the island are existent in records that go back at least five hundred years. The records used for this part of the study and the most important collections of Skyrian history are a) the archive of Antoniadis, partly published by the Skyros Association in 1990, b) the archive of Oikonomidis, unpublished, property of National Literature Archive, and c) the archive of museum Faltaits of Skyros, unpublished.

16. During the sixteenth and seventeenth centuries the governing body of Skyros was called *protogeri.* From 1607 to 1750 the political administration on the island was based on a body called *epitropi,* which means the commission. The local political administration during the nineteenth century was called *demogerontia,* and it was responsible for negotiations with each new political establishment and would decide for all legal and property affairs. (Zarkia 1991: 23). The council of *demogerontia* was constituted by three or sometimes four men over thirty-five years old, with each having a certain responsibility. There was a secretary (*grammatikos*), a president, and a person responsible for security in the countryside (*horafiaris*). These people were elected from the people of Skyros but had to be part of the local elite, the *arhontes* (Zarkia 1991: 23). The structure of *demogerontia* was formally abolished in 1833 by King Otto.

17. Western-style clothes were the Venetian-style clothes that appeared after the third crusade and during the fifteenth century when the island came under Venetian rule. A remnant of this mentality is the figure of *fragos* in the Carnival. *Fragos* literally means *Westerner,* and this figure is dressed up in what inhabitants consider ridiculous clothes.

18. The noblemen owned most of the land on the island, the best areas for pasturage, the farms, the olive plantations, and the vineyards. They also owned the windmills, the olive presses, and the cheese farms. Furthermore, the noblemen were the only ones who were allowed to be elected members of the political committees of the island. They were responsible for exports and imports, they represented the island in the Ottoman and European authorities, and they collected taxes (de Sike 1978: 69–78). In short, the noblemen held economic and political power on the island and were involved in many different social spheres. They would decide in most religious, property, economic, and legal matters. They had the most expensive clothes, which were usually imported, and they were also known as *megalostratites* because they lived in the area stretching from the *Kastro* to the area of *megali strata*. Their Byzantine names possibly reflect an association and descent from Byzantine noble families, but historical research is yet to examine this possibility. Until the beginning of the twentieth century, the life of the noblemen was dependent on the rent they received from the shepherds and farmers (Zarkia 1991: 36).

19. The *aloni* or *luni* is part of the dowry of each woman and is transmitted by mother to daughter. It includes what is known on Skyros as *palea,* such as porcelain or brass plates, pottery, embroidery, and other objects that decorate the interior of the house (Theoharidis 2009). It is considered inalienable wealth, and only in exceptional cases such as wars and extreme poverty are there diversions in the career of these objects. In addition, houses and pieces of land were regular gifts from the family of the bride. The groom was able to use the dowry but it was never totally his own property; this can be understood as a result of the matrilocal kinship system of the island. In many cases there was the condition that everything would be retained by the woman in case of divorce or separation. An example of a dowry agreement that dates back to 1616 states: "We give to Kali our daughter: first the mercy of God, and then God gives through us a house in the area of the *Kastro,* … another two houses, … one is given this day and the other one after my death, … the field in the area of *nifiri,* the fig trees close to the sea shore, the field next to the field of Christ in *ninon,* the vineyard in *kambos,* … another vineyard in *misokambia,* … another vineyard in *mavrounas,* … all our bees and the rents from our farms in the areas of *trahi, kalamia, psahra, sikamini, tremoutzi, lakkous, lole, bera kambo, hilidonia, aspous, paraskinia, ahili, kolithrous.* … And from our house four blankets, two made of silk and two imported bed sheet, ten pillows, … large and small towels, … two wooden bins, … a pan, a wine container, half the *louni (aloni)* of the house, … completed dowry agreement in November of the year 1616" (Antoniadis 1990: 36, document 17).

20. The distinct identity of each group was based on occupation/ownership, descent, and residence. However, residence was not a necessary requirement for inclusion, and wealth did not guarantee upward social mobility. In many instances people with higher incomes (such as seamen and successful shepherds) moved into the Kastro area, but their status did not change. Similarly, successful farmers tried to become shepherds but did not succeed in being accepted as such. On the other hand, *arhontes* who moved into neighborhoods where shepherds lived retained their status, and their spatial mobility did not affect their identity.

21. The inheritance of their land was solely based on descent. Interclass marriages sometimes took place, and in this way a part of the means of production was passed over to shepherds. Mixed marriages would more likely occur between shepherds and noblemen than noblemen and laborers. The main reason was that the shepherds had control over the goats

and sheep and were therefore situated in a higher position in relation to the laborers. The laborers were the lowest on the social scale and in many instances were exploited by the noblemen and the shepherds.

22. The distinctions between *kotsinogonati, xipoliti,* and *Kohiliani* are still used by the older generation of Skyrians. Such distinctions are not related to the segregation of social life but to hierarchical descent and property transmission. Nowadays intermarriage among the mentioned occupational groups is possible while the clear boundaries have been dissolved.

23. Booklet handed out during the commemoration of Georgios Labrou (1901–1965) on 20 August 2005, organized by the municipality of Skyros.

24. During the twentieth century two major processes influenced the hierarchical access to the means of production, which resulted in profound socioeconomic changes. Urban migration and gradual enrichment of the poorer social strata transformed the social categories of stratification and residence. Social space would no longer be related to social differentiation, and access to wealth would be the privilege of the migrants and the large shepherd lineages. More specifically, at the beginning of the century the majority of the local elite bought houses in Athens, sold their property on Skyros to sustain their lives in the city, married Athenians, and migrated to Athens. Most of these wealthy migrants received education and became lawyers, medical professionals, engineers, and writers. This educated diaspora decided to establish an association of Skyrians in Athens (*Silogos Skyrianon*) and publish a newspaper to maintain their ties with their native place. The newspaper *Skyriana Nea* was printed for the first time a few years before World War I and is still the major newspaper of the Skyrian diaspora.

25. The tragic influenza epidemic of 1917 had a dramatic effect on the island, resulting in hundreds of deaths, further reducing the number of noble names and decreasing the population in general.

26. After World War II, the political life of Skyros was not characterized by conflict and segmentation as in other areas of Greece. The left and the right were not major criteria of differentiation in local politics and during the civil war the islanders harshly criticized those who took sides or tried to take lives in the name of political ideology, as had happened in most areas of Greece.

27. The area of *Trahi,* where the airport was constructed, was the property of farmers and labourers; the majority of the property of shepherds was (and still is) in the village and in the south part of the island where goat herding takes place.

28. Before the first ferry boat was bought by SNE (Skyros shipping company) people were able to travel with fishing boats and a ferry boat of the Nomicos shipping group that would travel to the island once a week during the summer months.

29. By contrast, until recently the shepherds mostly lived off their own products and were self-sufficient. Ever since the sixteenth century, if they did not own any land they would rent from the *arhontes* and pay in cheese, animals, and other goods, in an economic relationship known as *trito.* In many cases they would also have small farms for the production of their own vegetables. The fact that they always had a stable income from their products played a major role in the durability of this way of life. Especially during the migration period in the 1960s and in the 1970s they were the only occupational group of the island who did not migrate to Athens or abroad. The profound relationship with the island in combination with the political power of these goat and sheep herding *soia* crystallized with

time into a mentality characterized by concepts of Skyrianness and traditionality as these were understood by folklorists and local historians.

30. The term Vlahos on the island of Skyros does relate to the ethnic group of Vlahs in the North of Greece. It is used in a pejorative manner by the Athenians and Skyrians and refers to a rural or local style of backwardness.

31. By contrast with the comments of du Boulay, Skyrians consider half-siblings from the same father to be real siblings, whereas half-siblings from the same mother are not so close and are called *muladerfia* (Du Boulay 1994: 258). The explanation I was given was the power of sperm, or the seeding, which has also been noted by various ethnographers in South-Eastern Europe such as Delaney (1991) and Papataxiarchis (1988), who have examined the monogenetic theory. In this context, men are viewed as having superior sexual powers. In addition, siblings from the same father have the same name and in that sense are considered to carry the family name, especially males.

32. The role of *nikokirio* has been elaborated by various ethnographers of Greece. It signifies "an economically and politically autonomous, corporate, conjugal household: this is the ideal social environment to which men and women can bring their distinct identities and abilities to create a new family" (Loizos and Papataxiarchis 1991a: 6).

33. As Papataxiarchis and Loizos have stressed, the household is particularly emphasized as a status symbol in communities where the church has taken on the role of political-cultural representation and leadership, especially during the Ottoman era, and has acted as a guarantor of customary law on marriage and kinship (1991a: 6). In the case of Skyros, all dowry agreements from the sixteenth century onward and possibly earlier took place under the supervision of a priest, and most documents incorporated religious elements.

34. The *iso* (ίσο), meaning *equal*, could be translated as *equivalence*, implying the equivalence of the bride with property. *Iso* is an informal dowry agreement, despite the fact more property is given after the *iso* has been signed. I should also mention that women are also allowed to propose marriage to the man. This involves a visit to the house of the groom by the bride accompanied by an old relative. Then the *iso* can be discussed and later can be written down.

35. Food is a major symbolic category that expresses various sociocultural relationships. As Sutton has illustrated, memory and food are interconnected in Kalimnos (1998) and gender is shaped by food habits (Herzfeld 1985, Cowan 1990).

36. Until recently most women from shepherd, farming, and fishing families were excluded from the production process, except for the women of laboring families (*Kohiliani*) who could be employed in farming. In all other spheres of production women were strictly restricted, and this is still the case with herding and fishing. Whereas in the past women would not appear often in the Skyros market unless they were employed as low-paid laborers, in recent years not only have women socialized in the market but many shops are run by women and they are named with female names. Women work in various businesses, including bars and *kafenio*, and they usually run them together with their husbands. Older women from the Kohilia area still work as low-skilled or unskilled laborers, such as cooks and cleaners in restaurants, whereas the younger generation is more likely to work in a bar or a shop. Generally speaking, women have more access to the island's market than in the past, and they are much more involved in business. However, the tasks of housekeeping and childcare are still performed solely by all women, as in the rest of Greece. The advantages of bilateral reckoning in combination with female matrimony and matrilocal

residence should not be overemphasized, as women still do a great deal of domestic labor. Other restrictions are still part of local life, such as the avoidance of appearing in public for long periods except in cases of communal rituals, religious festivals, and shopping. This absence is especially striking in the empty cold winter streets of the Agora and Kastro where people are rarely seen, and if they are seen they are more likely to be men.

37. While on fieldwork I collected several recipes for these liqueurs. Each recipe depends on the sweetness of the fruit, which is be adjusted with sugar. The quantity made is usually two liters of cognac mixed in a big glass bottle with one and a half kilo of sugar or more with the pits (fifty to a hundred) of the desired fruit. In the case of oranges, mandarins, or quinces, the peel (four or five fruits) is used to flavor the beverage.

38. The word *cognac* in Greek refers usually to Greek-made brandy, but as a term includes all kind of brandy. *Cognac* is a localized term, probably as a result of a French style of education and an adaptation of French words in modern Greek.

39. Kotsoni, for example, has illustrated the importance of the table in interfamily relationships in the South Aegean and how it is connected to various other aspects of social life (2001: 96–137).

40. Within forty days of a death, the family of the deceased offers wine to the external kin, friends, and neighbors for forgiveness. *Ouzo* usually accompanies the first dance of the married couple in the house. Brandy or Scotch is usually given after a funeral in the coffeehouse.

41. The ambassador's coffeehouse was located where Lefteris's travel agency is now. Ambassador was the owner's nickname because he always welcomed all types of different clients and was well dressed.

42. See Danforth (1997) and Karakasidou (1997).

43. *Kamaki* means the harpoon for spearing fish. It is used as a masculine metaphor for the art of seduction. *Kamaki* might take the form of a collective activity and might bring men into a club, an association for the advancement of *kamaki*. Such associations were widely established in several areas that faced massive tourism and institutionalized several rules of the proper ars erotica in relation to foreign women (Zinovieff 1992: 203–220). Nowadays the term might be used as a metaphor for the first interaction with women.

44. Various anthropologists have analyzed the institution since Campbell, including Herzfeld, Cowan, and Papataxiarchis.

45. It is the custom on the island to call the older people Uncle *Barbas* and Aunt *Thia.*

46. A term that is used on a popular level and is also part of the vocabulary of whisky drinkers on Skyros island is the term *katharo,* which literally means *clean.* The term has been used in opposition to so-called non-clean whiskies, which are home-brewed and illegally brewed spirits of unknown origin. However, it should be clear that the term *katharo* is also related to a mentality of purity existent since the linguistic debate in Greece (glossikon zitima), as Herzfeld has noted (1989). The obsession with the purity of the language (*katharevousa*), the purity of Greekness, pure Europeaness in opposition to unclean Turkishness and other such dichotomies should be understood within the context of disemia.

47. *Kaiki* is a particular type of fishing boat used in the Aegean Sea.

48. *Baraki* is also sometimes known as *orthadiko,* meaning a standing-bar, but the category also encompasses clubs or *clubakia.*

49. Cowan has elaborated on the emergence of the *kafeteria* in rural Greece (1990: 73–75), describing it as a hybrid establishment combining aspects of a bar and *zaharoplastio.*

Conclusion
Trajectories of Scotch Whisky, Realms of Localization

By following Scotch whisky through three distinct trajectories—the mediascapes of the cultural industry, the Athenian nightlife and entertainment, and the island drinking styles—this study demonstrated that the concept as well as the product has shifted between various meanings. The shifts in meaning from the cultural industry to various groups of consumers might be interpreted sometimes as complementary and sometimes as contradictory, making it clear that strategies of powerful institutions can face consumers' tactics. In that sense the material shows that consumers' tactics employ excessive opposition to resist the disciplining desires of the culture industry. Therefore, localization and resistance are understood as tactical practices shifting away from meanings of localization as a local dimension of globalization.

As Adorno and the critical theory scholars have argued, history is marked by progress, and humanity is improving itself by increasing its degree of emancipation (Horkheimer and Adorno 1947). Horkheimer and Adorno claimed that people's lives are based on an instrumental rationality, or, in other words, the use of the most efficient means to achieve the desired goal. This concept is interrelated not only with capitalism and the economy but also with politics and culture. Instrumental rationality is therefore understood as the capitalistic view of efficiency concerning the pursuit of profits, and it is associated with the concepts of mass production, specialization, and faith in progress. As a consequence, instrumental rationality is a set of implied values that influences the goal of human activity and in many instances goes against the values of other people, as the case of the rise of fascism in Europe in the 1940s. Within this context, the culture industry creates standardized products for its consumers and gives these consumers a false freedom of choice, when in fact the product is mass-produced. The consumers are led to believe that they have real individuality and are in control of their own decisions and actions, which in fact is a myth. Therefore, popular culture is viewed as an arena where choices are restricted and consumers are deceived (Adorno 1991: 98–107). This view corresponds to the Hegelian philosophy that views criticism as more than a negative judgment and takes an active role in detecting and unmasking existing forms of belief to enchase the emancipation of humans in modern society.

Although such critiques of capitalism have been very constructive for understanding social inequalities, this study takes a different stance to demonstrate that consumers are able to practice their own tactics to resist the strategies of the culture industry. As de Certeau has argued,

> A society is thus composed of certain foregrounded practices organizing its normative institutions and of innumerable other practices that remain "minor," always there but not organizing discourses and preserving the beginnings or remains of different (institutional, scientific) hypotheses for the society or for others. It is in this multifarious and silent "reserve" of procedures that we should look for "consumer" practices having the double characteristic pointed out by Foucault, of being able to organize both spaces and languages, whether on a minute or a vast scale. (1984: 48)

In this sense de Certeau offers, in contrast to critical theorists or other forms of Marxist theory, a theory of tactics that can resist, subvert, and make use of foregrounded power structures, as in the case of the Greek cultural industry. A reorientation from large-scale globalizing strategies to the everyday actions, movements, and sensations of the ordinary people (de Certeau 1984, Napolitano and Pratten 2007) is able to bring more insights into the disempowered space of consumption.

De Certeau has suggested that powerful strategies such as these practices of powerful industrialists and media producers do not necessarily dominate the contemporary consumers (1984). Strategies are practices calculated by capitalists, organizations, or bodies of expertise that have power over others and are able to claim a space of their own, such as the multinational whisky corporations. A tactic, by contrast, is a calculated practice of the disempowered and of those who do not have a protected space from which they can operate and are therefore forced to act within the territory of those who hold power (de Certeau 1984). Consumers in that sense have tactics in their everyday life.

Even more, the contrast between the material presented shows that the strategies of multinational capitalism and the cultural industry and the tactics of consumers in Athens and Skyros are not necessarily based on ideology or hegemony; on the contrary, consumers' practice in many cases can be autonomous and can be understood as their own cultural space because "the space of the tactic is the space of the other" (de Certeau 1984: 36–37). The ethnographies of whisky consumption in *bouzoukia* in Athens and competitive card playing and whisky drinking on the island of Skyros show that consumers use the mentality of excess as a tactic and negation. This excessive resistance goes against the argument of the culture industry (Adorno 1991) and shows that this is no triumph of instrumental rationality.

As Bataille has argued, this excessive mentality is a characteristic of humanity in general, and expenditure as well as spectacular transgression can be important in the social life of any group (1991). By adding to this theory of expenditure, the material in the first and second parts of the study shows that excess comes in at the national level, localized in the mediascapes of the culture industry and in the *bouzoukia* of Athens in a clear anti-thesis of the culture industry. This opposition is based on the imaginaries of Scotch in cinema, marketing, and advertising as a symbol of Western modern middle classness versus the anti-domestic Eastern discourse of *bouzoukia* and Greek contemporary popular music.

On the other hand, on the local scale of Skyros, Scotch opposes traditional matrifocal authority and shepherdness, which has occupied the political seats of power of national bureaucracy. Within this context, Scotch whisky is related to an excessive celebration of working-class positions of the former kohylians.

In all these contexts, Scotch emerges as a heterotopic beverage, as it is the dominant symbol in the heterotopias of *bouzoukia* and *kafenio* (Foucault and Miskoweic 1986), where the negation of discipline and modernity is mirrored in the position that the other occupies in them. While several practices in these spaces might seem deviant in relation to the required mean or norm, they form the spaces of otherness. Especially within the context of gambling, excessive consumption, and anti-domesticity, Scotch is also a form of deviation because the *nikokirio* values and the rational economic constructiveness are the rule.

Finally, these three trajectories show how Scotch has become a Greek fetish because as a strong drink it is replacing traditional wine, *tsipouro,* and *ouzo,* fitting into the use value of older consumption patterns. Rather than understanding the success of Scotch as a construction of needs from the multinational import corporations and the culture industry (simply as an imposition from above), this study argues that the commodification of alcohol has to be understood as a complex process that requires the histories of the importers and the culture industry in the region as well as the histories and tactics of the consumers both in Athens and Skyros. In this way Scotch encompasses both the presence of modernity and the excessive denial of modern discipline and traditional authority, all at once. Whisky consumption is thus a complex expression of independence from modernity. Its fetishistic attraction resides in the fact that both disrupts and exemplifies what Miller calls normal material frames within the context of the "humility of things" (Miller 2005: 4).[1]

Multinational Capitalism

The fact that the study deals with an imported beverage produced in Western Europe and more specifically in Scotland is due to a socioeconomic historical process that was intensified within the twentieth century and, more specifically, after the dictatorship in Greece. Since the whisky boom in Greece between the 1980s and the 1990s, Scotch whisky has been localized and deeply integrated in several aspects of the social life. This shift is also related to the gradual establishment of multinational capitalism in the sector of beverages in Greece and its expansion in the spheres of advertising, marketing, and popular culture. This shift has been followed by a gradual decrease in what has been thought of as traditional Greek-made beverages, including *ouzo* and retsina.

A major cause of this process was the contest between the small Greek importers and the large multination corporations, which ended in the total success of multinational capitalism. It is therefore important to state that the politics of commodity flow should be understood as the politics of contest between those in power.

These processes speeded up the processes of production and consumption and influenced the subcontracting and merging of Greek companies with the largest global multinationals in the alcohol business, namely the Diageo, Pernod Ricard, and Berry Bros. companies. These companies in turn gained control of almost 80 percent of the market within a few years, taking advantage of the local knowledge of their subcontractors and their associates in Greece. Within this context, multinational capitalism in the alcoholic beverages sector was established and became the leading force in the importation of Scotch whisky and other alcoholic beverages in Greece.

A Trajectory of Mediascapes

The first concrete trajectory of the localization process of Scotch whisky is related to the establishment of postwar Greek commercial cinema and marketing. In both mediascapes, Scotch became a central image around which cinematic scenarios, scripts, plots, and advertisements were constructed. These imaginaries became complex sets of metaphors that profoundly influenced the projected notions of modernity, tradition, globality, and locality. As a consequence, Scotch was projected as a symbol of Western modern middle classness.

More specifically, the commercial Greek cinema of the 1960s, which sold approximately 100 million tickets per year (Sotiropoulou 1989) although the population of the country was less than 7 million and had an average number of a hundred productions per year, was a booming industry (Soldatos 2002: 73). Within this context, a specific structure of feeling (Williams 1954) of the elite part of the culture industry was expressed through the cinematic scenarios that focused on consumerism and modernness, cosmopolitan and rural styles, internal and external migration, new commodities and social change, and an American way of life. In relation to Scotch whisky, the feelings of alienation, loss of innocence, and consumerism were portrayed in various scenarios. Conversely, the beverage came to represent the feeling of modernness, of optimism expressed in upward social mobility, and of celebratory companionship.

Such scenarios were approached as stories about possible, alternative imagined futures that integrate human diversity and uncertainty (Ginsburg, Abu-Lughgod, and Larkin 2002, Appadurai 1996) and as scripts circulated by mass communication in the public sphere (Habermas 1989). More specifically, the scenarios imagined a consumer society in which commoditization, individualization, alienation, and urbanization would characterize the most part of its social life. Within this context, whisky as well as other commodities expressed the imagined Americanization of the society, the alienation of the consumer, and the modernness associated with their consumption. Conversely, whisky was imagined as a symbol of success, urban style, and celebration. These contradictions remained part of the various scenarios until the decline of Greek commercial cinema and expressed the uncertainty about the outcome of this imagined modernity.

Moreover, in the cinematic scenarios of the 1950s and the 1960s, several conceptualizations in relation to whisky could be identified. Scotch was projected as a force that corrupts or decenters people and an evil drink that corrupts social relations. This alienation has been conceptualized as a form of division of the constructed self. Nevertheless, whisky came to represent modernity in a bottle consumed by the Greek-Americans or those who would identify with a modern way of life, by the wealthy cosmopolitan urbanites or those who would challenge the traditional family roles, including patriarchy, matchmaking, and the subordinate role of women.

By the time of the decline of the film industry during the dictatorship, a consumer culture characterized by mass culture and mass commodities would begin to emerge (Karapostolis 1984). That shift was accompanied by several other changes, such as rapid urbanization, increased numbers of women in university education, new youth movements, and an emergence of popular culture and music.

The decline of the Greek commercial cinema did not result in the decline of the cultural industry in general. In 1966, the Association of Advertising Companies, or EDEE, was founded and played a major role in promoting advertising in Greece. However, two clear differences emerged between the marketers and their predecessors in the film industry: they did not project whisky as an alienating force, and they would capitalize on the meanings of global and local. From the end of 1960s, marketing and advertising became institutionalized, the marketing companies multiplied, and commodification became intensive. During this period, several styles of projecting whisky in advertisements could be identified that correspond to different periods.

Distinction was used as a form of differentiating and reproducing class inequalities by emphasizing the association of Scotch with superiority, a cosmopolitanism, and a superior foreign influence that was expressed by the accent at the threshold of perception. Especially the use of the English language in marketing and advertising discourse has shown a long pattern of claiming higher status and has also been used politically. Furthermore, these conceptualizations were associated with an assertive sexuality, a gender emancipation, and a high-class style that was expanded to the sphere of art and culture. Haig, for example became the arty beverage, Johnnie Walker the science-oriented Scotch, and Cutty Sark the sporty and modern beverage.

Moreover, marketing and advertising used scale making to associate the concepts of national with Scotch whisky (Tsing 2000: 327–360). By investing in the meanings of national and Greek, scale making reproduced the conceptualizations of a Greek whisky, and the national connotations of Scotch whisky are expressed in advertisements that use national symbols and landmarks as a legitimate form of localization. This form of scale making became more active at the end of the 1990s and began to include national accomplishments such as the Athens metro, the new Olympic stadium designed by Santiago Calatrava for the Athens Olympics in 2004, and even the Greek flag. The nationalization of whisky through advertising demonstrates that despite the economic structures of multinational capitalism, the globalization of financescapes, and the standardized mass culture that has been emerging through the cultural industry, mediascapes reinforce the national imageries. Hence, it can be argued that mass media and, more importantly, the mediascapes continue to influence the formation of an imagined national community (Anderson 1983).

Moreover, the commodity of Scotch whisky transforms into a Greek gift in marketing and advertising discourse. More specifically, names can be engraved on the bottle of Scotch for name days (*giortes*) to individualize and personalize the gift. Scotch has also been projected as an ideal gift for Christmas and name days or birthdays in general, and it is almost always part of the ideal gift list of magazines and newspaper supplements.

Surprisingly enough, the cultural industry and the marketers did not capitalize on the symbolism of Scotch in Greek popular music with Eastern associations and the excessive character of the beverage. Therefore there are no advertisements of Scotch in relation to *bouzoukia* or *kafenio,* as that would contradict the Western modernity that the marketers have invested with various meanings.

A Trajectory of Popular Style and Entertainment

The relationships among Scotch whisky, popular style, and Greek popular music have to be understood within the context of commercialization, commoditization, and popularization of music and entertainment in general in postwar Athens. However, this popularization of music does not necessarily imply that the quality of the music or the associated practices of entertainment are not qualitative and the consumers are deceived, as the Frankfurt School of thought would argue. The emergence of *bouzoukia* and *skiladika* from a marginal scene from below and their modernization resulted in the establishment of Scotch whisky as a symbol of popular music and entertainment to the extent that the prices of these music venues are now represented in whisky. Moreover, this process of modernization resulted in a new aesthetic and in new consumption habits in night entertainment and *bouzoukia*. Live music became a trend, the orchestras multiplied and grew bigger, microphones were added, and the orchestras would perform on a stage where customers could also dance; food was not served anymore, and whisky was established as the main beverage of consumption. Excessive consumption was institutionalized with the breaking of plates and the throwing of flowers. Within this context, various artists had to make the choice to continue their performances in these commercialized conditions or retire from the nightclubs.

The genre of contemporary Greek popular music has been related to an excessive consumption that has been projected by the popular singers themselves and has influenced the notions of style of the social networks that I followed in Athens, who identify with contemporary Greek popular music. The style of the *parea* that I studied is identified with several excessive practices, even if the individuals are not always able to spend in these social contexts. This mentality includes opening a bottle of special, throwing baskets of flowers at singers, opening champagne, and paying enormous bills for a bottle of whisky. It follows that my interlocutors make themselves through the beverage and claim a relationship between Scotch and their identity.

The style of this audience expresses the construction of the conceptualization of modernity, which Argyrou has discussed (2005) and which might expand to various notions of modernness and traditionality, concepts that are constituted in relation to popular music, popular culture, and consumption in general. More particularly, a style invested with an aura of modernness might appropriate Scotch whisky or single malt depending on the knowledge of the consumers and the style they want to pursue. This appropriation can be further expressed in relation to a masculine style, even by women who want to challenge dominant conceptualizations of womanhood and femininity.

The Trajectory of North Aegean Alcohol Consumption

The modernness of whisky on Skyros Island in the North Aegean is associated with an imagined Athenian style, which opposes the values of shepherhood and domesticity and is widely shared by the laborers of the island. This process is related to the socioeconomic changes that took place during the twentieth century on the island of Skyros and resulted in the redistribution of social privileges among the occupational groups of the island. In particular, the *arhontes* (elite), who were the main owners of the means of production and the landowners, disappeared from the social landscape of Skyros. The shepherds were able to take a leading role in the economic and political life of the island and acquired the land and the old symbolic capital of the *arhontes*. The farmers as well as the Kohiliani who used to be the poorest strata of the Skyrian society became upwardly mobile in an economic sense during the 1970s and 1980s, the period during which wage labor expanded. Moreover, the laborers migrated *mesa* to Athens and abroad; then, upon returning to the island, they invested in small businesses and shops. However, their upward economic mobility did not bring any social and political recognition or privileges.

Upon their return to the island, the Kohiliani took the risk of opening bars during the 1980s. They were the first to invest in tourism and also were the ones who worked in manual labor and as a result were able to make their fortunes. As a consequence of their economic mobility and to be differentiated from the shepherds, the lower social strata intensified the consumption of imported commodities and imported beverages, and they adopted a cosmopolitan style, which allies itself with the urban Greek popular music of Athens. These laborers are attached to the *laiko* music scene, to the consumption of whisky, and to a style of dominant or assertive masculinity. Within these networks, assertive masculinity is a form of symbolic capital, which lies in opposition to the disciplined and ordered domesticity of manhood as expressed in the values of the matrilocal households of shepherds. Domesticated householders represent the mainstream values of the majority of the community, and they cannot afford economic excesses, gambling, drinking, or extended sexual relationships outside the context of marriage. Laborers, on the other hand, not only negotiate their masculine style through an assertive sexuality but also in some cases divorce. In addition, the *horiani* laborers drink whisky inside the village in opposition to most *eksohinous* shepherds, who drink wine outside the village. Likewise, laborers go regularly *mesa* (inside, to Athens) for their shopping or entertainment, in opposition to the shepherds, who spend most of their time *ekso* (outside, in the countryside).

Moreover, many laborers do not identify with the *soi*-based society of Skyros and the matrilocal obligations that such kinship relationships entail. They own their own houses, they are able to spend (*ksodepsoun*), and they have their own money. Shepherds, by contrast, do not own houses, as houses constitute part of the dowry. They are expected to do *oikonomia* (save money), and they do not have money of their own, as women are usually in control of the economics of the matrilocal household. By contrast, laborers perform an assertive masculinity; they may engage in courtship with *ksenes* from *eksoteriko* (foreign women from abroad); they do *eksoda;* they gamble; and they stay up late at night in bars drinking whisky or other imported beverages from *eksoteriko*. In these ways they can express their anti-domestic style or their breach with domesticity.

As Day, Papataxiarchis, and Stewart have argued, these oppositional identities can be found in marginal networks who wish to define themselves in opposition to the dominant cultural values of more powerful neighbors (1999: 1–24). For that reason, former Kohyliani replace the experience of dependency with the notion of cultural difference. In addition, such marginality has a focus on the luck of the present moment because any future transcendence, such as religious belief and practice, is associated with the dominant order (Day, Papataxiarchis, and Stewart 1999: 1–24).

One of the most important differences between laborers and shepherds in terms of the consumption of alcohol is within the context of their entertainment in *kafenion*. The shepherds, shop owners, and public servants socialize in the traditional *kafenion* of the upper market street and usually drink *tsipouro,* beer, or wine when they come together with their friends and *parees*. By contrast, the laborers socialize in the Makedonia and Synantisis *kafenion* on the margin of the town of Skyros. When the shepherds play cards they usually play *prefa* or *xeri*, games to be played among friends. The game of *xeri* has several basic differences with the game of *poka*, which is usually played by the laborers in the down part of the market street. The first and most important difference is that there are no money stakes in the game of *xeri* and no material interests involved but only drinking gifts. The second difference is that teams of two men usually play the game, and the third is that the rounds of the game are repeated over long periods. The losers of the game will be obliged to buy the *tsipouro* for the winners as an honorary gesture, a gift that requires no immediate return or future reciprocation.

In contrast, a minority of laborers plays the competitive game of *poka* (poker), and they put amounts of money and property at stake. Whisky is the main beverage of consumption in those cases, and the patrons of those heterotopic spaces identify with an Athenian style. In the game of *poka* only individuals can participate (in opposition to the teams of two in *xeri*) and only when they can afford the money stakes. Similar research in the Eastern Aegean has demonstrated that gambling is a form of ritual destruction of money that "purifies the male self and leaves *kefi* triumphant" (Papataxiarchis 1999: 158–175). Especially on Skyros, where the money is associated with the matrilocal obligations of domesticated shepherds, the squandering of money by laborers challenges the dominant cultural values of the dominant neighbors.

Participation in the game is limited to a few sessions a month, and sometimes long periods of time elapse between games, as the losers of the money stakes cannot afford to play very often. As a result, the formation of the group of *poka* changes regularly. During the game whisky is transformed into a gift; it is consumed in moderation to relax the players and in every session the winner is obliged to buy drinking gifts of whisky for the losers if they are willing to accept them. Within this context, Scotch is transformed into a symbol of *ksodema* that expresses an anti-domestic discourse as well as an upward economic mobility. However, this upward economic mobility of the laborers does not necessarily bring them political or social recognition within the hierarchical, *soi*-oriented, and hereditary society of Skyros.

Consequently, Scotch is for the *horianous* and for those who want to break apart from the matrilocal rules and extended matrifocal kinship obligations. It materializes the notions of Skyrian modernity and laborhood and opposes the values of domesticity. In addition, it expresses an outward movement as it comes from *eksoteriko* and is related to *ksodema* (spending-consuming) and to an Athenian style. Its localization is therefore tactical and cannot be understood without the kinship and matrilocal cultural values of the inhabitants of Skyros.

Notes

1. Personal communication with Peter Pels.

References

Abu-Lughod, L. 1995. "The Objects of *Soap Opera*: Egyptian Television and the Cultural Politics of Modernity." In *Worlds Apart: Modernity through the Prism of the Local*, ed. Daniel Miller, 190–210. London and New York: Routledge.

Adorno, T. W. 1991. *The Culture Industry*. London and New York: Routledge.

Agelopoulos, G. 2002. "Life Among Anthropologists in Greek Macedonia." *Social Anthropology* 11: 249–263.

Alexandris, T., Αλεξανδρής, Θ. 2000. *Αυτή η νύχτα μένει*. Athens: Periplous.

Allen, P. *1985*. "Appollo and Dionysus: Alcohol Use in Modern Greece." *East European Quarterly* XVIII, no. 4: 461–480.

Amanatidis, A. 2005. "Coming into Being Metaphors of Self and Becoming in Carnival, on the Aegean Island of Skyros." Ph.D. thesis, Department of Anthropology, The University of Adelaide.

Abatzi, L. 2010. Λ. Αμπατζή. *Ποτό για παρέα. Σεξουαλική διασκέδαση στη σύγχρονη Ελλάδα*. Athens: Kedros.

———. 2004. "Αμπατζή, Κ.Μ. 2004. Ποτό για Παρέα, Έφυλες σχέσεις, Σώμα και Συναίσθημα στη Σεξουαλική Εργασία. Διδακτορική διατριβή, Πανεπιστήμιο Αιγαίου, Τμήμα Κοινωνικής Ανθρωπολογίας και Ιστορίας." Ph.D. thesis, Lesbos.

Anderson, B. 1983. *Imagined Communities*. London and New York: Verso.

Andriakena, E. 1996. Ανδριάκαινα, Ε. "Η διαμάχη για το ρεμπέτικο." Στο Ν. Κοταρίδης, επιμ., *Ρεμπέτες και ρεμπέτικο Τραγούδι*, 9–33. Athens: Plethron.

Antoniadis, X. 1990. Αντωνιάδης, Ξ. *Αρχείο Εγγράφων Σκύρου*. Athens: Silogos Skyrianon.

Appadurai, A. 2005. "Materiality in the Future of Anthropology." In *Commodification: Things, Agency, and Identities: The Social Life of Things revisited*, eds. Wim van Binsbergen and Peter Geschiere, 55–62. Berlin and Zurich: LIT Verlag.

———. 2001. "Grassroots Globalization and the Research Imagination." In *Globalization*, ed. Arjun Appadurai, 1–21. London and New York: Duke University Press.

———. 1996. "Disjuncture and Difference in the Global Cultural Economy." In *Modernity at Large: Cultural Dimensions of Globalization*, ed. Arjun Appadurai, 27–47. Minneapolis: University of Minnesota Press.

———. 1986. "Introduction: Commodities and the Politics of Value." In *The Social Life of Things, Commodities in Cultural Perspective*, ed. Arjun Appadurai, 3–63. Cambridge: Cambridge University Press.

Archetti, E. 1999. *Masculinities. Football, Polo and the Tango in Argentina.* Oxford and New York: Berg.

Argyrou, V. 2005. *Tradition and Modernity in the Mediterranean: The Wedding as Symbolic Struggle.* Cambridge: Cambridge University Press.

Bakalaki, A. 2000. Μπακαλάκη, Α. "Γευστικά Ταξίδια, Συναντήσεις και διακρίσεις." Στο Ρωξάνη Καυταντζόγλου, & Μαρίνα Πετρονώτη, επιμ., *Όρια και Περιθώρια: Εντάξεις και Αποκλεισμοί.* Athens: EKKE.

Bampilis, T. 2012. "History of Consumption and Waste 1900s." In *The Encyclopedia of Consumption and Waste,* eds. Bill Rathje and Geoffrey Golson. London and New York: Sage.

Bampilis, T., and P. Ter Keurs, eds. 2013. *Social Matter(s): Recent Approaches to Materiality.* London and Berlin: LIT Verlag. (In Press).

Bampilis, T. 2002. *The Cyle of Death on Skyros Island.* MSc Dissertation, UCL, London.

Barber, B. 1995. *Jihad vs. McWorld.* New York: Times Books.

Bataille, G. 1991, *The Accursed Share: An Essay on General Economy.* New York: Zone Books.

———. 1990. "Hegel, Death and Sacrifice." *Yale French Studies* 78: 9–18.

Baudrillard, J. 1994. *Simulacra and Simulation.* Michigan: University of Michigan Press.

———. 1993. *The Transparency of Evil: Essays on Extreme Phenomena.* New York: Verso.

Bauman, Z. 2000. *Globalization: The Human Consequences.* New York: Columbia University Press.

Bender, B. 2001a. "Introduction." In *Contested Landscapes: Movement, Exile and Place,* eds. Barbara Bender and Margot Wine, 1–21. Oxford & New York: Berg Publishers.

———. 2001b. "Politics and Landscape." In *The Material Culture Reader,* ed. Victor Buchli, 135–140. Oxford and New York: Berg Publishers.

Bloch, M., and J. Parry. 1989. *Money and the Morality of Exchange.* Cambridge: Cambridge University Press.

Blum, E., and R. Blum. 1965. *Health and Healing in Rural Greece: A Study of Three Communities.* Stanford, CA: Stanford University Press.

Bott, E. [1987] 2003. "The Kava Ceremonial as a Dream Structure." In *Constructive Drinking: Perspectives on Drink from Anthropology,* ed. Mary Douglas, 182–203. London & New York: Routledge.

Bourdieu, P. 1984. *Distinction.* London and New York: Routledge.

———.1977. *Outline of a Theory of Practice.* Cambridge: Cambridge University Press.

Buchli, B. 2002. "Introduction." In *The Material Culture Reader,* ed. Victor Buchli, 1–22. Oxford and New York: Berg Publishers.

Burke, T. 1996. *Lifebuoy Men, Lux Women: Commodification, Consumption and Cleanliness in Modern Zimbabwe.* Durham and London: Duke University Press.

Caldwell, M. 2008. "The Taste of Nationalism: Food Politics in Postsocialist Moscow." *The Journal of the Royal Anthropological Institute* 14, no. 3: 590–608.

Calotychos, V. 2003. *Modern Greece: A Cultural Poetics.* Oxford and New York: Berg.

Campbell, J. 1964. *Honour, Family, and Patronage: A Study of Institutions and Moral Values in a Greek Mountain Community.* Oxford: Clarendon.

Carrier, J. 1995. *Gifts and Commodities: Exchange and Western Capitalism since 1700.* London and New York: Routledge.

Clifford, J., and G. Marcus. 1986. "Introduction: Partial Truths." In *Writing Culture: The Poetics and Politics of Ethnography,* eds. James Clifford and George E. Marcus, 1–26. Berkeley and Los Angeles: University of California Press.

Clogg, R. 1992. *A Concise History of Greece*. Cambridge: Cambridge University Press.

Close, D. 2002. *Greece Since 1945: Politics, Economy, and Society. The Postwar World*. London: Pearson Education.

Coe, Neil M., and Yong-Sook Lee. 2006. "The Strategic Localization of Transnational Retailers: The Case of Samsung-Tesco in South Korea." *Economic Geography* 82, no. 1: 61–88.

Comaroff, J. 1985. *Body of Power, Spirit of Resistance: the culture and history of a South African people*. Chicago: University of Chicago Press.

Comaroff, J., and J. L. Comaroff. 2003. "Ethnography on an Awkward Scale: Postcolonial Anthropology and the Violence of Abstraction." *Ethnography* 4, no. 2: 147–179.

―――. 2001. "Millennial Capitalism. First Thoughts on a Second Coming." In *Millennial Capitalism and the Culture of Neoliberalism*, eds. Jean Comaroff and John Comaroff, 1–56. Durham and London: Duke University Press.

Cowan, J. 1990. *Dance and the Body Politic in Northern Greece*. Princeton: Princeton University Press.

―――. 1992. "Going Out for Coffee? Contesting the Grounds of Gendered Pleasures in Everyday Sociability." In *Contested Identities: Gender and Kinship in Modern Greece*, eds. Peter Loizos and Akis Papataxiarchis, 180–202. Princeton: Princeton University Press.

Damer, S. 1988. "Legless in Sfakia: Drinking and Social Practice in Western Crete." *Journal of Modern Greek Studies* 6, 2: 291–310.

Damianakos, S. 2003. Δαμιανάκος, Σ. *Παράδοση Ανταρσίας και Λαϊκός Πολιτισμός*. Athens: Plethron.

Danforth, L. 1982. *The Death Rituals of Rural Greece*. Princeton: Princeton University Press.

Day, S., E. Papataxiarchis, and M. Stewart. 1999. "Introduction." In *Lilies of the Field: Marginal People Who Live for the Moment*, eds. Sophie Day, Evthymios Papataxiarchis, and Michael Stewart, 1–24. Boulder: Westview Press.

de Certeau, M. 1984. *The Practice of Everyday Life*. Berkeley: University of California Press.

de Moij, M. 2005. *Global Marketing and Advertising: Understanding Cultural Paradoxes*. Thousand Oaks, CA: Sage.

de Pina-Cabral, J. 2005. "The Future of Social Anthropology." *Social Anthropology* 13, no. 2: 119–128.

―――. 2000. "The Ethnographic Present Revisited." In *Social Anthropology* 8, no. 3: 341–348.

de Sike, Y. 1993. "Le carnaval *de Skyros*: un exemple *de* syncrétisme (note *de* recherche)." *Anthropologie et Sociétés* 17, 119–123.

―――. 1978. "Skyros. Aperçu d'une île grecque." *Objets et Mondes* 18, no. 1–2: 69–78.

Delaney, C. 1991. *The Seed and the Soil: Gender and Cosmology in Turkish Village Society, Volume 11 of Comparative Studies on Muslim Societies*. Berkeley: University of California Press.

Delveroudi, E., Δελβερούδι, E. 2004. *Οι Νέοι στις Κωμωδίες του Ελληνικού Κινηματογράφου 1948–1974*. Athens: Kentro Neoellinikon Erevnon.

Dimitriou Kotsoni, S., Δημητρίου Κοτσώνη. Σ. 2003. "Καταναλωτικες Πρακτικές και Συλλογικές Ταυτότητες." Στο Δήμητρα Γκέφου Μαδιανού, επιμ., *Εαυτός και Άλλος*, 305–342. Athens: Gutenberg.

Douglas, M. 1987. "A Distinctive Anthropological Perspective." In *Constructive Drinking: Perspectives on Drink from Anthropology*, ed. Mary Douglas, 3–15. London and New York: Routledge.

Douglas, M., and B. Isherwood. 1979. *The World of Goods: Toward an Anthropology of Consumption.* London and New York: Routledge.

Du Boulay, J. [1974] 1994. *Portrait of a Greek Mountain Village. Oxford Monographs on Social Anthropology.* Oxford: Oxford University Press.

Eriksen, T. H. 2001. *Small Places, Large Issues: An Introduction to Social and Cultural Anthropology.* London: Pluto Press.

Fabian, J. 1983. *Time and the Other: How Anthropology Makes Its Object.* New York: Columbia University Press.

Featherstone, M., ed. 1990. *Global Culture, Nationalism, Globalization and Modernity.* Thousand Oaks, CA: Sage.

Ferguson, J. 1999. *Expectations of Modernity. Myths and Meanings of Urban Life on the Zambian Copperbelt.* Berkeley: University of California Press.

Ferro, M. [1977] 1988. *Cinema and History, Contemporary Approaches to Scenario and Television Series.* Detroit: Wayne University Press.

Fischer, M. "What is Ethnography?" *Anthropological Theory* 2, no. 3 (2002).

Foster, R. 2008. *Coca Globalization. Following Soft Drinks from New York to New Guinea.* New York: Palgrave Macmillan.

———. 2002. *Materializing the Nation: Commodities, Consumption, and Media in Papua New Guinea.* Bloomington: Indiana University Press.

Foucault, M., and J. Miskoweic. 1986. "Of Other Spaces." *Diacritics* 16, no. 1: 22–27.

Friedl, E. 1962. *Vasilika: A Village in Modern Greece. Case Studies in Cultural Anthropology.* New York: Holt, Rinehart and Winston.

Gallant, T. 2001. *Modern Greece.* New York: Arnold & Oxford University Press.

Gandoulou, J. 1984. *Entre Paris et Bacongo.* Paris : Centre Georges Pompidou.

Gately, I. 2002. *Tobacco: The Story of How Tobacco Seduced the World.* New York: Grove Press.

Geertz, C. [1973] 2000. "Thick Description: Toward an Interpretive Theory of Culture." In *The Interpretation of Cultures,* 3–32. New York: Basic Books.

Gefou-Madianou, D. 1992. "Exclusion and Unity, Retsina and Sweet Wine: Commensality and Gender in a Greek Agro-Town." In Dimitra Gefou Madianou, eds., *Alcohol, Gender and Culture,* ed. Dimitra Gefou Madianou, 108–136. Oxon and New York: Routledge.

Gell, A. 1998. *Art and Agency.* Oxford: Oxford University Press.

Georgakopoulou, A. 2000. "On the Sociolinguistics of Popular Films: Funny Characters, Funny Voices." *Journal of Modern Greek Studies* 18: 119–133.

Giddens, A. 1991. *Modernity and Self-Identity: Self and Society in the Late Modern Age.* Stanford: Stanford University Press.

Ginsburg, F. D., L. Abu-Lughod, and B. Larkin. 2002. "Introduction." In *Media Worlds: Anthropology on New Terrain,* eds. Faye D. Ginsburg, Lila Abu-Lughod, and Brian Larkin, 1–37. Berkeley: University of California Press.

Gregory, C. 1980. "Gifts to Men and Gifts to God: Gift Exchange and Capital Accumulation in Contemporary Papua." *Man* 15: 626–652.

Gusfield, J. [1987] 2003. *"Passage to Play:* Rituals of Drinking Time in American Society." In *Constructive Drinking: Perspectives on Drink from Anthropology,* ed. Mary Douglas, 73–90. Oxon & New York: Routledge.

Habermas, J. 1989. *The Structural Transformation of the Public Sphere: An Inquiry into a Category of Bourgeois Society.* Cambridge: Polity.

Hannerz, U. 1996. *Transnational Connections: Culture, People, Places.* Oxon and New York: Routledge.

———. 1989. "Notes on the Global Ecumene." *Public Culture* 1, no. 2: 66–75.

Harvey, D. 1989. *The Condition of Postmodernity.* Oxford: Blackwell.

Hatziiosif, H. Χατζηιωσήφ, X. 2003. "Η Πολιτική Οικονομία της Μεταπολεμικής Ελλάδας, 1944-1996". Στο Βασίλης Κρεμμυδάς, (Επιμ.). *Εισαγωγή στη Νεοελληνική Οικονομική Ιστορία. 18ος-20ος. Αιώνας.* Athens: Tipothito.

Herzfeld, M. 2005. *Cultural Intimacy: Social Poetics in the Nation-State.* Oxon and New York: Routledge.

———.1989. *Anthropology through the Looking Glass: Critical Ethnography in the Margins of Europe.* Cambridge: University of Cambridge Press.

———. 1985. *The Poetics of Manhood: Contest and Identity on a Cretan Mountain Village.* Princeton New Jersey: Princeton University Press.

———.1982. *Ours Once More: Folklore, Ideology, and the Making of Modern Greece.* Austin Texas: University of Texas Press.

Horkheimer, M., and T. Adorno. [1947] 1997. *Dialectic of Enlightenment.* London and New York: Verso.

Hughes, G. 1998. *Imagining Welfare Futures.* London and New York: Routledge.

Inda, J. X., and R. Rosaldo. [2002] 2008. "Tracking Global Flows." In *The Anthropology of Globalization: A Reader,* eds. Jonathan Xavier Inda and Renato Rosaldo, 3–46. Oxford: Blackwell Publishing.

Ioannou, A., Ιωάννου, A. 2001. "Η σκυλότητα ενος σκυλάδικου. Κατανάλωση και ταυτότητες στην παραλιακή του Πειραιά." *Δοκιμές* 09–10: 239–262.

Iossifides, M. 1992. "Wine: Life's Blood and Spiritual Essence in a Greek Orthodox Convent." In *Alcohol, Gender and Culture,* ed. Dimitra Gefou Madianou, 80–100. Oxon and New York: Routledge.

Jackson, M. 1998. *Whisky: The Definitive World Guide to Scotch, Bourbon and Whiskey.* New York: Hudson, Dorling Kindersley.

Just, R. 1994. "The Reformation of Class." *Journal of Modern Greek Studies* 12, no. 1: 37–56.

Kapsomenos, E., Καψωμένος, E. 1990. *Κώδικες και Σημασίες.* Athens Arsenidis.

Karakasidou, A., and F. Tsibiridou. 2006. "Mirrors, Myths and Metaphors: Ethnography-ing Greece in Late Modernity, Introductory Reflections." *Journal of Modern Greek Studies* 24: 217–228.

Karapostoli, V., Καραποστόλη, B. 1984. *Η Καταναλωτική Συμπεριφορά στην Ελληνική κοινωνία 1960-1975.* Athens: EKKE.

Kartalou, A. 2000. "Gender, Professional, and Class Identities in *Miss Director and Modern Cinderella.*" *Journal of Modern Greek Studies* 18: 105–118.

Keane, W. 2008. "The Evidence of the Senses and the Materiality of Religion." *Journal of the Royal Anthropological Institute* 14, no. 1: 110–127.

———. 2003. "Self-Interpretation, Agency, and the Objects of Anthropology: Reflections on a Genealogy." *Comparative Studies in Society and History* 45, no. 2: 222–248.

———. 1998. "Calvin in the Tropics: Objects and Subjects at the Religious Frontier." In *Border Fetishisms: Material Objects in Unstable Spaces,* ed. Patricia Spyer, 13–34. Oxon and New York: Routledge.

Kerofilas, G., Καιροφύλας, Γ. 1997. *Η Αθήνα στη δεκαετία του '60.* Athens: Filipoti.

Klein, N. 2000. *No Logo.* New York: Picador.

Koliopoulos, J., and T. Veremis. 2002. *Greece: The Modern Sequel: From 1821 to the Present.* London: Hurst.

Kontogiorgis, G., Κοντογιώργης, Γ. 2006. *Έθνος και Εκσυγχρονιστική Νεωτερικότητα.* Athens: Enalaktikes Ekdosis.

Kopytoff, I. 1986. "The Cultural Biography of Things: Commoditization as Proces." In *The Social Life of Things, Commodities in Cultural Perspective,* ed. Arjun Appadurai, 64–91. Cambridge: Cambridge University Press.

Kotaridis, N., Κοταρίδης, N. 1996. "Εισαγωγη." Στο *Ρεμπέτες και Ρεμπέτικο Τραγούδι,* 9–33. Athens: Plethron.

Kremidas, V. Κρεμμυδάς, Β. 2003. *Εισαγωγή στη Νεοελληνική Οικονομική Ιστορία. 18ος-20ος. Αιώνας.* Athens: Tipothito.

Küchler, S. 2002. "Binding in the Pacific: Between Loops and Knots." In *The Material Culture Reader,* ed. Victor Buchli, 63–80. Oxford and New York: Berg Publishers.

Kurlansky, M. 2002. *Salt: A World History.* New York: Penguin.

———. 1997. *Cod: A Biography of the Fish That Changed the World.* New York: Penguin.

Larkin, B. 2008. "Itineraries of Indian Cinema: African Videos, Bollywood, and Global Media." In *The Anthropology of Globalization: A Reader,* eds. Jonathan Xavier Inda and Renato Rosaldo, 334–351. Oxford: Blackwell Publishing.

Latour, B. [1991] 1993. *We Have Never Been Modern.* New York: Harvard University Press.

Lien, M. 1997. *Marketing and Modernity. An Ethnography of Marketing Practice.* Oxford and New York: Berg Publishers.

Loizos, P., and E. Papataxiarchis. 1991a. "Introduction." In *Contested Identities, Gender and Kinship in Modern Greece,* eds. Peter Loizos and Evthymios Papataxiarchis, 3–25. Princeton: Princeton University Press.

———. 1991b. "Gender, Sexuality and the Person in Greek Culture." In *Contested Identities, Gender and Kinship in Modern Greece,* eds. Peter Loizos and Evthymios Papataxiarchis, 221–234. Princeton: Princeton University Press.

Malaby, T. 2003. *Gambling Life: Dealing in Contingency in a Greek City.* Urbana and Chicago: University of Illinois Press.

Marcus, G. 1998. *Ethnography through Thick and Thin.* Princeton: Princeton University Press.

———. 1995. "Ethnography in/of the World System: The Emergence of Multi-Sited Ethnography." *Annual Review of Anthropology* 24: 95–117.

Marx, K. [1867] 1974. *Das Kapital: Kritik der Politischen Ökonomie, Vol.1.* Berlin: Dietz Verlag.

Mauss, M. [1954] 2002. *The Gift: The Form and Reason for Exchange in Archaic Societies.* Oxon and New York: Routledge.

Mazzarella, W. 2003. "Very Bombay: Contending with the Global in an Advertising Agency." *Cultural Anthropology* 18: 33–71.

McLuhan, M. 1964. *Understanding Media: The Extensions of Man.* New York: McGraw Hill.

Meyer, B., and P. Geschiere. 1999. "Introduction." In *Globalization and Identity: Dialectics of Flow and Closure,* eds. Birgit Meyer and Peter Geschiere, 1–15. Oxford: Blackwell Publishers.

Michaels, E. 2002. "Hollywood Iconography. A Walpiri Reading." In *The Anthropology of Globalization: A Reader,* eds. Jonathan Xavier Inda and Renato Rosaldo, 311–324. Oxford: Blackwell Publishing.

Miller, D. 1995a. "Consumption and Commodities." *Annual Review of Anthropology* 24: 141–161.

————. 1994. *Modernity an Ethnographic Approach: Dualism and Mass Consumption in Trinidad.* Oxford and New York: Berg.

————. 1987. *Material Culture and Mass Consumption.* Oxford: Basil Blackwell.

————. 2005. "Introduction." In *Materiality,* ed. Daniel Miller, 1–50. London and New York: Duke University Press.

————. 1998. "Coca-Cola: A Black Sweet Drink from Trinidad." In *Material Cultures: Why Some Things Matter,* ed. Daniel Miller, 169–188. London: UCL Press.

————. 1995b. "Introduction: Anthropology, Modernity and Consumption." In *Worlds Apart, Modernity through the Prism of the Local,* ed. Daniel Miller, 1–22. Oxon and New York: Routledge.

Mintz, S. 1985. *Sweetness and Power: The Place of Sugar in Modern History.* New York: Viking Penguin.

Mitchell, T. 2000. "The Stage of Modernity." In *Questions of Modernity,* ed. Timothy Mitchell, 1–34. Minneapolis: University of Minnesota Press.

Moeran, B. 1996. *A Japanese Advertising Agency: An Anthropology of Media and Markets.* Honolulu: University of Hawaii Press.

Moxham, R. 2003. *Tea: Addiction, Exploitation and Empire.* London: Constable.

Napolitano, V., and D. Pratten. 2007. "Michael de Certeau: Ethnography and the Challenge of Plurality." *Social Anthropology* 15: 1–12.

O'Hanlon, M. 1993. *Paradise: Portraying the New Guinea Highlands.* London: The British Museum.

Oikonomou, L., Οικονόμου, Λ. 2012. "Το ρεμπέτικο και λαϊκό τραγούδι. Μια εισαγωγή στη μελέτη και τη μυθολογία της λαϊκής ανατολικής μουσικής παράδοσης", υπό δημοσίευση στο Χ. Δεμερτζόπουλος και Γ. Παπαθεοδώρου (επιμ.), *Συνηθισμένοι άνθρωποι. Προσεγγίσεις στη Λαϊκή Κουλτούρα και την Εμπειρία της Καθημερινότητας.* Athens: Gutenberg and Open University of Cyprus.

————. 2010. "Λαϊκά και σκυλάδικα στη δεκαετία του 1980." Στο Βασίλης Βαμβακάς— Παναγής Παναγιωτόπουλος *Η Ελλάδα στη δεκαετία του '80. κοινωνικό, πολιτικό, πολιτισμικό λεξικό.* Athens: To Perasma.

————. 2005. "Ρεμπέτικα, λαϊκά και σκυλάδικα. Όρια και ετατοπίσεις στην πρόσληψη της λαϊκής μουσικής του 20ου αιώνα." *Δοκιμές,* 13–14: 361–398.

Ortiz, F. 1940. *Contrapunteo Cubano del Tabaco y el Azúcar.* La Habana, Cuba: Jesús Montero Editor.

Panourgia, N. 1995. *Fragments of Death, Fables of Identity: An Athenian Anthropography.* Madison: University of Wisconsin Press.

Papagaroufali, E. 1992. "Uses of Alcohol Among Women: Games of Resistance, Power and Pleasure." In *Alcohol, Gender and Culture,* ed. Dimitra Gefou Madianou, 48–70. London and New York: Routledge.

Papanikolaou, T., Παπανικολάου, Θ. 1996. *Slogans.* Athens: Barberopoulos.

Papataxiarchis, E. 2006. Παπαταξιάρχης, Ε. "Εισαγωγή." Στο *Τα άχθη της Ετερότητας, Η Παραγωγή της Πολιτισμικής Διαφοράς Στη Σημερινή Ελλάδα.* Athens: Alexandria.

————. 1999. "A Contest with Money: Gambling and the Politics of Disinterested Sociality in Aegean Greece." In *Lilies of the Field: Marginal People Who Live for the Moment,* eds. Sophie Day, Evthymios Papataxiarchis, and Michael Stewart, 158–175. Boulder: Westview Press.

―――. 1998. "Ο κόσμος του καφενείου. Ταυτότητα και ανταλλαγή στον ανδρικό συμποσιασμό." Στο Ευθύμιος Παπαταξιάρχης Θεόδωρος Παραδέλης, επιμ., *Ταυτότητες και φύλλο στην σύγχρονη Ελλάδα.* Αθήνα: Εκδόσεις Αλεξάνδρεια.

―――. 1991. "Friends of the Heart: Male Commensal Solidarity, Gender and Kinship in Aegean Greece." In *Contested Identities, Gender and Kinship in Modern Greece,* eds. Peter Loizos and Evthymios Papataxiarchis, 156–179. Princeton: Princeton University Press.

―――. 1988. "Worlds Apart: Women and Men in Greek Aegean Household and Coffeeshop." Ph.D. thesis, London School of Economics.

Papazahariou, Zahos, E.. Παπαζαχαρίου, Ζάχος, E. 1980. *Η Πιάτσα.* Athens: Kaktos.

Pels, P. 2002. "The Confessional Ethic and the Spirits of the Screen: Reflections on the Modern Fear of Alienation." *Etnofoor* 15, no. 1/2: 91–119.

―――. 2003. "Introduction: Magic and Modernity." In *Magic and Modernity: Interfaces of Revelation and Concealment,* eds. Birgit Meyer and Peter Pels, 1–38. Stanford: Stanford University Press.

―――. 1998. "The Spirit of Matter: On Fetish, Rarity, Fact and Fancy." In *Border Fetishisms,* ed. Patricia Spyer, 91–121. Oxon and New York: Routledge.

Perpiniadis, V., Περπινιάδης, Β. 2001. *Πρίν το Τέλος.* Αθήνα: Εκδόσεις Προσκήνιο.

Persidis, V. Περσίδης, Β. 1984. "Πια η παράδοση και η αξία της." *Σκυριανά Νέα,* 7–9.

Petridou, E., Πετρίδου, E. 2006. ΄Τυρί και Έθνος, Εθνικές διεκδικήσεις στην Ευρωπαϊκή Ένωση΄ στο Ευθύμιος Παπαταξιάρχης *Τα άχθη της Ετερότητας, Η Παραγωγή της Πολιτισμικής Διαφοράς Στη Σημερινή Ελλάδα.* Athens: Alexandria.

―――. 2001. "Milk Ties. A Commodity Chain Approach to Greek Culture." Ph.D. thesis, Department of Anthropology, University College London (UCL).

Petropoulos, I. Πετρόπουλος, I. 1987. *Το Άγιο Χασισάκι.* Αθήνα: Νεφέλη.

Playboy Magazine. 1990. "Το αλκοόλ τρόπος ζωής." January: 136–141.

Riginos, M., Ρηγίνος, M. 2002. "Η ελληνική βιομηχανία 1900–1940." Στο Κρεμμυδάς Β. Επιμ., *Εισαγωγή στη Νεοελληνική Οικονομική Ιστορία. 18ος-20ος αιώνας.* Athens: Tipothito.

Ritzer, G. 2004. *The McDonaldization of Society.* Thousand Oaks, CA: Sage.

Rowlands, M. 2002. "The Power of Origins: Questions of Cultural Rights." In *The Material Culture Reader,* ed. Victor Buchli, 115–133. Oxford and New York: Berg Publishers.

Seremetakis, N. 1996. *The Senses Still. Perception and Memory as Material Culture in Modernity.* Chicago: The University of Chicago Press.

Sihroni Diafimisi Magazine, Περιοδικό Σύγχρονη Διαφήμιση, 1992, v. 528, 17–23.

Skopetea, E., Σκοπετέα, E. 1992. *Η Δύση της Ανατολής. Εικόνες από το Τέλος της Οθωμανικής Αυτοκρατορίας.* Athens: Gnosi.

Skoumpourdi, A., Σκουμπουρδή, A. 2002. *Καφενεία της παλιάς Αθήνας.* Athens: Politistikos Organismos Dimou Athinaion.

Soldatos, G., Σολδάτος, Γ. 2002. *Η Ιστορία του Ελληνικού Κινηματογράφου.* vol. 1–4. Athens: Aigokeros.

Sotiropoulou, H., Σωτηροπούλου, Χ. 1989. *Ελληνική Κινηματογραφία 1965–1975: Θεσμικό Πλαίσιο- Οικονομική Κατάσταση.* Athens: Themelio.

Souliotis, N., Ν. Σουλιώτης. 2001. "Ο αστικός χώρος ώς συμβολικό αγαθό. Τα μπάρ των Εξαρχείων και του Κολωνακίου." *Δοκιμές* 09-10: 211–238.

Spyer, P. 2000. *The Memory of Trade: Modernity's Entanglements on an Eastern Indonesian Island.* London and New York: Duke University Press.

———. 1998. "Introduction." In *Border Fetishisms: Material Objects in Unstable Spaces,* ed. Patricia Spyer, 1–12. Oxon & New York: Routledge.

Stathakis, G. 2007. "Η χούντα στο μεταίχμειο ανάμεσα στην αγροτική και την αστική Ελλάδα." Working paper.

Stewart, C. 1991. *Demons and the Devil: Moral Imagination in Modern Greek Culture.* Princeton: Princeton University Press.

———. 1989, "Hegemony or Rationality? The Position of Supernatural in Modern Greece." *Journal of Modern Greek Studies* 7, no. 1: 77–104.

Sutton, D. 2008. "Tradition and Modernity Revisited: Existential Memory Work on a Greek Island." *History and Memory* 20: 84–105.

———. 2001. *Remembrance of Repasts: An Anthropology of Food and Memory. Materializing Culture.* Oxford and New York: Berg Publishers.

Taussig, M. 1980. *The Devil and Commodity Fetishism in South America.* Chapel Hill: University of North Carolina Press.

Theoharidis, A., Θεοχαρίδης, A. 2009. "Υλικός Πολιτισμός, Κοινωνική Οργάνωση και Μνήμη. Κειμήλια και αντικείμενα "λαϊκής τέχνης και χειροτεχνίας" στη Σκύρο και η κυκλοφορία τους μέσα και έξω από τα όρια του τοπικού. Διδακτορική διατριβή, Πανεπιστήμιο Αιγαίου, Τμήμα Κοινωνικής Ανθρωπολογίας και Ιστορίας, Μυτιλήνη." Ph.D. thesis, University of Aegean.

Tilley, C. 2006. "Theoretical Perspectives." In *Handbook of Material Culture,* eds. Christopher Tilley, Webb Keane, and Patricia Spyer, 7–12. Thousand Oaks, CA: Sage.

———. 2001. "Ethnography and Material Culture." In *The Handbook of Ethnography,* eds. Paul Atkinson, Amanda Coffey, Shara Delamont, John Lofland, and Lyn Lofland, 258–272. Thousand Oaks, CA: Sage.

Traganou, J. 2008. "Shades of Blue: Debating Greek Identity through Santiago Calatrava's Design for the Athens Olympic Stadium." *Journal of Modern Greek Studies* 26, no. 1: 185–214.

Trouillot, M, R. 2003. *Global Transformations, Anthropology and the Modern World.* New York: Palgrave Macmillan.

Tsing, A. [2000] 2008. "The Global Situation." In *The Anthropology of Globalization,* eds. Jonathan Xavier Inda and Renato Rosaldo, 327–360. Oxford: Wiley-Blackwell.

Tsitsopoulou, V. 2000. "Greekness, Gender Stereotypes, and the Hollywood Musical in Jules Dassin's Never on Sunday." *Journal of Modern Greek Studies* 18: 79–93.

Tziovas, D., Τζιόβας, Δ. 2006. *Οι μεταμορφώσεις του Εθνισμού και το Ιδεολόγημα της Ελληνικότητας στο Μεσοπόλεμο.* Athens: Odysseas.

Tziovas, D. 1994, "Heteroglossia and the defeat of regionalism in Greece", *Kambos* 2: 95-120

Varouhaki, S., Βαρουχάκη, Σ. 2005. "Μαζική Κουλτούρα και Σύγχρονο Λαϊκό Τραγούδι, 1974–2000. Διδακτορική Διατριβή, Τμήμα Κοινωνιολογίας, Πάντειο Πανεπιστήμιο." Athens: Ph.D. thesis, Panteion University.

Wallerstein, E., 2004. *World Systems Analysis.* London and New York: Duke University Press.

Watson, J. L. 1997. *Golden Arches East: McDonald's in East Asia.* Stanford: Stanford University Press.

Weiner, A. 1992. *Inalienable Possessions: The Paradox of Keeping-While-Giving.* Berkeley and Los Angeles: University of California Press.

Weiss, B. 1996. *The Making and Unmaking of the Haya Lived World: Consumption, Commoditi-zation and Everyday Practice*. Durham and London: Duke University Press.

Wilk, R. 1995. "Learning to be Local in Belize: Global Systems of Local Difference." In *Worlds Apart. Modernity Through The Prism of the Local*, ed. Daniel Miller, 110–133. Oxon and New York: Routledge.

Williams, R. 1965. *The Long Revolution*. Baltimore: Penguin.

———. 1997. *Marxism and Literature*, Marxist Introductions Series. London and New York: Oxford University Press.

Williams, R., and M. Orrom. 1954. *Preface to Film*. London: Film Drama Limited.

Yalouri, E. 2001. *The Acropolis, Global Fame, Local Claim*. Oxford and New York: Berg.

Yiakoumaki, V. 2006. "'Local,' 'Ethnic,' and 'Rural' Food: On the Emergence of 'Cultural Diversity' in Greece since its Integration in the European Union." *Journal of Modern Greek Studies* 24, no. 2: 415–445.

Zarkia, C. 1996. "*Philoxenia* Receiving Tourists—but not Guests—on a Greek Island." In *Coping with Tourists: European Reactions to Mass Tourism*, ed. J. Boissevain, 143–173. Oxford and Providence: Berghahn Books.

———. 1991. "Societe *et espace* dans 1' *ile* de *Skyros*." These de Doctoral EHESS, Paris.

Zinovieff, S. 1992. "Hunters and Hunted: Kamaki and the Ambiguities of Sexual Predation in a Greek Town." In *Contested Identities, Gender and Kinship in Modern Greece*, eds. Peter Loizos and Evthymios Papataxiarchis, 203–220. Princeton: Princeton University Press.

Zuckerman, L. 1998. *The Potato: How the Humble Spud Rescued the Western World*. New York: North Point Press.

Reports

Εθνική Στατιστική Υπηρεσία Ελλάδος (ΕΣΥΕ), 2007. Οικογενειακοί Προϋπολογισμοί (National Statistical Service of Greece, Family Budgets).

Εθνικό Σχέδιο Δράσης για τον Περιορισμό των Βλαπτικών Συνεπειών του Αλκοόλ στην Υγεία 2008—2012 του υπουργείου Υγείας και Κοινωνικής Αλληλεγγύης, 2008 (National Scheme for Alcohol effects, Ministry of Health).

Foundation of Economic and Industrial Research of Greece (IOBE), 1993. Report on the Greek alcohol industry and the sector of beverages.

The Scotch Whisky Association, 2007. Scotch whisky export markets and consumption levels.

Index

✛ ✛ ✛